THE COMPANY I'VE KEPT

Hugh MacDiarmid

HUGH MacDIARMID
(Christopher Murray Grieve)

The Company I've Kept

HUTCHINSON OF LONDON

HUTCHINSON & CO (*Publishers*) LTD
178–202 Great Portland Street, London W1

London Melbourne Sydney
Auckland Bombay Toronto
Johannesburg New York

First published 1966

*This book has been set in Scotch Roman, printed in Great Britain
on Antique Wove paper by Anchor Press, and
bound by Wm. Brendon, both of Tiptree, Essex*

For my daughter Christine and my sons Walter and Michael, and her husband and their wives, and for my grandchildren, Elspeth, Donald, Alison, and Roderick McIntosh, Judith, Angela and Jane Grieve and Christopher and Lucien Grieve

Contents

Contents

Illustrations

Acknowledgements

Ever since I was a boy I have been an incessant and omnivorous reader and lived in 'a strong solution of books'. There are accordingly many quotations in this volume and some of these I have been unable to trace to their sources, though every effort has been made to do this. If I have trespassed unwittingly and quoted copyright material without having secured the necessary permission, I trust that I may be forgiven.

Acknowledgements are due to the following:

To Philip Mairet and Messrs. Lund Humphries for quotations from *Pioneer of Sociology. The Life and Letters of Patrick Geddes*.

To Dr. George Elder Davie and Edinburgh University Press for quotations from *The Democratic Intellect*.

To the executors of the late William Gallacher and to Messrs. Lawrence and Wishart for quotations from *Revolt on the Clyde*.

To Edward Conze and Messrs. Victor Gollancz for quotations from *Spain Today*.

To Abe Moffat and Messrs. Lawrence and Wishart for quotations from *My Life with the Miners*.

To J. S. Collis and Messrs. Cassell & Co. Ltd. for quotations from *Farewell to Argument*.

To Philip Mairet and Messrs. J. M. Dent & Sons Ltd. for quotations from *A. R. Orage. A Memoir*.

To the executors of Major C. H. Douglas and Messrs. Cecil Palmer for quotations from *Economic Democracy*.

To the executors of the late Dr. Thomas Robertson and Messrs. Wm. Maclellan, Glasgow, for quotations from *Human Ecology*.

To J. D. Scott and the editor and publishers of *Horizon* for extract from article about Scottish novelists.

To Thomas McGrath and the editor and publishers of *National Guardian* (New York) for review of the author's *Collected Poems*.

And to the editors of the *New Statesman*, *The Spectator*, *The Western Mail* (Cardiff), *The Saltire Review*, *The Daily Worker*, and *Marxism Today*, in respect of extracts from articles originally published in their columns.

Hugh MacDiarmid

Brownsbank
Biggar
Lanarkshire

'A man needs a thin skin to be a writer, and mostly needs a thick skin to put up with the consequences.'

Frank Dalby Davison

'Art is the joy of the intelligence which sees the universe clearly and re-creates by illumination of the consciousness. Art is the sublime of man, since it is the exercise of thought which seeks to understand the world and to make others understand it.'

Auguste Rodin (translated by Katharine Susannah Prichard)

'There is no self, no individual. There is a continuation of thought.'

David Hume

'That merciless and mercenary gang of cold-blooded slaves and assassins, called, in the ordinary prostitution of language, "friends" '.

Thomas Love Peacock

'Be friendly with the folks you know. If it weren't for them, you'd be a total stranger.'

New York World-Telegram

1

My friends

I HAD my seventy-third birthday recently. About thirty years ago I published a volume of autobiography entitled *Lucky Poet*. It has been long out of print and is extremely difficult to find, yet I am continually astonished by testimonies to the extraordinary influence it has had, and continues to have, on individuals all over the world. Owing to wartime exigencies, the paper shortage, etc., that book was only a fifth of the original manuscipt, and I promised in my Introductory Note that the other four-fifths would appear as separate volumes in due course. But that has proved impossible. Circumstances have changed, and I with them. Many, probably most, of the people about whom I wrote then are now dead, and in many ways I would find it necessary to express myself very differently now about them and about my relations with them and my opinions generally than I did in these abandoned writings. In the intervening years, however, readers all over the world have written to me asking me to redeem my promise and publish the other volumes.

Lucky Poet, while a very personal book, was little concerned with what most people regard as a life-story. It was certainly—if at all—a very uncommon sort of *apologia pro vita mea*, being almost wholly concerned with the course of my intellectual and aesthetic development and the ways that had been affected by my omnivorous reading, schools of thought I had encountered, and political considerations. I am not disposed to be any more forthcoming in the present book with regard to intimate personal matters. I agree with W. H. Auden that 'knowledge of an artist's life, temperament, and opinions is unimportant to an understanding of his art', and it was almost exclusively what seemed to me to be important to that in my own case I sought to elucidate in the earlier work. But here I am concerned with a host of other people, and only with myself in so far as my personality—or rather my significance as a poet and politician—is reflected in my relations with them.

What, then, are friends? It has been written of me that I 'seemed to have read everything and to know everybody', and there can be no doubt, I think, that the circle of my acquaintanceship is vastly greater than that of most people. Greater—and far more various. There can be few alive who have known and been on friendly terms with W. B. Yeats, T. S. Eliot, and Dylan Thomas, to name only three of the best-known of a multitude of poets I have known. In regard to the theatre I have known Sean O'Casey, 'James Bridie', Bernard Shaw, John Galsworthy, Joan Littlewood, Ewan McColl, Arnold Wesker, Brendan Behan, and have had the honour of kissing Helene Weigall and corresponding with Stefan Brecht. Sir J. M. Barrie is one of the few Scottish authors who lived in my time I did not know personally, although he was one of the signatories to a remarkable tribute to me in the 'thirties. But I knew William Archer, R. B. Cunninghame Graham, John Buchan (who introduced my first volume of poems), and, above all, Compton Mackenzie, who wrote me a year or two ago that we had known each other for forty years without ever being at variance, and who was one of the godfathers of my son Walter. In science I name only Sir Ronald Ross, Ronald Campbell Macfie, Sir Edward Appleton, Jr., Logie Baird, and, above all, Sir Patrick Geddes. If next to the last named I was asked who had made the profoundest impression upon me of all the men I have known I would say the Welsh Nationalist leader, Saunders Lewis.

In politics my principal friends have been Keir Hardie, William Gallacher, James Maxton, Jim Larkin, Tom Mann,

J. R. Campbell, and the present General Secretary of the
Communist Party of Great Britain, John Gollan—and
immediately I have said that I remember my association
in the Peace Movement with Dr. Hewlett Johnson, D. N.
Pritt, Paul Robeson, Gordon Schaeffer, Bertrand Russell—
and a score of others.

It will be noticed that I have named only men so far,
but I am no misogynist, and at once I think of Christabel
Pankhurst, Annie Kenny, Sarah Purser, Sara Allgood, Sybil
Thorndike, Naomi Mitchison, and, above all, the woman
responsible for raising the fund that keeps the *Daily
Worker* going, Barbara Niven. Even so, I have not mentioned the women writers I have known best, Mary Webb,
May Sinclair, Rebecca West, Violet Jacob, Marion Angus,
and Helen Burness Cruickshank. But one woman I remember with special gratitude—Mrs. Winnie Challis (*née*
Manners), who was my assistant when I was London
Editor of Compton Mackenzie's short-lived radio-critical
journal *Vox* in 1929. She had a wonderful wit and a knack
of most diverting light journalism. She used to do profiles
for me of radio personalities, and I still laugh when I think
of one she did of Victoria Sackville-West—captioned 'Wry
Vita'! She went abroad, I think, in 1930 or 1931, and to my
great regret I lost touch with her entirely. Another lady I
must mention is Comtesse Eileen de Vismes. I was listening
to the orators one day at Speakers' Corner in Hyde Park
when this lady got into conversation with me. When the
speechifying was over, and the crowd was dispersing, she
said, 'Well, aren't you going to take me somewhere for
tea?' 'I am afraid that is impossible,' I replied, 'I don't
think I have enough money on me.' I searched my trouser
pockets and came up with the grand total of ninepence.
'Just lend me that, then,' she said. 'I can't,' I said, 'I
must keep a few pennies to get to the house I'm living in.'
So I divided the money and lent her fivepence. I couldn't
get in touch with her again, as I had forgotten to ask her
her address. Years later in the *News of the World* I saw an
advertisement from a firm of lawyers in Sydney, Australia,

B

asking her to get in touch with them. It seemed she was
due to inherit a very considerable fortune, I hope she did.
Not till eighteen years after our encounter did I hear from
her or of her again. Then, in 1962, on the occasion of my
seventieth birthday, I received a greetings telegram from
her—but it gave no clue to her address.

In art I remember Augustus John, Pittendrigh Mac-
Gillivray, J. D. Fergusson, Victor Pasmore, Benno Schotz,
Josef Hermann, and the cartoonist Will Dyson. I could
multiply these names, and add others not in the cate-
gories I have given, of political, literary, and artist friends,
and in, say, religion (where I think of the Very Reverend
Dr. George F. MacLeod of the Iona Community, Professor
Martin Buber, Father Vincent McNab, Father Dineen, the
Irish Gaelic lexicographer, Father John MacMillan, the
great authority on Gaelic songs, Rev. John McKechnie,
who knows all the Gaelic languages and is a member of
both the Welsh and the Cornish Gorsedd, and Father
Anthony Ross, the Dominican chaplain to Edinburgh
University). But it will be seen that I have not amongst
all these names included several of those to whom I have
given extended consideration in this book—A. R. Orage
of the *New Age*, Major C. H. Douglas of the Social Credit
proposals, Professor Denis Saurat, the composers Kaikhosru
Shapurji Sorabji and Francis George Scott, and co-workers
in the field of Scottish letters like Robert Maclellan and
Alex Reid, the dramatists, and fellow-poets like Norman
McCaig, Sydney Goodsir Smith, Sorley MacLean, and
George Campbell Hay, with whom I have been closely
associated. I have known many foreign poets too—Kuo-
mo-jo in China, Uys Krige, the Africaans poet, Nazim
Hikmet, Pablo Neruda, Tristan Tzara, Eugeni Yevtushenko,
Eugenio Montale, Salvatore Quasimodo, Boutens in
Holland and Nezval in Prague, among them (and the poets
in whose work I have been most interested in recent years,
the Swedish Harry Martensen, the Rumanian Tudor
Arghesi, and the Hungarian Josef Attila). 'A multitude of
poets,' I say. I have known or wanted to know few novelists

—few British novelists at any rate. I will write later about
Neil Gunn, one of my earliest and closest associates in the
Scottish Literary Movement and a man for whom I had a
great affection though, as will appear, as with all novels
except detective stories, I can read little of his work. Against
the strong vigour of Scottish life, almost all our novels of
this century are flimsy constructions of cardboard. Lewis
Grassic Gibbon's novels are almost the only exception.
The writers are not alone to blame, of course. As W. B.
Yeats in his 1909 diary complained of Ireland, so it must
be said of Scotland today that it is 'ruined by abstractions'
and that only an 'ill-breeding of the mind' is prevalent
among Scots—'every thought made in some manufactory
and with the mark upon it of its wholesale origin'. A land,
in short, where every sprig of promise is 'crushed by the
mechanical logic and commonplace eloquence which give
power to the most empty mind, because, being "something
other than human life", they have no use for distinguished
feeling or individual thought'.

The long-neglected problem which suddenly confronted
Scottish writers with special urgency between 1918 and
1930—and, since it was never properly tackled, let alone
solved, confronts us now more desperately than ever—is
simply the problem of the writer's faithfulness to his calling,
without which he is of no use to his nation. A brilliant,
living, too-little-known Scottish writer, Richard Curle, in
his book *The Last Twelve Years of Joseph Conrad*, defines
it by saying that, for a literary artist, 'nothing walks or
creeps or grows or exists which must not in turn arise and
walk before him as exponent of his meaning'. Emerson
expressed it in his speech on *Literary Ethics* when he said:
'The perpetual admonition of nature to us is: "The World
is new, untried. Do not believe the past. I give you the
universe a virgin today." '
The brochure put out by the Scottish B.B.C. in connection with their Annals of Scotland series tells us that
Scottish Literature lacks innovators. In other words, it has

ignored the injuction to sing a *new* song to the Lord—where
(as Ezra Pound has always insisted, with his slogan to all
artists: 'Make it new') the operative word is *new*. Scottish
fiction is static or regressive; content that dynamic, if any,
should be generated elsewhere. Most of our writers are
backward-looking, consumed by a repetition complex,
afraid to face up to and grapple with contemporary realities,
writing to purely artificial formulae. The Polish poet,
Mickiewicz, paraphrased Emerson when he counselled
writers: 'Act from yourself, be faithful to yourself, have
self-trust. Don't be a leaning willow; you must detach
yourself and become your own power.' Have any modern
Scottish writers done that? I am afraid the very sound of
the word 'power' in relation to almost all of them is a complete give-away of their pretensions.

It seems to me a very serious matter if the stream of
our imaginative prose cannot rise to the level of, and carry
with it, the great Scottish figures who have contributed
so splendidly to science and philosophy, but neglects the
link between scientific thought and humanism personified
in these men; and it will, I think, be very grave for the
future of our culture if this underestimation of the scientific
investigation of the problem of culture proves more than
a temporary phenomenon. As matters stand, compared
with the way in which our national genius has expressed
itself in science, philosophy, economics, engineering and
industrial organisation, all that our novelists are achieving
seems to me to resemble nothing so much as the yammering
of a man without a roof to his mouth or that feminine
twittering which led a man to say of one such woman that
he would as soon think of marrying a canary.

'As matters stand we are condemned', wrote R. L.
Stevenson, 'to avoid half the life that passes us by. . . .
They give us a little box of toys and we play with that and
avoid real life—except in private.' So has every subsequent
Scottish writer and the great majority of writers of every
other country too.

Highbrowism is not tolerated, of course. I remember

one Benjamin Swift who contributed to the *New Age*.
Benjamin Swift was the pseudonym of a Glasgow writer,
William Romaine Paterson (b. 1871), but all J. H. Millar
says about him in his *Literary History of Scotland* is that
he 'successfully contrived to stifle considerable natural
abilities in the frantic effort to be "clever" at all costs'.
Just in the same way Dr. Millar says of David Storrar
Meldrum's novel, *The Conquest of Charlotte*, published in
1902: 'It is sufficiently provoking in many ways. It is not
by any means a "plain tale" from Kirkcaldy, and sometimes the style is *plus-quam-Meredithian* in its allusive-
ness and obscurity. But it has temperament and atmosphere; and in the character of Rab Cook, the author,
despite himself, as it sometimes appears, has achieved a
triumph.'

Entirely excepted from these strictures, of course, is the
work of two modern Scottish writers—R. B. Cunninghame
Graham and Norman Douglas—and I would also commend as of a higher value than almost all the other
Scottish fiction of our period two books not included in the
B.B.C.'s Annals of Scotland series—namely, Fred Urquhart's
Edinburgh novel, with its wonderfully faithful seizure of
the demotic idiom, and Sydney Goodsir Smith's *Carotid
Cornucopius* (dealt with in another chapter), which revives
to contemporary purpose much of the manner and matter
of Urquhart's Rabelais and does for Edinburgh something
like what Joyce's *Ulysses* did for Dublin. Also exempt from
my strictures—and also omitted from the Annals series—
are Fionn MacColla's (Thomas Douglas MacDonald's) two
novels, *The Albannaich* and *And the Cock Crew*, which
move on a higher intellectual plane than ninety per cent
of our fiction. But the novelist I recall with special pleasure
is Chris Massey—and not because of any of his novels,
but on account of an early book, *Confessions of a Journalist*,
which I read in Edinburgh Central Public Library in 1908
or 1909 and have never forgotten. It was full of splendid
stories of literary and journalistic characters in New York.
The Edinburgh copy seems to have disappeared long ago.

It is no longer there. In Liverpool in 1930 I met Massey, who was living on Canvey Island. Philip Jordan, Attlee's P.R.O., was with us. Massey told me he had never met anyone else who had ever heard of the book. I wish somebody would re-issue it.

Again, it must be obvious that I have named only people of some public reputation, yet I have had—and have—a great number of friends who are entirely private persons, hardly known to anyone save their own domestic circles and their fellow-workers. It is not intellectual snobbery that prevents me from writing about these men and women. One must draw the line somewhere. If I began to write about these friends I would have to name hundreds, if I were to avoid being invidious.

I am aware that name-giving can mean little and must be tiresome to many of my readers, yet I cannot forbear another name or two. There was the polar explorer and artist, W. G. Burn-Murdoch, to whose hospitable house in Edinburgh most of us, and notably such writers as Eric Linklater and Moray Maclaren, used to go for 'feasts of reason and flow of soul' thirty years ago, and there is happily still with us, Major Hume Sleigh—a wonderful character, though not in quite the same sense as two remarkable figures, Alastair Cameron, ex-roadman, Justice of the Peace, Fellow of the Society of Antiquaries, and author of books about Sunart and Moidart; and Davie Glen, who promised if he came back from the First World War that he would lead parties of young people to see the sunrise from the summit of Lochnagar and has done so faithfully seventeen times, in addition to himself climbing the tops of 500 Scottish mountains. ('I don't believe,' he said in a recent interview, 'in getting involved in this Munro business about summits over 3000 feet. That makes mountaineering competitive which, to my mind, is asking for trouble.') Where do you live? he was asked, and replied: 'In a railway carriage at Bachnagairn, Tealing, near Dundee. It's not exactly a palace, but it's all I need. I've a coal stove, paraffin lamps lighting, and a gas cooker using liquid gas. And I'll no' starve as long as I've got a tin of Baxter's Royal Game Soup. I like to be my own gaffer. I'm independent of any man. All the walking and climbing I've done in my older days keeps me in fine fettle. I've been at death's door with spinal meningitis, and I've had an ulcer for years. So keeping hardy keeps me alive, you might say.' Do you ever sleep out of doors? 'Many's the time. Sometimes I just use a sleeping bag. Often I build a bracken shelter like an igloo. But in winter I always make sure I'll reach a bothy before dark. Not long ago a man came from the Canadian Broadcasting Corporation. He was gathering Scottish material and managed to track me down. I filled two tapes for him of Scots songs, bothy ballads, diddling and whistling. I've had a couple of cheques since, so I must have been broadcast on his network.'

How did I acquire so many friends of all social levels and nationalities? They just happened to me as Topsy 'growed'. One leads to another. If I mention Sorabji, for instance, he was, when I met him first, already on friendly terms with Denis Saurat, A. R. Orage, and Francis George Scott, all of whom became very close friends of mine too. Orage and A.E. (George Russell) were good friends, and it was through A.E. that I met Yeats and Oliver St. John Gogarty. And so the process went on in every connection. Most people seem to be puzzled by how little I know of any of these friends, colleagues, acquaintances—whatever they may be called—and by how little curiosity I have, or have ever had, about the kind of particulars concerning them that apparently constitute the very essence of such relationships for most people. That may be counterbalanced by my conviction that I know about them what matters most, or the only things that really matter, and can therefore afford to dispense with any knowledge of the personal details about them by which so much store is commonly set.

Whether I am right or wrong about that is perhaps arguable, but I am not attempting to justify my attitude,

merely describe it. As Paul Valéry said, the problem is
how to enjoy the pleasures of social contacts and extract
nourishment from them without losing one's integrity.
'The business of an artist is not to respond to the favour
bestowed on him by any modification of his manner which
might increase that favour.' In a recent controversy in *The
Scotsman*, when I had occasion to accuse Sir William
Mactaggart, President of the Royal Scottish Academy, of
'social climbing', he replied that there were other causes for
my losing friends than my Communism. But the fact is
that I have practically never lost a friend. I have held to
Valéry's precept all along the line, and that is what a
writer in *The Guardian* had in mind when he wrote of me
'as a driving, angular, uncompromisingly extreme intellectual in poetry, rather nobly refusing to make peace either
with the world or his own talents. The final impression
one is left with is of a poetic personality that commands
respect, and that proudly does not ask to be loved or
liked.'

I am the son of a rural postman who died when I was a
student in my early teens. I had no advantages by birth
to account for the number and variety of the friends I have
made, but one of the reasons is, of course, that for many
years I was a newspaper reporter—and on weekly local
papers at that. I preferred these because in that way one is
involved in every element of a community's life and gets
to know practically everybody in the area in question. That
was certainly the case with me in Clydebank, Ebbw Vale,
Cupar-Fife, Forfar, and finally Montrose. Prior to the
First World War, too, a type of journalist flourished
in such places alive to every move on the board of local
affairs, and I still recall with gratitude my association with
such men as David Esplin in Cupar-Fife, Herbert Duncan
in Forfar, John Drummond Smith in Montrose, and Wallace
Ferguson in Clydebank. I do not know whether such types
survive in the changed conditions of journalism today, but
these were splendid fellows and are still remembered in the
communities in question.

Alastair Cameron, the old roadman author and historian, says: 'There is no advantage I can think of in living far from towns, with all their civilising influences. On the other hand there are many things I do not like. Television, I despise. How can people *talk* with *that* going on?' But he speaks of a spirit he feels is all but gone from the Highlands, of days when, he says, people *really* lived in unison. Of a time when help needed was help given, without asking. 'If the man in the next croft was putting up a fence you automatically helped him with the work. It was something that didn't need thinking about. They didn't have community centres then either. Social life was in the home. A light shining in the farmhouse window of an evening was the only invitation you needed to call in.' He mourns the passing of that era and points out sadly: 'People keep more to themselves nowadays. They don't want to know what is happening to their neighbour.'

I am different from Alastair Cameron, however. I have lived for the last forty-five years (with a brief interval during the Second World War) in country places, where I have had no immediate neighbours, and it would now be utter torture for me to live in any city or even any town. They would affect me, as Valéry said to Lefèvre about his life in Paris: 'You can't imagine how horribly I suffer from this dispersion, this disintegration forced upon me by the conditions of existence in Paris. Not to belong to oneself any more, or rather, not to belong to one's best moments, is the torture of a mental inferno which has never yet been described. It is a place of torment peopled with interrupted thoughts, abandoned ideas, desires arrested and petrified— left powerless in the very attitude of power.' There is the misery of futile activity and the deadly numb state of exhaustion. 'I have', he continues, 'noticed one rather odd effect of this "molecular bombardment" on myself. Sometimes the number of requests, engagements, etc., is so great, the cross-fire of questions so thick, that they become practically equal and although there are in fact considerable differences in the importance of the interests involved in these various activities, the differences are wiped out. Everything takes on the same value of distraction, interruption, fatigue, and one's days, taken together, seem like the confused hubbub of a public meeting where everyone is speaking at once.'

As Auden has put it: 'A democracy in which each citizen is as fully conscious and capable of making a rational choice, as in the past has been possible only for the wealthier few, is the only kind of society which in the future is likely to survive for long. In such a society, and in such alone, will it be possible for the poet, without sacrificing any of his subtleties of sensibility or his integrity, to write poetry which is simple, clear and gay. But we do have to choose, every one of us. We have the misfortune or good luck to be living in one of the great critical historical periods, when the whole structure of our society and its cultural and metaphysical values are undergoing a radical change. Our only choice lies between an external and false necessity passively accepted and an internal necessity consciously decided, but that is the difference between slavery and freedom.'

So of course I chose as Valéry did. He remained exposed to the bombardment. 'Once having abandoned the masterly inaction of Teste, Valéry was bound to respond to every summons of the external world.' That is what has happened to me too.

I am frequently told that I am wasting my time being an active member of all sorts of societies, and lecturing to small groups of people all over the United Kingdom and in other countries. I am, in fact, held in a cat's-cradle of such activities and in the last ten years my involvement has become greater and greater. Surely, it is argued, I am dispersing my energies and should rather concentrate them, above all on my poetry. It is true that age is beginning to tell, but I recall that all my best early poetry was written when I was holding down an exacting journalistic post and at the same time functioning as a Town Councillor, Parish Councillor, member of the Education Authority, and a

Magistrate, and I am convinced that I still work best in a press of diverse activities and that to have less to do than I have would not be a good thing and certainly would not enable me to write more or better poetry.

Although I live in a cottage on a hill-farm I get a great many visitors. I had no fewer than twelve American professors (all concerned with different matters) one week last year. My most interesting recent visitors were probably Colin Wilson and Philip O'Connor, Professor Roger Assillineau, who had just published his study of Walt Whitman, Ian Milner of the English Seminar at the Charles University in Prague, Michael Peto the photographer, Hugh Gordon Porteus, Iain Hamilton (ex-editor of *The Spectator*), the American poets Louis Simpson and Muriel Rukeyser and her son Bill. So it goes on. Just before I wrote the last few sentences I was 'invaded'—very agreeably—by the American poets Jonathan Williams and Ronald Johnson, and the artist R. B. Kitaj. But I have had an exceptionally busy year (1964–5). I stood in the General Election as Communist candidate in Kinross and West Perth against Sir Alec Douglas-Home, gave poetry readings at Newcastle upon Tyne, Aberystwyth, Leeds, Manchester, and Cambridge, took part in a televised debate in the Oxford Union against Humphrey Berkeley, M.P., and Lord Stonham, with, on my side, Malcolm X, who was shortly afterwards assassinated. He was a brilliant speaker and to my mind an extremely able and attractive personality.

In recent years I have also done a great deal of lecturing on Scottish Literature for Glasgow University Extra-Mural Department, and for Edinburgh and Leeds Universities too, as well as conducting classes in Edinburgh and elsewhere for the Workers' Educational Association. I even did a series of lectures in South Wales for the W.E.A. These were usually held in Miners' Institutes, which are licensed, and the bar was always open and drinks being served while I spoke, but the miners are very generous and with each round put up a pint for me as well, so that at

the end of the two hours' session I had always about a
dozen pints standing on the table, waiting for me to
polish them off, which as a point of honour I, of course,
did.

A poet's life in the modern world can be a very arduous
one. The above is only one of the occupational hazards.
That I should know a host of people in all walks of life and
in many countries is an inevitable consequence of the
range of my interests, which are well defined by Professor
David Daiches in a recent article in *Library Review* where
he says: 'What have the consequences of the Union of 1707
proved to be? What has Scotland become, culturally,
nationally, psychologically? Is there a viable Scottish
identity available to nourish the artist and to provide a
vantage point from which to look out on the world? How
is Scotland's present related to her past and to her future?
And what sort of Scottish future do we want anyway? If
Scotsmen of intelligence and imagination have been asking
these questions, and other questions of the same kind,
more and more fiercely throughout the last forty years,
Hugh MacDiarmid must take a considerable share of the
responsibility. His work for a Scottish Renaissance was
not simply a literary endeavour: it was bound up with questions of Scottish identity which had for the most part
been slumbering for nearly two centuries when he came
upon the scene. And not only with questions of Scottish
identity, for the question of the quality of modern industrial
democratic society, which prevails over the whole western
world, is also involved. The Anglicisation of Scotland is
part of the general *Gleichshaltung* of all western culture,
and an investigation of its nature and causes is therefore
bound up with social and political—and economic—ideas.
Arguments about the use of Lallans or the relative merits
of Burns and Dunbar or the place of Gaelic in Scottish
culture could not therefore, in the context of any adequately
conceived Scottish Renaissance movement, be merely
arguments about a literary trend or skirmishes preliminary
to the emergence of something parallel to the Pre-Raphae-

lite movement or the publishing of the *Yellow Book*. They were in the last resort not only about the meaning of culture, of nationality, or history; they were, to put it quite simply, about the meaning of life, and that is what Hugh MacDiarmid's poems are about. He could have settled for less. He could have stayed at the head of a Scottish literary revival and become a respected Allan Ramsay type of figure, writing introductions to Saltire editions of older Scottish writers and blessing the Lallans-writing young. And indeed he played some of the parts played by Ramsay. Like Ramsay, he has edited an anthology of Scottish poetry and combined creative with historical and editorial interests. But his driving vision of the fulfilled man in the fulfilled society—a vision which is as much responsible for his choice of language, his kind of imagery and the course of his poetic career from lyricist to discursive epic encyclopaedist as it is for his ever-shifting syntheses between nationalism and communism—would not leave him alone. He puzzles, distracts and annoys many of his greatest admirers. When he wrote those magnificent early Scots lyrics, rightly hailed as the finest things in Scottish poetry at least since Burns, he was expected to continue in that vein. He didn't. He turned to English and, to make matters worse, turned after a while to a special kind of Whitmanesque (up to a point) catalogue poetry whose essential principle of order escaped most critics. There *is*, it should be at once added, an essential principle of order in those long encyclopaedic poems, but it is related to MacDiarmid's vision of reality (both human and natural) rather than to his kind of Scottish nationalism or his role as a Scottish nationalist poet. A major concern of his has long been the search for what Hopkins, following Duns Scotus, called *haeccitas*, the 'thisness' and individuating reality of things and of human response to things. Nationalism for him is only superficially a political programme. At bottom, its object is to provide a means of responding properly to experience. His verse catalogues, like Whitman's, are suggestions of objects to be responded to put forward in such a way as to indicate the reason for and the manner of the proper response.'

It occurs to me at this point that I have not properly introduced myself and that many readers may have little or no knowledge of my work. And, lacking that, may even be unable to make much of Professor Daiches's remarks. In the immense number of articles which appeared in papers and periodicals in practically every so-called civilised country in the world on the occasion of my seventieth birthday in 1962, it seems to me that by far the best to serve as such an introduction is the following by Thomas McGrath, which appeared in the *National Guardian* (U.S.A.). It certainly presents the image of myself by which I hope to be known, and covers the whole field of my poetic output accurately, and I am glad to be allowed to reproduce it here, since I am surely my best—or one of my best—friend.

'Hugh MacDiarmid's poems [*Collected Poems*, by Hugh MacDiarmid. Macmillan Co., New York, 498 pp.] make up not so much a book as they do a literary movement; and the writer is not only a poet of the first rank but a culture hero, a political activist, and, as far as I am concerned, a magician. As culture hero he created a tradition in Scots poetry which has managed to "digest" Burns without the malign sentimentality of the Burns cult; as a revolutionary he was a founder of the Scottish Nationalist Party without losing his revolutionary credentials; and as a magician— the best evidence is in the poems themselves, where a powerful, wide-ranging, *reconciling* imagination is capable of making poetry sometimes simple, sometimes complex (lyrical, meditative, or didactic) out of the most diverse elements—work where Lenin and Rilke can exist in the same poem.

'MacDiarmid's work begins conventionally enough, but almost immediately he begins a long war against the decayed and perverted tradition of Burns. This satirical view of the "poet intestinal" is aimed not at the poet but at the Burns idolators who have forgotten the revolutionary content of Burns' work and who remember him only as an occasion for maudlin, drunken, "intestinal" celebrations.

'The energy which MacDiarmid put into this battle can only be estimated when we think that the Burns of "A fig for those by law protected!" must have been a heroic figure to the later poet. In a sense we might make a parallel with the Whitman problem in the United States. Our disciples of the good gray poet have generally got caught in the machinery of his rhetoric, dragged in and disembowelled; others, more wary, have turned away and taken shelter in the tall timber of academic verse; meanwhile the Whitman juggernaut goes charging across the plains of American poetic sensibility—making hay while the moon shines.

'In a considerable degree MacDiarmid managed to revive and purify the radical traditions of Burns. At the same time he was in a sense recreating the Lallans dialect— changing and adding to it—and making it an instrument for not only his own song but for a whole movement of Scots poets who moved along with him. In a sense this Lallans was both a signal of new Scottish nationalist feeling and an instrument for the creation of that feeling and these two aspects are nowhere more clearly evident than in Mac-Diarmid's poem, "The Barren Fig": "O Scotland is / THE barren fig. / Up, carles, up / and round it jig. / Auld Moses took / A dry stick and / Instantly it / Floo'ered in his hand / Pu' Scotland up / And wha can say / It winna bud / And blossom tae. / A miracle's / Oor only chance. / Up, carles, up / And let us dance."

'The use of Lallans moves from the nationalist poems through *A Drunk Man Looks at the Thistle* (the thistle becomes a prime symbol for the poet, like Yeats's rose, but more contradictory and complex, a symbol finally for the world that must be worked with) to the volumes *First Hymn to Lenin*, and *Second Hymn to Lenin*.

'It is in this area that MacDiarmid's work is best known in this country. One remembers "the eternal lightning of Lenin's bones" and that poem for the unknown soldier "At the Cenotaph", with its ferocious ending: "Keep going to your wars, you fools, as of yore; / I'm the civilisation you're fighting for".

'Here, too, Lallans begins to be discarded for a more direct and often a more abstract language, and the rhythms are less related to traditional song than to open speech. Now he can write a gloss on A. E. Housman's "Epitaph on an Army of Mercenaries" like this: "It is a God-damned lie to say that these / Saved, or knew, anything worth any man's pride . . .". Or he can set a soldier to speculating about what he would be if he were not a soldier. Probably, the soldier concludes, he'd be "The slave of a licensed thief— / One of the criminals I'm shielding now: Or perhaps he'd be out of work 'And that would make me a Red as well / Till I rose with the rest and was batoned or shot / By some cowardly brute—such as I am now'!"

'It is impossible to indicate here the full range of Mac-Diarmid's work either as to subject or method. From the kind of poetry we have described so far he went on to poems using a lot of Gaelic words and phrases, and, in *In Memoriam James Joyce*, to what might be called an "international" language full of quotations from many tongues. And he went back again, never content to fix on one style or subject matter. His poetry is in the truest sense experimental. I do not mean in the way of American "traditional" experiment where a back-broken free verse is often regarded as the limit of search. I mean it in the sense that for a true poet every poem is a unique experience to be worked out in some part at least in its own terms.

'In "The Kind of Poetry I Want" MacDiarmid puts it this way: "A poetry the quality of which / Is a stand made against intellectual apathy, / Its material founded, like Gray's on difficult knowledge, / And its metres those of a poet / who has studied Pindar and Welsh poetry . . . / In photographic language, 'wide-angle' poems / Taking in the whole which explains the part . . . A poetry that is— to use the terms of Red Dog— / High, low, jack and the goddam game . . .".

'This gives to the poet's work a radical, unregenerate, and, to my way of thinking, life-giving "impurity". This is the poetry of the whole man, and an involved man at that. There are very few such poets, willing to take the whole of a life's activity rather than a few special moments or themes as the ground of their work. It is no wonder that this "impurity" has been the despair of some of his friends and critics.

'MacDiarmid says: "I write now in English and now in Scots / To the despair of friends who plead / For consistency: sometimes achieve the true lyric cry, / Next but chopped-up prose . . .". But he goes on to remind them that it is the nightingale's song which most moves us, the nightingale "whose thin high call / And that deep throb . . . seem to come from different birds".'

In a box in the middle of Mr. McGrath's article appeared the following under the caption, 'The sitting duck that raised the roof': 'Almost everyone took a swipe at Hugh MacDiarmid, the seventy-year-old poet, who offered himself as a sitting duck by announcing that he was committed to Communism. John Amirthanayagen attending from Ceylon, asked: "How can such a wonderful poet be such a political simpleton?" Lawrence Durrell, bland on the platform, showed great irritability towards MacDiarmid in a B.B.C. recording. Muriel Spark giggled her agreement, adding that MacDiarmid was a marvellous poet, all the same' (from Roslyn Rosen's account of an International Writers' Conference, held in Edinburgh in August 1962, published in the New York *Nation*, 22nd September).

The 'trouble' was that some wag had put on the speakers' table what we all took to be a carafe of water but which actually held pure malt whisky with which in the course of the proceedings we refreshed ourselves copiously. Still, that was a great deal better than Sir Compton Mackenzie's account of a splendid practical joke told in Ulick O'Connor's biography of Oliver St. John Gogarty. At the Tailltean Games in 1924 Augustus John was a guest of the late Lord Dunsany in County Meath. Gogarty informed

C

Dunsany that John was a passionate teetotaller, then told John the same about Dunsany. So two of the most convivial men in Ireland spent joyless hours, John stood it for a bit until Dunsany tried to teach him to play the great Irish Harp. This was too much without a drink. The painter climbed over the wall of Dunsany Castle and walked all the way to Dublin. In our case it wasn't us but all the Moral Rearmers and other sour-pusses in Scotland who were 'sent' up and over the wall! Unfortunately the wall was not topped with jagged bits of broken bottles embedded in concrete—the only 'concrete poetry' in which I am ever likely to be interested!

With regard to the contest against Sir Alec Douglas-Home, I have been interested to find that at Templehof airport near Berlin, in London, and elsewhere, people come up to me and say 'You must be the man who fought against Douglas-Home'. They had seen me on TV. Throughout the campaign the French National TV and the Belgian TV followed me and televised many of my meetings. We were not of course allowed to appear on B.B.C. TV, or to give political broadcasts on sound radio, but at the very inception of the Election I had made recordings for half a dozen European radio systems and we got tremendous world publicity. This was repeated when after the Election I brought an action before an Electoral Court in Edinburgh in which I sought to unseat Sir Alec because he had been given—and used—B.B.C. and ITV broadcasting and telecasting facilities when these had been denied to me. It was the first time such an action had been brought and it created immense interest throughout the world. I lost the action of course—but morally won it, since the B.B.C. and I.T.A. have since agreed to give political broadcasting and telecasting time to two of the smaller political parties, namely the Scottish Nationalists and the Welsh Nationalists. They have not yet conceded it to the Communists, however. A friend of mine told me the other day that he had met someone connected with the case who remarked: 'The verdict ought to have gone to MacDiarmid, of course.' 'Well,' the reply came back, 'I suppose so really, but think of the repercussions.' That throws a curious light on the conception of even-handed justice. It is true that if a verdict had been given in my favour, not only Sir Alec but a lot of M.P.s, including the Prime Minister (Harold Wilson), would have been unseated. That would never do! On this occasion at least it was too much to expect their Lordships to act on the principle: *fiat justitia, ruat coelum.*

The Kinross and West Perth Constituency, lying in some 8000 square miles of the loveliest scenery in Scotland, has an incredibly feudal electorate. They are still at the stage of touching their forelocks to their betters. An American woman journalist I met in Crieff who was following Sir Alec told me that one day on a country road Sir Alec espied a couple of gundogs in the hedgerow. So he stopped his car and got out and patted them on the head. Always the perfect gentleman! The next man with whom the lady spoke was an old estate gardener. 'Aye, lassie,' he said to her, 'this is a queer constituency. If they were putting up a retriever dog as a candidate it would go in with a thumping majority!'

One of the questions I was most frequently asked was why the Communist Party put me up when they had no organisation or membership in the area at all and I was certain to lose my deposit and only receive a very low vote. I always replied that the fact that the constituency had never been contested by a Communist before, and most of the electorate had never seen one, was reason enough, but I went on: 'Whether we like it or not, it cannot be denied that Sir Alec must be opposed, since he is one of the key figures in this Election—if only a skeleton key!'

Since I wrote the preceding paragraph my wife and I have been to Edinburgh to meet Eileen O'Casey, the widow of Sean O'Casey, who was one of my best friends. She told us how when Sean was in hospital, and under an anaesthetic, a journalist had tried to see him but was told he was too ill and in any case unconscious as a consequence of sedation. But the journalist, inspired with the idea that 'the public has a right to know', climbed up a drain-pipe and got into Sean's room on the second floor. The nurse in charge was temporarily out of the room, but when she came back the journalist had actually raised Sean to a sitting position and was shaking him vigorously to bring him to a condition when he could be questioned.

Again prior to his going into hospital, another journalist called to see him at home. Eileen said he was too ill to be interviewed. A little later the journalist phoned, and when she replied berated her for coming between Sean and the public. 'Who the h—— did she think she was?' and so on.

Among the books on Sean now being published, Eileen said, there were objectionable elements. The simple facts of Sean's slum upbringing were not enough, but had to be exaggerated. One told how one day Sean was to be seen hugging a hunk of dirty bread he had salved from some rubbish-bin, and crying, 'Thank you, God, oh! thank you.' Nobody who ever had a word with Sean could possibly believe such a story. It wasn't in Sean's nature from the beginning to the end of his life to do or say anything of the sort, and the pity of it is that he wasn't alive and in possession of such a hunk of bread to throw it with all his force in the face of the writer in question.

We went to one of my favourite 'howffs', Milne's Bar in Hanover Street in Edinburgh, which has on its walls a collection of portraits and drawings, photographs and caricatures of me and of some of my fellow-poets and is our regular meeting place. Here Sydney Goodsir Smith, son of Sir Sydney Smith, the famous Professor of Forensic Medicine, soon joined us. He had with him a splendid street scene of Old Edinburgh depicting 'the Deil's awa' wi' the exciseman'. He had just had it cleaned and a magnificent job they had made of it. The Deil was represented by a spirited black horse on the back of which the exciseman, dressed in clothes reminiscent of those in which Burns is conventionally portrayed, was being borne away. The frenzy of that horse has to be seen to be believed. We talk about the Edinburgh Festival nowadays. It is a poor thing compared with the wild abandon of that painting: and just when we were exclaiming over it with enthusiasm, in came two other friends of ours, Dr. Jessie Kocsmanova (*née* Scott) of Brno University, and her husband Vincenz Kocsman, who had been a distinguished Czech airman in the Second World War. Such encounters—or *rencontres*—happen constantly in Milne's Bar; it is part of the real Edinburgh, not that whited sepulchre, which most people know, and know only.

2

Kaikhosru Shapurji Sorabji

No MATTER how many friends I wish to write about in this book I feel I must give pride of place to Sorabji. Few readers will have so much as heard his name. But I met him in the early 'twenties at the house in Chingford of the poet George Reston Malloch, and we have been friends ever since and merely to think of him, let alone see him, still gives me the same thrill I experienced when we first met.

Another composer-friend of mine, Ronald Stevenson, and the pianist John Ogdon and I, planned the other year to do a *Festschrift* in Sorabji's honour. We met in Stevenson's house in West Linton to make a recording of a discussion between us which might form the final chapter of such a book. I wrote an essay on Sorabji as a critic which I append here, and which is the essay Stevenson and Ogdon refer to in their remarks. But first of all, who is Sorabji?

Kaikhosru Shapurji Sorabji (b. 1892). English-born composer, son of a Parsi father and a Spanish-Sicilian mother. Also pianist and writer on music. Works include *Opus Clavicembalisticum* for piano—in three parts, twelve sub-divisions, 252 pages, taking two hours to perform—described by the composer as 'the most important work for piano since "The Art of Fugue".' Has banned public performance of his works. His real name is Leon Dudley Sorabji. And what has he to say for himself? He writes:

'I am not a "modern" composer in the inverted commas sense. I utterly and indignantly repudiate that epithet as being in any way applicable to me. I write very long, very elaborate works that are entirely alien and antipathetic to the fashionable tendencies prompted, publicised and plugged by the various "establishments" revolving around this or that modern composer.

'Why do I neither seek nor encourage performance of my works? Because they are neither intended for, nor suitable for it under present, or indeed any forseeable conditions: no performance at all is vastly preferable to an obscene travesty. Fortunately for me I have the pleasantest memories of two public performances, one by the admirable editor of *Musical Times* of a "Fragment" (a sort of musical sample) in a recital of his many years ago at the Aeolian Hall, and the other of the fugal movement of my First Organ Symphony by that superb organist, the late E. Emlyn Davies. I have always been deeply convinced of the vastly greater general musical intelligence of organists vis-à-vis other performers and E.E.D. was a shining example of this. Why do I write as I do? Why did (and do) the artists-craftsmen of Iran, India, China, Byzantine-Arabic Sicily (in the first and last of which are my own ancestral roots) produce the sort of elaborate highly wrought work they did? That was their way. It is also mine. If you don't like it, because it isn't the present-day done thing, that is just too bad, but not for *me*, who couldn't care less. In fact, to me your disapproval is an indirect compliment and much less of an insult than your applause, when I consider some of your idols.'

The tape of our symposium reads as follows:

RONALD STEVENSON: The purpose of our discussion is to gather together some of the loose threads in the book we have thus far written on Sorabji and to attempt to draw some sort of conclusion about him. For this purpose, I propose that we consider three questions: the first, Sorabji's racial and national aspects; second, his catholicity or—*au contraire*—his bigotry as a critic; and third, his place in the contemporary scene.

Sorabji's position is the reverse of Beethoven's in one sense: all the musical world heard Beethoven's music, which his deafness prevented him from hearing himself; no one hears Sorabji's music because his ban on performance virtually makes him his own sole audience. I invoke the name Beethoven because the case of his dedication of the 'Eroica' Symphony seems relative to the idea of dedicating or devoting a book to one man—in this case, Sorabji. Beethoven dedicated, as is well known, the 'Eroica' originally to Napoleon, but, when his symbol of an heroic destiny declared himself Emperor in May 1804, Beethoven destroyed that dedication. Instead he left the work to the memory of a great man. It may be questioned whether dedications are of any consequence at all, if they can be reversed, whilst the music which expresses them must remain the same. Now the idea of dedicating a *Festschrift* to an artist is by definition bedevilled with hagiography. This, unlike Beethoven's dedication of his 'Eroica', seems unchangeable. I would change it. As the saint's nimbus acquires a non-ecclesiastic tilt when he aspires to artistic expression (the halo that threatened to laureate the brow of Gerard Manley Hopkins became a dog-collar and threatened to choke him as a poet while it dignified him as a priest); as very few saints have ranked as great artists (one thinks of Jerome's Vulgate and the poems of St. John of the Cross); so hagiography would appear as ill to befit an artist, who is always on the side of the devils, as Freudian analysis would ill befit a saint, who is notoriously and inevitably on the side of the angels. Therefore, while I would consider it jejune and, furthermore, an insult to Sorabji to find him flawless, I would find it fitting and worthy, even as we have paid our tributes to him, so to wonder about, and maybe unravel, some of the ways in which he might reasonably be criticised. Cromwell had his warts and even the sun has his spots. Sorabji is no *guru*.

This book on Sorabji dawned with the East. I considered Sorabji as a great Eastern tributary swelling the main-stream of European music. Considering Sorabji's multiple

racial background in Iran, Spain, and Sicily, it may at
first be found surprising—disconcerting, even—that he upholds nationalism so strongly as to say, on a postcard to
me, that for him 'borders are frontiers'. In strong contrast
with this view, I found in Romain Rolland's book on Gandhi
a quotation from Tagore which I should like to cite.
Tagore says: 'It is logical that Mahatma Gandhi, weak of
body and without material resources, should prove the unconquerable strength of the meek and humble hidden in
the heart of the outraged and destitute humanity of India.
India's destiny is bound up in *Narayana* and not in *Nara-
yani-sena*, in soul force and not muscle. It must uplift
human history, transport it from the confused valley of
material struggles to the high plateaux of spiritual battles.
Although we may delude ourselves through phrases
acquired from the vocabulary of the West, *Swaraj*, home
rule, is not really our goal. Our battle is a spiritual battle,
a fight for humanity. We must emancipate man from the
meshes he has woven around him, free him from the
organisations of national selfishness. We must persuade
the butterfly that the freedom of the sky is better than the
shelter of the cocoon. In India we have no word for
"nation". When we loan the word from other peoples it is
not suited to us, for we should ally ourselves with *Narayana*,
the Supreme Being, and our victory will be the victory
for God's world . . .'. Now, Dr. Grieve, I should like to ask
you whether you can resolve the statement of Tagore's—
'In India we have no word for nation'—with Sorabji's
slogan, 'Borders are FRONTIERS'.

HUGH MACDIARMID (DR. C. M. GRIEVE): Well, I regard
Sorabji as a refutation in person of the statement that
'East is East and West is West and never the twain shall
meet'. They *have* met, most effectively in Sorabji. But I
don't regard the quotation which Mr. Stevenson has just
given us from Tagore as apposite in this case, because
Sorabji again and again has very violently reacted against
any suggestion that he was in any sense Indian.

STEVENSON: I took the Tagore quotation as universally valid—

MACDIARMID: Sorabji is not Indian. Spanish, Sicilian, Persian,—yes, but not Indian. And in the history—in the modern history, at any rate—of the arts, most of the practitioners from the near or far East, no matter how superlatively endowed they may have been, seemed to Europeans to have at least a trace of the babu about them. There's no trace of the babu at all about Sorabji. He has the distinction, in contrast to any others who have come into Europe from the Near East or the Far East, of being *au fait* with the whole range of European culture, understanding it perfectly, able to converse on the highest level with any practitioner of the arts in the West. The difference is that he has an intellectuality, a dialectical ability which, to my mind, far outranges the dialectical ability that the Communists in Russia, or elsewhere, boast they have. It's a much subtler dialectic. And it's that dialectic that has impelled him progressively for the last forty years, in his composing, to go for big forms. It's easy enough for all kinds of musicians with ability as composers to acquire a certain technique and, in an imitative or derivative way, do small things. But when you address yourself to huge compositions, such as the major compositions of Sorabji are, it's a very different matter. Many years ago now—forty years perhaps—he was involved in one of the common controversies in *The New Age*, when people who were baffled by his big works said, 'Let him give some proof of his ability by doing a few song settings or something of that kind—something within our own compass.' I strongly advised him not to do anything of the kind, if he was tempted at all. He wasn't tempted, but I strongly advised him, on the contrary, to go for bigger and bigger forms and not in any way at all to play down to the masses. He has kept on doing that. I think he was right. I estimate him extremely highly for the simple reason that he stands in such radical opposition to the whole tendency of the age, where you've got the emphasis on mass man, on the desirability of being comprehensible to the mob and so on. There's nothing like that about Sorabji, and that's the virtue of the man. He's essentially, despite his Sicilian or Spanish elements, an oriental aristocrat, with all the autocracy that that involves. But remember that in the finest reaches of materialistic Eastern philosophy, you've got the same phenomenon that you had centuries ago in the West, where the utmost intellectuality, the utmost difficulty of form, the most intricate elements in any of the arts, were yet comprehensible to all levels of society in a way that has long ceased to be true. Now that is the element, the Eastern, the oriental element in Sorabji that I attach major importance to. It seems out of reach to the modern masses. Well, there's no royal road at all: you only get from the arts in proportion to what you bring to them. And it's because he takes his stand on that utmost pinnacle of technical expertise, that I am confident that, in the long run (and it may be a very long run, the way the world's going today) Sorabji will be manifested as one of the great composers and one unique in the sense that he has built the bridge between the best of oriental art and the best of European art.

JOHN OGDON: I feel that, in another way, Sorabji is hardly covered by the quotation from Tagore, in the sense that his tremendous instinct to fight and not lie down under any sort of injustice is exemplified in that he does not personify any sort of *Narayana*.

Apropos the question of dedication, it is a little off the point but I think it interesting that Scriabin would never dedicate a piece to anybody; and thus never had to contradict himself.

STEVENSON: Did he not say that every one of his works was dedicated to God, and how therefore could it be dedicated to anyone else?

OGDON: Yes.

MACDIARMID: In the same sense that Dylan Thomas's poems were dedicated to the glory of God, but not in any definitely religious sense. I shouldn't say that Sorabji is a religious man at all.

OGDON: I'm glad, too, that Dr. Grieve has touched upon the question of size. There seems to be a common fallacy that it is easier to compose a big work than a small work. I don't particularly agree with this. I remember hearing a very short *avant garde* work for orchestra that lasted possibly at the most ten minutes. A very well-known critic reviewing it said, 'This is surely a good sign, that a composer would write a short work for orchestra without starting off by trying to write a symphony.' Well, I would have thought that, with the tremendous examples of the early symphonies of Mendelssohn and Berlioz, this would actually be an extremely bad sign. Surely ambitions should also be encouraged. Certainly the tremendous scope of Sorabji's work has kept pace with his ever-increasing mastery of the medium that he uses.

STEVENSON: Perhaps we may pass to the second point now, which was whether Sorabji as a critic gives proof of catholicity or bigotry of opinion. Dr. Grieve, in his essay 'Sorabji, the man and the critic', praises Sorabji's catholicity. Now, in certain cases, I would question this. Here is a quotation from Sorabji's book *Mi contra Fa*, a criticism of Shostakovich: 'Shostakovich's own account of his "conversion" to a better frame of mind more in accordance with the taste, or lack of it, of his Sovietical betters—is breathtaking in its abjectness, its slavish prostration to authority, and is such as no musician in the "bourgeois" capitalist West was perhaps ever known to be guilty of before a moneyed or aristocratic patron'.

That last idea may be refuted outright by the following

account, from *Grove's Dictionary*, of the monstrously ill-mannered treatment meted out to Mozart at the hands of his patron, the Archbishop Hieronymus of Salzburg: 'At the Archbishop's private concert Mozart excited the greatest enthusiasm though he was often addressed in that very house as *"Gassenbube"* (low fellow of the streets) . . . At his next audience he was greeted with *"Lump"*, *"Laus-bube"*, and *"Fex"* (Lout, lousy rascal and teddy boy). . . . *"Fex!* there is the door; I will have nothing more to do with such a vile wretch (*"elenden Buben"*). "Nor I with you,' retorted Mozart, and turned on his heel. Not having received an answer to his application for his discharge, Mozart drew up a fresh memorial, with which he presented himself in the ante-chamber of this Prince of the Church; but as a culmination to all the brutal treatment he had already received, Count Arco, the high-steward, addressed him as *"Flegel"* (clown), *"Bursch"* (fellow), etc., *and kicked him out of the room.* This took place on the 8th of June, 1781. Mozart was now free, though he had not received his formal dismissal; "I will never have anything more to do with Salzburg," he wrote to his father, "I hate the Arch-bishop almost to fury." '

Sorabji, in his diatribe against the Russian composer, says that Shostakovich concludes that music can be made, indeed *must* be made, to express an ideological programme, and that it can have no existence apart from such a pro-gramme. According to Sorabji, Shostakovich, writing of the old masters, says, 'Whether they knew it or not, they were bolstering the rule of the upper classes.' Personally, I agree with Shostakovich there. Of the old masters, Beethoven seems the only one who directed his music to humanity and not to some spiritual or temporal master.

Then Sorabji begins an explosive polemic in which he speaks of Shostakovich in terms of 'nonconformist Peck-sniffery gone mad' . . . 'this pretentious dunderhead, this ideology-besotted prig' . . . 'this preposterous personage' . . . 'this platitude-monger, this universal provider of the

commonplace'. To me this reads like the *Daily Express* at
its worst. Sorabji doesn't often practise palinody, but I
wish he would in this instance. I wish he would say *'mea
culpa'* to what he has written on Shostakovich, to repudiate
and disavow it as he did—to use his own words—'some
exceedingly ill-judged, foolish and unjust remarks I made
about Fauré in my *Around Music'*.

MACDIARMID: I don't know that you are doing justice to
yourself or Sorabji in that respect. When he made those
remarks about Shostakovich he probably was influenced
by two things: by the fact that he only knew earlier works
of Shostakovich; also by the fact that the Soviet authorities
had denounced more recent work of Shostakovich—he
was in trouble with the Soviet authorities. But I think the
thing goes deeper than that. When I referred to the
catholicity of Sorabji I meant, of course, a catholic acceptance of everything that was above a certain level in his own
art. But I wasn't taking account at all of anything below
that level. In other words, I'm perfectly certain that one
of the mainsprings of Sorabji's whole position is agreement
with my own belief that the good is the enemy of the best;
that talent is always opposed to genius; and that for any
major artists, it is only the best, the apex of the pinnacle,
it is only genius that finally matters. I know Sorabji well
enough—I've known him for about forty years—to know
that he is fully *au fait* with everything that has happened
in the history of European music. It used to be the case—
I suppose it still is—that, when a composer did something
difficult, a little incomprehensible to the 'man-in-the-
street', that he was apt to be told, 'Why don't you write
something that we can understand, something simple?'
What these sort of people failed to understand, of course,
was that a composer who was doing that particular kind of
work that they couldn't understand, had necessarily to
come right up through the whole development, the whole
evolution of modern music, before he was able to make his
particular departure. Because it is true that, as with an

apple, the development of the arts is not from the core but from the periphery. It's the periphery that accounts for Sorabji's particular quality, because he has got the whole core behind him and he's developing from the periphery. That accounts for his development and for the complexity of it. I know that as well as in music, he has a wonderfully wide-ranging, penetrating knowledge of literature and the other arts, and I'm sure that he would agree with what the American poet, Walt Whitman, said when he wrote that no poetry had yet been written that, in its magnitude and limitlessness corresponded to the potentialities of mankind today. These potentialities can't be put into headlines for one of the popular national newspapers, but it's these potentialities—the potentialities of mankind as a whole at this great turning point in history—that it seems to me that Sorabji is manifesting in his own particular art and in his own particular way; and that's why I attribute to him a catholicity that places him among the giants—creative giants—of the contemporary world.

OGDON: I'm not surprised at Mr. Stevenson's reactions to Sorabji's remarks on Shostakovich. My own were similar.

Then I thought: Sorabji has the habit, it seems to me, of making 'snap' judgements of composers, often on slender evidence, or only on that of a 'general' impression; there is the recantation on *Fauré* in *Mi contra Fa*.

When he admires a composer, his judgement is based on passionate inquiry and careful evaluation of individual works (e.g. Medtner's minor Sonata, the first Szymanovsky Violin Concerto). When he dislikes a composer he falls back on generalisations, sometimes *a priori*.

Certain works of Shostakovich—e.g. the 9th Symphony —may foster a facile generalisation against his work. Certain other works—e.g. the 'Cello Sonata—can sound absolutely inspired, as the 'Cello Sonata did when I heard it. Sorabji never goes to concerts—do these works *look* inspired in the seclusion of his study? Does the simplicity appeal to one of such complexity?

I am only trying to understand this strange cataract on Sorabji's vision—for I think I have seen him imply that, much as he hates Boulez, he hates Shostakovich even more (in an article in *The Musical Times*) . . .

STEVENSON: Shame!—

OGDON: . . . and this does *not* tally with his love for Rachmaninoff and Medtner.

Is there anything in Shostakovich's music to support Sorabji's thesis? I think not. The 24th Fugue, in D minor, does not seem to me as conspicuously original as some of Shostakovich's work, but even so is preceded by a *superb* prelude, which irresistibly called forth in my mind a visual image of Napoleon brooding on the field of Borodino.

Do you think there are elements in Sorabji that are actually superficial and unthinking? It seems heresy, yet . . .

MACDIARMID: It doesn't seem to me that it's the duty of a critic to anticipate the verdict of posterity. There seems to me to be a real value in the current expressions of the prejudices, the limitations, even, of a great man, and I would defend even the most preposterous (as they might seem) criticisms on these grounds. But taking his work as a whole—after all, isolated instances don't make good law —I don't think that either you or Mr. Stevenson would contest with me at all that Sorabji has shown a wonderful range of appreciation, a catholicity in that sense, a real *nous*, a real understanding of all that has gone to the building up of the European musical tradition at its very highest.

OGDON: Yes. And we should certainly remember the tremendous amount he has done for fostering interest in the music of Medtner, Rachmaninoff, Szymanovsky, Godovsky and others.

STEVENSON: That reference to contemporary composers suggests a smooth modulation into the third question, that of Sorabji's place in the contemporary scene.

In connection with that, I have been surprised and intrigued by two apparently contradictory comments on Sorabji's music, one positive, one negative, one in Dr. Grieve's essay, 'Sorabji; the critic and the man'; the other, in an essay on Sorabji by Frank Holliday. Dr. Grieve, in his essay, says: 'I can think of one other achievement on a similar scale [that is, to Sorabji's music] by another man who has gone on with his work despite the hostility of the Establishment and the mob: I refer to the sequence of 180 drawings, mostly in Indian ink, though some in wash, some in coloured chalks, and some heightened with water colour, which Picasso made between the middle of December, 1953 and the beginning of the following February . . . which take their place among the great drawings of all time. . . .'

Now, put by the side of that a quotation from Frank Holliday's essay on Sorabji: 'As for that music which reaches its peak with our modish composers; that painting that reaches its apex in Picasso and, of course, began in nineteenth-century France; that Freudianism that is the last word on the human mind; that logic that can know no higher goal than in the negative illogicalities of logical positivism; that functionalism of contemporary packing-box architecture; as for all these—what have they to do with Sorabji?'

How on earth can those two views on Sorabji—both by friends of his—be reconciled? I confess I'm stumped—completely stumped! Can you offer a solution to this?

MACDIARMID: I think it's quite easy to offer a solution. When I compared Sorabji's later extraordinary output with that period of Picasso's creative activity, I wasn't thinking

D

of the nature of content of Picasso's work. I was thinking
purely of that fury of creativity that led him to such an
astonishing output in a short time; and there is the same
fury of creation on Sorabji. It doesn't matter if Sorabji is
antipathetic to Picasso's work, as it doesn't if Picasso, as
a communist, might be antipathetic to Sorabji's work. The
ultimate reconciliation doesn't lie with us. It lies with time.
I'm convinced that they are both great artists in their own
particular media, but I think that they have one thing in
common (and it seems to me to be the very core of Sorabji's
position); and that is the recognition of the fact that the
good is the enemy of the best. As soon as you make allow-
ances—'Well, he was a poor man' or 'He had his limitations'
or 'He was living in an antipathetic country' or whatever
it may be—then you are opening the floodgate for mediocrity and they pile in on you and you are submerged
under a tide of subhumanity. Now, I'm perfectly certain
that both Picasso and Sorabji have been actuated by a
sovereign contempt for the mob. They have been concentrating on the apex of the pyramid of artistic creation, and
only in so far as they have done and succeeded in doing
that would they interest each other or do they interest me.
I'm not interested in mediocrity, in people who attempt to
do things. The final artistic judgement can only rely upon
what has been done and its quality. And from that point
of view, no matter how different they are, Picasso and
Sorabji seem to me in their work to have justified the very
different genius that inspired both of them. The ultimate
reconciliation is a matter of complete indifference. But I'm
perfectly sure, that apart from that impatience with contemporary fashions, so-called 'modernism' in art and so on,
I'm perfectly sure that on sober reflection, surveying the
enormous output of Picasso, Sorabji would agree that he
was a very, very great artist, no matter how different from
anything that Sorabji might have wished would emerge in
a world of genius. And I think Picasso also—I don't know
if he is a musical man or not—but I'm quite sure that he
too would come to a recognition of Sorabji's genius, in the

sense of an aspiration towards the apex of achievement. An enormous concentration, based upon adequate knowledge, and working without any regard for popular appeal, for monetary success or any other form of success; solely concerned with the service of the Muse; I'm quite sure that they would both be reconciled on that level.

OGDON: Well, I do agree with Dr. Grieve that it is in the fury of creative artistry that one can find the common link between Sorabji and Picasso.

I felt that Dr. Grieve's quotation from Wagner was very apropos: that music blots out civilisation as sunshine does lamplight. On my only meeting with Sorabji I asked him who, in the composers of the past, he felt the greatest affinity with; and he did feel that, in spite of many things in Wagner that he did object to, the side of Wagner that Joyce would call 'kinetic', he did feel a great affinity with the long melodic lines and the tremendous large-scale architecture of Wagner. And I think, also, in the directions which Sorabji gives for the performance of his music— —such as 'oscure', 'sordamente', 'catastofico', etc.—one may feel something perhaps of the pessimistic anarchist which one can feel in Wagner at times. Possibly it's also hidden deep in Sorabji at certain times. In the finest parts of his music there is an almost Parsifal-like solemnity. Again the directions give the clue: 'con solemnita', 'pontificale', 'grave e severo'.

Reverting to the question of Picasso, I feel the musician with whom he might best be compared is Stravinsky; though I think Picasso is the more considerable figure.

STEVENSON: I'm wondering how we can reconcile the idea of Sorabji and Picasso as two contemporary figures who seem to be in mutual opposition, with the quotation from Orage in Dr. Grieve's essay: the comparison between the critic and the judge and the suggestion that it is as possible for a fine critic to reach as certain a conclusion as a fine judge. Dr. Grieve and Mr. Holliday are both discerning critics, yet they arrive at diametrically different conclusions respecting Sorabji's alleged affinity with or antipathy to Picasso. And I remember just now that Van Dieren, who was a much respected and even revered friend of Sorabji (a friend whose opinions Sorabji also respected and revered), also writes with great praise of Picasso in one of his books —either in his Epstein Monograph or in his essays, *Down among the Deadmen.*

The same kind of situation cropped up when I was writing the chapter on Sorabji's affinities. I discovered that, while Sorabji and Van Dieren were kindred spirits, Sorabji emptied basketfuls of praise on Max Reger while Van Dieren had nothing but scorn for Reger, characterising his music as 'flat-footed'.

OGDON: It does strike me that Sorabji instances what must be one of Reger's greatest works, the B minor Variations for piano on a theme of Bach; and if Van Dieren had in mind perhaps the orchestral Variations and Fugue on a theme by Mozart by Reger, one does see the flat-footedness coming through, whereas, in the greater solemnity of the work based on Bach, it does seem to work much better.

MACDIARMID: The tests that we bring to these things—if you imagine that you find a certain contradictoriness in the statements—can't be the tests of mere logicality. There are no co-ordinates. We're talking, I presume, in all these cases—Picasso, Sorabji, Reger, Van Dieren—of genius. Naturally, they may have certain things in common. They may have others which are utterly opposed to each other. But then, that is only evidence of the enormous fertility of human genius. It isn't necessarily proceeding— no matter how far you extend it—to any uniformity. There's no reason why it should, unless you happen to be an accountant or something. And Sorabji is just as far removed from accountancy as I am—or Mr. Stevenson or Mr. Ogdon!

STEVENSON: Well, the student of Sorabji's scores must certainly be an accountant in musical notes, if not in pound notes! And, however staunchly Sorabji upholds the Social Credit theory, society gets little credit as far as his music is concerned. Sorabji—by all accounts (though I confess I am no accountant!) the most generous of men—has in his possession the richest hoard of densely covered music-paper, the blackest and most bristling manuscripts, that any composer can boast today.

Are these mammoth scores, with their millions of notes, in any way characteristic of the twentieth century? I wonder. Their prodigiousness seems all the more pheno-menal in an age of Eton crops, short skirts, bikinis, abbreviated titles of organisations and business companies, of commercial TV catch-words and other symbols of the modern madhouse. One could argue, though, that Sorabji's vast scores continue the tradition initiated in the first decade of the present century by Busoni, in his Piano Concerto, and Mahler in his symphonies; a tradition that, by virtue of its requirements (summed up in encylcopaedic knowledge of what is necessary to the completion of a monumental work for huge orchestral forces), automatically ensures that its adherents will be few indeed. Other con-temporary composers who have maintained the monu-mental tradition include Shostakovich and Havergal Brian, as symphonists. The genius required for work of such an order is the species spoken of (all too glibly!) in the popular definition of genius which parrots the formula about 'infinite capacity for taking pains'. That capacity, in Sorab-ji's case, must be shared by his aspiring appreciator: just as James Joyce, who spent seventeen years writing *Finnegans Wake*, nonchalantly expected his reader to devote the same number of years to mastering the book.

To revert to *Opus Clavicembalisticum*. A work of three hours' duration in the 'black and white' sonorities of the piano keyboard, without recourse to the more exotic palette of the full orchestra, is a conception of colossal ambition. Its monochrome, in such vast stretches, makes it extremely difficult to grasp as a whole. And in the composition of the thing, miscalculations must become well-nigh unavoidable. But, of course (and thank heaven!), one can admire and enjoy a work in spite of miscalculations.

OGDON: One admires the 'Goldberg' Variations in spite of the fact that Busoni felt it necessary to cut ten of the thirty variations in performance.

MACDIARMID: The assumption that underlies that question raises the question that's so often raised today in discussion of this kind: the problem of communication. If it's a question of appealing to the public, Sorabji's out from the word 'go'. But then he's not conceiving of that. Why should he? If his public is only an idea of himself alone, that's adequate for his particular work. There's no particular reason why he should want to communicate beyond that. And certainly in so far as I know Sorabji, he would only want to communicate with his own intellectual and spiritual peers. Why should he lower his standard to make himself popular with people of less perception, less receptivity? Of course not.

STEVENSON: But I do feel that this is a 'sunspot' in Sorabji's work. And by using the word 'sunspot' I imply admiration as well as criticism. His musical speech does not know the vernacular. Yet I recall that some of the profoundest statements have been uttered in the vernacular: even Christ spoke a dialect. In the music of the twentieth century the common speech of folk song has enriched the work of such fine composers as Bartok and Janacek; and even Busoni, for whose Piano Concerto Sorabji has expressed unqualified admiration, has in that work employed Italian popular airs with brilliant effect. This popular aspect can be found in so many—I was going to say, so many great ones; but there aren't many great ones; 'the few great ones' should have been the phrase. Dozens of phrases from Shakespeare have been absorbed into common parlance in Britain; the same can be said for Dante in Italy; the difference is that in Britain most people don't know it's Shakespeare they're quoting, whereas in Italy they do know it is Dante. A few years ago, on O'Connell Bridge in Dublin, an Irish tramp quoted Yeats to me. I said, 'Could you direct me to the Abbey Theatre, please?' and he replied, correcting me with kindly reproof, 'You mean Yeats's theatre'; and he proceeded to quote Yeats to me. That old tramp wasn't drunk—except with the spirit of old Eire. Within Britain, it takes drink to make people uninhibited enough to wax poetical. Yeats—who by no means played to galleryites or groundlings—penetrated to the proletarian. Sorabji doesn't. His peculiar lunar aloofness appeals to me—appeals to us three—but does not appeal to many. Perhaps it's because of Sorabji's amphibious birthright that he lacks a popular aspect, which always seems to stem from a definite national element. (One thinks of Robert Burns and other national and, at the same time, international artists.)

MACDIARMID: It's impossible for him, of course, to have the immediate nationalist appeal, which by analogy can be accepted by people of other nationalities. His origins were, as you've said, very mixed: Spanish, Sicilian, Persian, and so on. But I think there's something else divides him, and that's the sheer intellectuality of his work. The great mass of people hate that like anything. Yet it seems to me at the present time, at this great turning-point in history, we are just at a point where the arts may be coming into their own. The drones everywhere are going down the drain; through automation, cybernetics, there's going to be no work in the future for the stupid. There must be an enormous mutation of the human species, and that mutation can only be towards higher intellectuality. You've cited Shakespeare, Dante, and others, the acknowledged and great names in their particular media. They had this communicability, this popular element. Exactly. That's been the historical process. But the argument is a circular argument, invalid in logic, just for that reason. No, I think Sorabji is on the right lines, in view of the future. I mean, he's not going to win recognition at the present time. There's too much bastard democracy about, too much hypocrisy. But I think he's on the right line for recognition in the future. I've never had the slightest qualms about the advice I was privileged to give him forty years ago or so, to go for bigger and bigger works. I'm all for GIANTISM in the arts. Everything that means the expansion of creative genius to a point where all the little people simply can't comprehend it and are excluded automatically.

OGDON: Perhaps, as Mr. Stevenson says, the amphibious birthright goes some way to explain why Sorabji has not got, in the best sense, an appeal to the people. For instance, I think that an Indian *raga*, when performed in India, might have this appeal. In England, of course, it is esoteric, 'Third Programme'; a thesis could be written on it. Similarly, perhaps, if one performed *Opus Clavicemballisticum* in Tokyo—who knows? I think the only part of Sorabji's work that I know where one can, perhaps, see him desiring this appeal, is in the Third Piano Sonata, where he does, on certain occasions, put the indication *en dansant* (in the style of a dance). And there's also, of course, the *Fantasia Hespanica*, which might indeed have had a certain popularity with more frequent performance.

This ended our recording, and if it seems that some of my arguments are inconsistent and that I brushed aside some contradictions very cavalierly, the reason is simply that I never forget what Conrad says: 'The part of the inexplicable should be allowed for in appraising the conduct of men in a world where no explanation is final.'

My essay is concerned particularly with Sorabji as a critic and great musicologist.

'There is delight in singing, tho' none
Hear beside the singer . . .'
W. S. Landor: *To Robert Browning*

'His volant touch,
Instinct through all proportions low and high,
Fled and pursued transverse the resonant fugue'.
Milton: *Paradise Lost*

'Music,' said Wagner, 'blots out our
entire civilisation, as sunshine does lamplight.'

Paul Valéry was right when he wrote: '*Tout veritable poète est necessairement un critique de premier ordre.*' That is still truer of composers of consequences, in the course of their own work at least, if fewer of them have given us critical writings, and far fewer still, critical writings that did them any sort of justice. Sorabji, however, is unquestionably '*un critique de premier ordre*'. As with our mutual friend, the late Denis Saurat, '*mon admiration pour Sorabji est totale*' and it is largely due to community of insight—to the fact that faced with what Jacques Barzun says ('One need not be a practitioner to see that "Artists" have painted themselves into a corner. There is nothing left for them to "say" in any manner that relies on mind. Every conceivable stance, all imaginable devices have been tried, combined and parodied. The heedless prolongations into our century of the several Romantic styles, their dilution, over-development, or self-conscious avoidance, have driven our most gifted men literally out of their minds and into the realm of gesture, where the most random is the truest.') Nor is this situation confined to the plastic arts. An experienced critic of new music, who is also a composer and a musicologist, Mr. Richard Goldman supplies in a critique of Stravinsky's latest work a confirmation of the view that the arts have come to rest in a Grand Central Terminal. Speaking of Stravinsky's long search through the past for musical substance that might be fertile, Mr.

Goldman concedes 'the inevitability, in our anxious and
history-conscious age, of the artistic ransacking of the past
in search of a companionship that Mozart and Beethoven
no longer provide. They are not only too big for us, on a
different scale, but represent a different relation to civilisation.' And he considers the likelihood that 'harmony is
dead, that the composers of the eighteenth and nineteenth
centuries have explored all the possibilities of what we
have come to call traditional harmony, and that the
composer today can add nothing to what they have left us.'
'This relation of past to present, taken together with
enormous verbalism that goes with the slightest of new
works, leads the critic to conclude: "I fear that (like Weber
who so analysed music that only style remains) enough like-
minded activists on the periphery of art will succeed in
analysing music out of existence." ' Mr. Goldman mentions
in passing that Stravinsky may wind up exploring electronic music. The remark is a clue to the logical course
dictated by the exhaustion of the past. It tells us of the
abolitionists' second purpose, which is to develop a new
consciousness, pure and unheard of. So far the sounds of
electronic music are meaningless, like the drippings and
droppings of the abstract expressionists and action painters,
like the words and images that the beat poets seek to capture
with a tape-recorder during their mindless monologues or
in the trances of drug-taking. The search is for materials
absolutely disinfected from Art and ideas. Each kind of
artist wants to come upon, overhear, or summon forth something that shall in no way be remembered literature, music
or painting. The suspension of intent is to preclude in the
'act' any habitual choosing of the material or censoring of
the sensibility. The aim is to flee from the previously
actualised and also from the prescient foreshadowing. It
is a sacrificial effort, a true anti-mental education; we react
in precisely like fashion.

Even if Messrs. Barzun and Goldman were right—even
if 'The Eye' (significantly the name of Sorabji's house near

Cerne-Abbas in Dorset, and an eye with an ample, not to say most exceptionally extensive, panoramic purview of past and present) should fail in these circumstances to telegraph me a sly wink—I am certain that Sorabji's response would be, as Oliver St. John Gogarty expressed it in these lines:

> 'Our friends go with us as we go
> Down the long path where Beauty wends,
> Where all we love forgathers, so
> Why should we fear to join our friends?
>
> Who would survive them to outlast
> His children; to outwear his fame—
> Left when the triumph has gone past—
> To win from Age, not Time, a name?
>
> Then do not shudder at the knife
> That Death's indifferent hand drives home,
> But with the Strivers leave the Strife,
> Nor, after Caesar, skulk in Rome.'

No matter what efforts may be made to make our flesh creep at the news of a painting-machine like Jean Tinguely's to produce unexpected designs, or of the recording of factory noises as the makings of music, like the composers of *musique concrete* or of poets, painters, and serial composers feeling impelled to rely on chance motions, scattered points or number systems as a means of avoiding the *déjà vue*, Sorabji is incapable of being affected in the sense of deflected from his tremendous and unremitting output by so-called 'critics' or prophets of woe who point to the overwhelming trend of the times, that is, what the 'emancipated masses' want, any more than the trustees of a well-endowed and well-patronised museum of twentieth-century art managed to impress its director with their anxieties about the public 'approval' of the collection—he simply gave up his job on finding that the trustees had hired a polling agency to ascertain whether the unabating flood of visitors 'really liked' what they saw. In the same way (and not just yesterday, but over twenty years ago!) Sorabji simply cut himself off from the whole racket and forbade any public performance of his work. And I wrote in one of my poems:

'These things will pass. "The world will come to an end
But love and music will last for ever."
Sumeria is buried in the desert sands,
Atlantis in the ocean waves—happier are these
Than our world, for all is gone, no travesty
Of their ancient glories lives
On the lips of their degenerate sons as here.
That is what is hard to bear; the decivilised have every
    grace
As the antecedent of the vulgarities,
Every distinction as the precedent of their mediocrities,
No silly tune but has the excuse
That the feint was suggested, made easy,
By some once living sweetness . . .
Is not the rich fruit of the Arbor Vitae
Which is all antiquity and no decay
Rejected because of its rough concealing rind
By the forest pigs, though it contains meat
Of heart-succouring savour and drink of brain-renewing
    power?
Beside it, Tartar-like, sits the times' civility
And eats its dead dog off a golden dish.
The abomination of desolation is always in the holy
    places.'

In a typical recent letter to me, Sorabji wrote: 'Yes, thank you, I am very well indeed, in fact better than I've been all my life, though the corpus of my work has grown vastly since I last wrote to you. Five immense piano works have been completed, all of them as big or even bigger than Opus Clavicembalisticum, i.e. the Opus Archimagicum, the Tantrik Symphony, the Sequentia Cyclia, the

Second Symphony for Piano, and now the Third, on which I am actually working. All these works are *enormous*. The Tantrik Symphony has seven movements each named after the Chakra. The Opus Archimagicum has two enormous sections named respectively the lesser and great Arcana (allusions to Tarot lore). The Sequentia Cyclica, which, with your[1] Opus Clavicembalisticum, the Tantrik Symphony, and the Second Piano Symphony, I regard as my most mature and important piano works, consists of twenty-seven movements each based on Dies Irae. Then there is also the vast Jami Symphony for very large orchestra, two five part wordless choruses and a high baritone soloist in the final Cantico movement. He is the only person in the whole crowd who has any words to sing . . . and he sings Edward Brown's translation of a mystical poem of Jami ("In solitude where Being signless dwells apart from all duality"). Also there is the third Organ Symphony, likewise a vast recent work, and a more recent work for piano and orchestra dedicated to my near and great friend John Ireland, Opus Clavisymphonicum, a sort of symphony with a very important piano part. It's not all that vast, the full score being only 300 pp., modest compared with the Jami Symphony which is nearly 1000 pp. . . . Utterly out of the fashion, aren't I? And *glory in being so*! By the way, I was asked by a friend who has been asked to do a short study on me to give him my artistic Credo as you might say. It may amuse you to have a copy, viz. For the present-day idols, the Stravinskys, the Hindemiths, the Schonberg lickspittles, offshoots and toadies, I have nothing but loathing, execration and contempt. As for serialism . . . well! This is nothing but jigsaw in terms of notes instead of words. They are always prattling of the intense logic of it all . . . Ebbene . . . it is possible to conduct an argument that is syllogistically flawless from premises that are inherently nonsensical, reaching a logically sound conclusion but one that is factually nonsensical. So it is with

1. This refers to the fact that Sorabji did the present writer the honour of dedicating Opus Clavembalisticum to him.

the tone-rowers, serialists, and all the rest of them. One
of them shatteringly exposed himself recently when he
said that he had adopted serial technique 'because he was
repeating himself' when writing in a more reasonable and
traditional manner. The implication you see being that
this wouldn't be so noticeable when what he is pleased to
call his musical "thought" is tricked out in serial twaddle!
and, another priceless give-away, *The Times* recently blew
the *gaffe* even more shatteringly on the whole tawdry set-up
when it said that you have to be a much better composer
deliberately to turn your back on fashionable "developments"—again the implications being that if you bedizen
yourself with tone-rows, serialism, and the rest of it it
isn't likely to be so immediately obvious that you are a
fraud. Can you beat it? But there, as Goethe said, Gegen
Dummheit streben die Gutterselbst vergebens . . . and we
live in probably one of the silliest epochs of all time.'

When I think of Sorabji accomplishing this stupendous
tale of work in his Dorset retreat—a little island surrounded with the wild waters of the new 'barbarism', the
rising tide of sub-humanity, when the very sky seems
darkening in an eclipse of human hope—I can only think of
one other contemporary achievement on a similar scale,
by another man who has gone on with his work despite the
hostility of the Establishment and the mob. I refer to the
sequence of 180 drawings,[1] mostly in Indian ink, though
some are wash drawings, some in coloured chalks, and some
heightened with water-colour, which Picasso made between
the middle of December 1953 and the beginning of the following February, a period of personal unhappiness. I agree
about this wonderful sequence (made in a fury of production
—eighteen drawings in one day, and a weekly average of
thirty) that although some of the drawings are less good
than others, there are many which take their place among
the great drawings of all time, and in any case the whole
sequence is unique. 'Here', as another writer has said, 'is

1. They were published by *Verve*, the French Review of Art, Vol.
VIII, Nos. 29/30.

yet another proof of how ridiculous it is to accuse Picasso of lack of humanity or of charlatanry. Judged by the highest standards, these drawings are the creations of a supreme craftsman, and no one looking through them can fail to be moved by their human appeal.'

There is nothing new about Sorabji's position vis-à-vis mass men. Kierkegaard was right when he said that a man can find acceptance so long as he is content to be (or lets it be assumed that he is) just 'one of the boys'—all 'much of a muchness', but he will be sent to Coventry, driven out, crucified immediately he claims to be (or it becomes obvious that he is) above the ruck. This phenomenon has long been well known and in a poem of mine dealing with it I quote Pascal and Rilke to the same effect, viz. '*L'extrême esprit est accusé de folie comme l'extrême defaut. Rien que la médiocrité est bon. C'est sortir de L'humanité que de sortie du milieu*', and

'*Und wir, die an steigendes Gluck denken, empfenden die Ruhrung die uns beihah besturgt wenn ein Gluckliches fallt.*'

It has been a constant source of encouragement to me for over half my lifetime to think of Sorabji:

'Imperturbable, inscrutable, in the world and yet not in it,
Silent under the torments it inflicts upon us,
    With a constant centre,
With a single inspiration, foundations firm and invariable;
    By what immense exercise of will,
Inconceivable discipline, courage and endurance,
    Self-purification and anti-humanity,
        Adamantime and inexorable?
It will be ever increasingly necessary to find
    In the interests of all mankind
Men capable of rejecting all that all other men
        Think, as a stone remains
Essential to the world, inseparable from it,
        And rejects all other life yet.
Great work cannot be combined with surrender to the
        crowd.'

Sorabji as a critic—no self-seeking whatever, no expression of any personal grudge, or meanness or pettiness of any kind, outspoken contempt for all the 'helot usurpers of the true kingdon of awareness', for the trash culture and usurer-society of the present time, for hypocrites, pretenders, violators of the temple, but on the other hand boundless generosity, a readiness to share his immense stores of knowledge and insight and creative experience with all genuine seekers, the patience of a great teacher, 'blazing', as the *Bhagavid-Gita* puts it, 'with spiritual energy'. Those who have read passages of scathing invective from his pen, or again those who have developed an inferiority complex on seeing the tremendous range and exactitude of his knowledge, or who put the wrong construction on his self-sufficiency and detachment from the habits of the herd, may find it impossible to believe that Sorabji is the man I portray in the following pen-picture; but then I know him and they don't—even the few who have heard of him are mostly in the position of Tennyson in relation to Whitman: 'aware of his existence: he is a vast monster of some sort'. Here it is, and I vouch for its accuracy, viz. 'Candour and sensibility and catholic humanism are his chief characteristics. Keenly sensitive to the injustices he stumbles across in his wanderings, he is at once rebellious, irreverent, humble and acutely civilised. There is about him a perpetual tension, a trigger-ready quality that may explode at any moment. He is imbued with a reckless courage and a furious lust for life—the most unfettered man imaginable, disinclined to play anything safe, scorning money as a staff of security. He says what he thinks and lives the way he wants to live. There's nothing false about him. His honesty is almost shocking. And what he prizes most—and simply cannot do without—is always an unmuzzled articulation of ideas.'

No intelligent and honest-minded reader of his two volumes of criticism—*Around Music* and *Mi Contra Fa*—can fail to realise that Sorabji is indeed, as Pachmann once said of Liszt, 'alone on a mountain top'. From what other

stance could he have such a view as this: 'It is often said
by those whose livelihood is gained by mass-sycophancy and
who are, therefore, under an immoral obligation to lick the
foot of the public, that in the long run it is the best works
that are the most popular. We are in all seriousness asked
to believe this frantic nonsense in the face of the vastly
greater popularity of the *Moonlight* compared with that of
the *Hammerklavier* or Opus III, the *Tannhäuser* Overture
with the Prelude to Act III of *Siegfried*, the *Valse Triste*
with the same composer's Fourth Symphony, the E flat
with the A major piano Concerto of Liszt, or the same
composer's A flat *Liebestraum* with his B minor Ballade,
the second with the third Rachmaninoff piano Concertos;
Debussy's *Petite Suite* with his three Nocturnes; Elgar's
"Pomp and Circumstance" Marches, and *Cockaigne* with
Falstaff or the violin Concerto. After this, instances which
could be multiplied ten thousand-fold in every imaginable
department of every art, what becomes of the twaddle-
some sentimentalities about trusting the ultimate judgement and good sense of the public and all the rest of the
spurious, optimistic, discreditable, sycophantic clap-trap?
Let him listen, who would still try and believe it, to that
archetype of the "democratic" audiences, the Promenaders,
and hear them as they enthusiastically applaud some
wretched woman's miserable singing of abject trash as fine
playing of a great work, like Egon Petri's of a Mozart
piano Concerto, as I myself have heard them do times
without number.'

Again, think of Sorabji's sheer knowledge and immense
power of 'distinguishing and dividing' exemplified in this
passage: 'Except for the great Sonata and for the few virtu-
oso pieces which no more represent Liszt than "Salut
d'Amour" represents Elgar, or the "Romance" Sibelius,
Liszt is largely unknown to our audiences. The ignorant,
with their usual impudence and that obstinacy against
which, as we say in my country, the gods themselves fight
in vain, on the strength of a possible knowledge of one or
two rhapsodies, a Liebestraum or so, dismiss Liszt with the

E

derision and ridicule that is, in fact, the highest compliment such as they can pay. The superb Fantasia and Fugue on B-A-C-H, the masterly "Weinen Klagen" Variations, the great B minor Ballade, the Haganini Etudes, the *Années de Pelerinage*, the *Harmonies Postiques et Religieuses*, the great "Dante" and "Faust" Symphonies are scarcely heard once in years. Among the smaller piano works there are some numbers of the Consolations, the Valse Impromptu, the Valses Oubliées (one of which in F contains the origin of Scriabin's later harmonic methods), and the exquisite Berceuse that, within my knowledge, have never been seen on a London programme. The solo cantatas of Bach are scarcely ever touched—with good reason perhaps, since hardly anyone can sing them, or for that matter any Bach, properly. The magnificent "Jauchzet Gott in Allen Landen" —a genuine specimen of that instrumental or concerted type of music for voice and accompanying instruments for modern examples of which Mr. Newman pleaded some years ago, under the name of vocal concerto, as superb opportunity for great singing and fine musicianship, had one complete and by no means worthy performance in London during fifteen years. Miss Carrie Tubb, who was the only English soprano of her time, or later, who had the spirit of the matter in her and anything like the necessary voice and technique for singing Bach, once or twice sang the closing Allelujah so finely that it is a matter for acute regret that she never, so far as I am aware, sang it in its complete form. The very beautiful Schumann *Faust* I have never yet seen on any London programme, nor *L'Enfance du Christ* of Berlioz: and surely those whose mania is to root out the "odd" and "queer" might let us hear that very curious and interesting pendant to the *Symphonie Fantastique*, *Lélio*. Surely one performance less of the gimcrack "New World" Symphony is not too much to pay for such a privilege, and if the treacle-eaters must have their dose of soothing syrup, why not the Dvorak piano Concerto for a change.'

Where else in any book published in Britain, or in any British periodical, in the last half-century will you find

musical criticism of this quality? It has an unmatched
authority, derived from the fact that the writer under-
stands the creative process from inside, and has himself
made great contributions to the art or arts he writes about
and is on a level with the greatest of those he criticises.
Just consider its directness and force—the crushing and
indisputable piling up of examples, giving immediate proof
of the writer's competence and concern. As A. R. Orage
said, critical writing cannot be too simple and unaffected.
'It is a common practice for a critic to approximate his
style to the style of his subject; for example, to write about
poetry poetically, about a "grand, impassioned writer" in
a grand and impassioned manner. By so doing it is supposed
that a critic shows his sympathy and his understanding of
his subject. But the method is wrong. Criticism is not a
fine art. The conversational tone is its proper medium, and
it should be an absolute rule never to write in criticism
what cannot be imagined as being easily said.' I do not
believe that Sorabji ever once violated that rule. 'Easily
said'—but by whom? Sorabji is a superb conversationalist
—though not of the type who think they are exchanging
ideas when they are merely gossiping—and I can imagine
without difficulty his saying in the course of conversation
anything in his published critical writings.

Elsewhere Orage said: 'To abandon the aim of finality of
judgement is to let the jungle into the cultivated world of
art; it is to invite Tom, Dick and Harry to offer their
opinions as of equal value with the opinions of the cultivated. It is no escape from this conclusion to inquire into
the mentality of the critic and to attach importance to his
judgement as his mentality is or is not interesting. In
appraising a judgement I am not concerned with the
mentality, interesting or otherwise, of the judge who delivers
it. My concern is not with him, but with the work before us;
nor is the remark to be made upon his verdict the personal
comment, "How interesting" but the critical comment,
"How true" or "How false". Personal preferences turn the
attention in the nature of the case from the object criticised

to the critic himself. The method substitutes for the criticism
of art the criticism of psychology. In a word, it is not art
criticism at all. It may be said that if we dismiss personal
preference as a criterion of art judgement, there is nothing
left or only some "scientific" standard which has no
relevance to aesthetics. It is the common plea of the
idiosyncrats that, inconclusive as their opinions must be,
and anything but universally valid, no other method
within the world of art is possible. I dissent. A "final"
judgement is as possible of a work of art as of any other
manifestation of the spirit of man; there is nothing in the
nature of things to prevent men from arriving at a universally valid (that is, universally accepted) judgement of
a book, a picture, a sonata, a statue or a building, any more
than there is to prevent a legal judge from arriving at a
right judgement concerning any other human act; and,
what is more, such judgements of art are not only made
daily, but in the end they actually prevail and constitute
in their totality the tradition of art. The test is not scientific,
but as little is it merely personal. Its essential character is
simply that it is right; right however arrived at, and right
whoever arrives at it. That the judge in question may or
may not have "studied" the history of the art-work he is
judging is a matter of indifference. Neither his learning nor
his natural ignorance is of any importance. That he is or is
not this, that, or the other, is likewise of no concern. All
that matters is that his judgement, when delivered, should
be "right". But who is to settle this, it may be asked?
Who is to confirm a right judgement or to dispute a wrong
one? The answer is contained in the true interpretation of
the misunderstood saying, *De gustibus non est disputandum.*
The proof of right taste is that there is no real dispute
about its judgement; its finality is evident by the cessation
of debate. The truth may be simply stated; a judge—that
is to say, a true judge—is he with whom everybody is
compelled to agree, not because he says it, but because it
is so.'

No wonder Orage said: 'I have learned, in fact, to take

Mr. Sorabji as my guide in music; and I do not remember that he has ever failed me.'

No one concerned with music should fail to read Sorabji's essays on Charles Henri Victorian Morhange (Alkan), *The Voice in Contemporary Composition,* Medtner, *Leopold Godowsky as Creative Transcriber,* Bernard Van Dieren, and Karol Szymanovsky; and when they do they will of necessity agree with me that in him we have a phenomenon different not only in degree but in kind from every other writer on musical matters in Britain today, and that, if Jacques Barzun or anyone else tells of the actual or imminent extinction of the Arts today under the rising tide of the 'emancipated' masses and all the individuals and interests concerned to give the public 'what the public wants'—to say nothing of the complete annihilation of human life in a possible nuclear war—the proper reply of the creative spirit, as exemplified so splendidly in Sorabji if in anyone at all in any of the arts in these islands today, is Havelock Ellis's, who, communing with the ageless seer across the centuries, went right back to the vision of Heraclitus, who saw life as the sustained upleaping of a Fountain of Fire, and found that Vision is essentially unchanging. 'For after all', as Ellis wrote, 'we cannot go beyond the ancient image of Heraclitus, the "Ever-living Flame, kindled in due measure, and in like measure extinguished". That translucent and mysterious Flame shines undyingly before our eyes, never for two moments the same, and always miraculously incalculable, an everflowing stream of fire. The world is moving, men tell us, to this, to that, to the other. Do not believe them! Men have never known what the world is moving to. Who foresaw—to say nothing of older and vaster events—the Crucifixion? What Greek or Roman in his most fantastic moments prefigured our thirteenth century? What Christian foresaw the Renaissance? Who ever really expected the French Revolution? We cannot be too bold, for we are ever at the incipient point of some new manifestation far more overwhelming than all our dreams. No one can foresee the next aspect of the Fountain of Life. And all the time the Pillar of that Flame is burning at exactly the same height it has always been burning at!'

A great composer, a great critic, and a prince among men, I know nothing about Sorabji (none of the particulars men usually know of each other, family affairs, education, hobbies, etc.)—nothing, but I think everything that matters, everything, as Jeeves would say, that is 'of the essence'.

3

Patrick Geddes, Francis George Scott and William Johnstone

'Intellect is invisible to the man who has none'
                                        Schopenhauer

WHILE I believe I never went out of my way to meet and seek friendship with anyone, and the vast number of people with whom I have been on 'friendly terms' and with whom I have associated over the years in some of my cultural, political, and social activities simply accrued to me as it seemed accidentally, nevertheless an underlying plan discloses itself in retrospect and there must have been a selective principle at work which I did not realise at the time.

Just as Judge Ferdinand Pecora, in *Wall Street Under Oath*, says, 'the laxness of the State Authorities borders on the fantastic', so in every direction in which we can turn today we find equally fantastic spectacles which, like short-selling, are, as the late Otto Kahn stigmatised that operation, 'Inherently repellent to a right-thinking man', and it is in this general milieu of insanity that one makes one's friends—and finds them (and oneself) so riddled with absurdities that a decent human relationship is seldom possible, and the best friendship—like the curate's egg—only good in parts.

One should remember too that, as Francis Bacon said, 'there is little friendship in the world, especially between equals'.

My relations with my friends may be explained if I recall

how Major Yeats-Brown on one occasion tells of his
impressions of a French cavalry officers' mess. The talk
was infinitely more intelligent than one would ever hear
in any British officers' mess, but Major Yeats-Brown was
distressed by the absence of the *camaraderie* characteristic
of the latter—'there was no cosy intimacy, apparently
these French officers had little or no genuine liking or respect for each other. . . .'

I am with the French all the way in this respect as against
the British. I can dispense with any amount of jolly good-
fellowship for the sake of a little additional intelligence
and a somewhat higher level of conversation. But my
general position can be better shown perhaps by saying
that I am at one with Lao Tzu when he says: 'To speak of
loving all is a foolish exaggeration and to make up one's
mind to be impartial is a kind of partiality. If you indeed
want the men of the world not to lose the qualities that
are natural to them, you had best study how it is that
Heaven and Earth maintain their eternal course, that the
sun and the moon maintain their light, the stars their
serried ranks . . . the trees and shrubs their station. Then
you too shall learn to guide your steps by inward power, to
follow the course the Way of Nature sets; and soon you
will reach a goal where you will no longer need to go round
laboriously advertising goodness and duty, like a town-crier
with his drum, seeking for news of a lost child. No sire!
What you are doing is to disjoint men's natures!'

As I have said in one of the poems in my autobiography
Lucky Poet, apropos a Berwickshire friend, the Scots when
they are good talkers are the best talkers in the world.
With F. G. Scott, Neil Gunn the novelist, and Norman
McCaig the poet, in particular, all of whom have a Russian-
like capacity for long-sustained talking, not at random but
to a purpose—a thorough threshing out of ideas—I have
many a time talked from supper one night till breakfast
the next morning—ten or twelve solid hours of it—and
these spates have released a lot of our best work. (As
Logan points out in *The Scottish Gael* the pre-Union Scots

like the Russians were great talkers and all-night 'cracks' were nothing out of the common. The later reputation of the Scots for being dour, taciturn, and limited in conversation to a few ayes, ums, and imphms is purely a post-Union product, as is the loss of the old gaiety and abandon and the development in lieu thereof of the appalling modern dullness and social gaucherie.)

Worst of all is the way Scottish comics seem to have infected a great part of the population with a resultant incapacity for anything but brainless giggling and uproarious noise. The real Scottish comedians are, of course, quite different—men like Duncan Macrae, for example, or the late Tommy Lorne. But the whole abominable jocosity associated with the names of Sir Harry Lauder and Will Fyfe—and brought to a worse depth by Andy Stewart and Jimmie Logan—has spread like a monstrous blight and you have to pick your company very carefully to escape it. In Glasgow in particular it forces itself upon you at every turn.

I agree with my friend Neil McCallum when he says, in his book *It's an Old Scottish Custom*: 'In a profitable way the Scot has prostituted his Scottishness. Extirpated from his Highland glens and Lowland valleys, confined within a brick box in a city suburb, his values have changed. He has come to worship the meretricious in his nation. In a theatre he applauds the most grotesque modern travesty of a Scotsman—the Scots comedian. Where Scottishness remains true to type, in the rural areas, a Scots comedian would find a stony unappreciative audience. In the Highlands where he dare not trespass with his ill-fitting kilt and his cosmetic inebriation he would be ignored, which is the politest insult of all. The Scots comedian is the symbol of the way in which robust natural traditions become perverted and sentimentalised when they are cultivated in cities. The symbol of national pride and vigour—the peer of John Bull, Uncle Sam, and Marianne—is a Scottish professional figure of fun, an unsteady scarecrow on a stage. (The true comedians of Scotland are of a different tradition of vigorous and glorious theatre, in a class far apart from the second-rate funsters with whisky bottles and tottering steps.)'

Living for long periods as I have done in out-of-the-way places I have sometimes gone for months at a time without seeing anyone with whom to exchange a word, outside my own household. Yet what I missed most was not company and the conversation of my fellow-men (which, except in about one case in every half-million perhaps I would, if I had it, find for the most part only a maddening waste of time, a mud-bath of ignorance), but a heartening professional chat. But that is difficult to find anywhere—almost as difficult in Edinburgh or Glasgow or London as on a little Shetland island; and for the rest I became increasingly impatient with the waste of time 'bunkering up' to amateurs, and experience more and more in all my contacts the utter exasperation of the professional confronted with the tyro. I want (and can never content myself with anything else) a thorough mental appreciation and the stimulus of a good argumentative brain.

I have no doubt if David Hume had been writing to me, as he wrote to Adam Smith, he would have said: 'My dear Hugh MacDiarmid, have patience: Compose yourself to tranquillity: Show yourself a Philosopher in practice as well as profession: Think on the emptiness, and rashness, and futility of the common judgements of men: How little they are regulated by reason in any subject, much more in philosophical subjects, which so far exceed the comprehension of the Vulgar, *Non si quid improba Roma, Elevet, accedas examenque improbum in illa, Perpendas trutina, nec te quaesiveris extra.* A wise man's Kingdom is his own breast: or, if he ever looks further, it will only be to the Judgement of a select few, who are free from prejudices, and capable of examining his work. Nothing indeed can be a stronger presumption of falsehood than the approbation of the Multitude; and Phocion, you know, always suspected himself of some blunder, when he was attended with the applauses of the Populace.'

I was extremely fortunate, however, at the very outset of my work in getting into close touch with a number of men of exceptional brilliance—Denis Saurat, Patrick Geddes, R. B. Cunninghame Graham, Compton Mackenzie, and others—with some of whom I have retained close friendship ever since. Of all these men Denis Saurat, Kaikhosru Sorabji, Francis George Scott, and A. R. Orage are, I have no hesitation in saying, by far the most remarkable of all the men I have had the pleasure and privilege of knowing and associating with. To each of them may be applied the *Bhagavid-Gita* phrase—'blazing with spiritual energy', and what Ramiro de Maeztu said of Orage in the Literary Supplement of *La Prensa* of Buenos Aires is certainly true of these four. 'Alfred Richard Orage', he said, 'was one of the most influential spirits in England although not one Englishman in ten thousand would know his name—because Orage only influenced influential people. He had no other public but writers.'

In this connection I agree entirely with what my friend J. S. Collis says in the 'Tribute to Havelock Ellis' in his book *Farewell to Argument*. Calling Ellis 'the greatest living English writer; one of the greatest since Beowulf up to the present day', he says: 'By all the laws of life that we know of intellectually or by intuitive grasp, it is impossible that in occupying that position his stature could be generally recognised; for to be greater than the great and lauded ones calls for the possession of qualities that cannot even be seen by the multitude.'

So, naturally, Orage is known only to a few, while people like J. B. Priestley, Herbert Morrison, or Lord Beaverbrook are known to almost everybody, and, in Scotland, F. G. Scott is virtually unknown while Tom Johnston was regarded as 'perhaps the greatest Scotsman of his day', and, in music, while people like Benjamin Britten have an international vogue, and people like Ernest Newman and Percy Scholes are accounted great commentators on music and profoundly informed musicologists, Kaikhosru Sorabji goes for nothing at all; and, in philosophy, no one hears a

word about Denis Saurat, but the names of Sir James Jeans
and Sir Arthur Eddington were, for a time, almost household words, and even men like Earl Balfour and Lord
Haldane had wide reputations as philosophers. And, as
soon as one begins to 'distinguish and divide' and claim that
a man like Scott is not to be grouped with so-and-so as one
of 'our contemporary Scottish composers', and that,
indeed, with Saurat and Sorabji, his place is so high that
he is out of sight of the mob altogether and cannot possibly
have the widespread recognition accorded to a whole host
of 'famous' composers, and to the Beatles, none of whom
are fit to tie the latchets of his shoes, one is on that deadliest
of all grounds of contention which is also in such connections
the only one worth fighting on, and has against one all the
cohorts of mediocrities, led by the serried ranks of these
practitioners of 'the good which is the worst enemy of the
best'.

For it is precisely what these four friends of mine have
(or had—for three of them are now dead, only Sorabji still
alive) in common—an inability to suffer fools gladly or at
all; an utter incapacity for the brainless chit-chat which
passes almost everywhere else for an 'interest in' literature
or music or philosophy or what not, and is in fact intolerable to anyone who has a real interest in these matters or
indeed in anything, just as most writers and speakers on
spiritual matters may begin well, but slump swiftly into
platitude and commonplace, and, to be precise, it is these
commonplaces that are utterly intolerable in the treatment
of any higher human activity; these friends I have named
had a concentration on their own creative processes which
insulates them from the majority of people, and which,
indeed, infuriates the majority of people whenever they
encounter it, just as household pets are apt at times to
resent people who are always reading or writing or playing
the piano, instead of paying attention to *them*.

It is, therefore, not in the least surprising that four such
very different men should have been great friends of each
other. Saurat was one of the editors, along with Sir Herbert

Read, of Orage's posthumously collected *Selected Essays and Critical Writings*, and he was one of F. G. Scott's closest friends for many years; Sorabji contributed a great deal of musical criticism to Orage's two papers, first the *New Age* and then the *New English Weekly* for nearly twenty years, and he, too, was one of F. G. Scott's oldest friends—though neither in Saurat's case nor in Sorabji's was Orage the catalyst who brought the others into contact: Scott's friendships with them had been independently formed, and mine with them were formed *via* Scott, though I had met Sorabji independently before. After an intermission of about fifteen years—from my schooldays until the end of the 1914–18 war; a period during which I lost touch with Scott again; but in my case I certainly knew of Sorabji first (a different matter from knowing him) through Orage's *New Age*, of which I was a regular reader from 1908 onwards and, later, a regular and voluminous contributor.

But it is certainly no mere chance that there should have been these interrelations between these men; they are, in many ways, of a kind. And it was precisely on the same ground that I met most of my best friends—A.E., Will Dyson, T. S. Eliot (whose first wife was a Scotswoman from Glasgow), and Augustus John were also all friends of Orage's (though, except for the last-named I did not meet any of them through him, but quite independently). Indeed, my best friends are all part of an intellectual élite whose members are nearly all known in some degree to each other.

In the same way it is not surprising to find Sir Herbert Read (whom I have known since he was Professor of Fine Arts in Edinburgh University and shared the plinth in Trafalgar Square with as a co-speaker on behalf of Earl Russell's Committee of 100), dealing in his *The Origins of Form in Art*, with the phenomenon I dealt with in the conclusion of my chapter on Sorabji and saying, in the final chapters in which the spirit of our own age is examined: 'In their boredom and restless urge to action frustrated youth seeks to hurt, to destroy, for destruction, as Bakunin said, is also creation.' More exactly, it is a substitute for creation. This attitude, Sir Herbert goes on to show, is to be explained as the result of a failure to combine physical preoccupations of a creative kind with the development of mental activity. We have much to learn from Rousseau's dictum: 'Keep the child dependent on things only.' 'The cultivation of the arts,' Sir Herbert goes on to say, 'is an education of sensibilities, and if we are not given an education of this kind, if our hands remain empty and our perception of form is unexercised, then in idleness and vacancy we revert to violence and crime. When there is no will for creation the death instinct takes over and wills endless, gratuitous destruction.'

Pop-art, or, as Sir Herbert would prefer to call it, ante-art (or, as I call it, anti-art), is to a great extent the outcome of this state of affairs, for the pop artist does not address any audience, does not represent any point of view; he has staked everything on nothingness. And this leads him to pose the final question, which is not so much 'that of the role of the artist in society or the proper use of leisure in an affluent society, but rather the general problem of the decadence of our civilisation'. And he concludes that though pop-art may be only a passing phase, 'the social conditions that determine the emergence of such a kind of anti-art are not ephemeral; they are with us in increasing and frightening intensity. Until we can halt these processes of destruction and standardisation, of materialism and mass communication, art will always be subject to the threat of disintegration. The genuine arts of today are engaged in a heroic struggle against mediocrity and mass values, and if they lose, then art, in any meaningful sense, is dead. If art dies, then the spirit of man becomes impotent and the world relapses into barbarism.'

If 'art is the mirror of its age' it is an appalling thought that Scotland in this respect may give back nothing but the visage of Ian Hamilton Findlay (of whom *The Times Literary Supplement* makes much), who naturally finds my work boring and entirely unrepresentative of the true 'voice of Scotland today', and attempted to arrange a demonstration against me at the Edinburgh Festival Writers' Conference on the ground that he, and not I, should have been chosen to represent Scotland—a demonstration that to my regret was forbidden by the police.

I had to think twice before I gave Sorabji pride of place in these reminiscences rather than Sir Patrick Geddes (1854–1932)—he died at the Scots College at Montpellier on 17th April 1932 at the age of seventy-eight. Sir Patrick was a friend of Orage and other friends of mine too, and I was on terms of friendship with him for nearly ten years before his death. Lewis Mumford—whom I met at Geddes's Outlook Tower in Edinburgh—wrote that Geddes 'practiced synthesis in an age of specialism', the very practice that has been the theme of all my later poetry and work as a teacher and publicist, and, as the young Edinburgh Communist poet Alan Bold has said, that, along with his refusal to indulge in any form of careerism, has had much to do with Geddes's neglect. Sir Patrick's son, Dr. Arthur Geddes of Edinburgh University, said in a recent letter: 'I well remember the day in Montpellier when in *Les Nouvelles Litteraires*, we first read a few of MacDiarmid's poems and my father wrote to him straightaway; the friendship began with poems and response to them!'

Prophets are proverbially without honour in their own country, but even so the neglect or ignorance of Sir Patrick Geddes in Scotland goes to an uncommon degree and throws a very disconcerting light on our whole national condition, since he was one of the outstanding thinkers of his generation, not merely in Britain but in the world, and not only one of the greatest Scotsmen of the past century but in our entire history. The position is, I think, that his name at least, with some slight notion of his achievements is known to a small minority of our people, while mention of the name 'Geddes' only conjures up in many cases the personalities and careers of Sir Eric Geddes and Sir Auckland Geddes, but to most people simply that far older and

probably apocryphal case of Jenny Geddes as a hang-over
from the schooldays.

These three, though far more widely known, if only by
their bare names, are of no importance whatever in comparison with Sir Patrick. In one way modern Scotland's
obliviousness to some of its greatest sons is preferable to
the way in which other countries commemorate some of
theirs. A London novelist friend of mine in one of his books
has a passage about the statue to John Hanning Speke, the
African explorer, in which he says: 'Where the nursemaids
of Brompton and Bayswater gossiped stood the greasy
obelisk, with the one forgotten word Speke deep in its
compressed-beef granite. Than this emanation of the
London mist Africa had nothing more sad and mysterious.'

Scotland has no statue to Sir Patrick, but what I wish
is not that it should have any, but that something of his
stature and significance should enter into our national consciousness and enable us to share his wide-ranging and
indefatigable spirit and profit by his foresight of the future.
When the centenary of another great Scot, Sir J. G.
Fraser, was celebrated in many distinguished tributes all
over the world, I had hoped—in vain—that Sir Patrick
Geddes's might evoke a like recognition of his magnificent
contribution to the whole range of mankind's most crucial
problems and towards the support and strengthening of
'man's unconquerable mind' to equip it for the ever-greater
tasks which confront it.

This, alas, has not been the case. Yet in these perilous
times there can be no better tonic than a glimpse of Geddes's
great visions of the need for the benefits of the tremendous
change in our conceptual apparatus he called for and the
importance of the organic approach he so tirelessly advo-
cated. The humane arts of the physician and the psychologist and the architect, the hygienist and the community
planner have begun during the last few decades to displace
the mechanical arts from their hitherto central position in
our economy and our life.

Form, pattern, configuration, organism, historical filia-

tion, ecological relationship and concepts that work up
and down the ladder of the sciences; the aesthetic structure
and the social relations are as real as the primary physical
qualities that the sciences were once content to isolate.
This conceptual change is a widespread movement that is
going on in every part of society; in part it arises out of
the general resurgence of life—the care of children, the
culture of sex, the return to wild nature, and the renewed
worship of the sun—and in turn it gives intellectual re-
inforcement to these spontaneous movements and activities.

This reawakening of the vital and the organic in every
department undermines the authority of the purely mechanical. Geddes's prime significance lies in the fact that he
was one of the greatest prophets and pioneers of this
change. 'Everything I have done', he once said at Scots
College, 'has been biocentric; for and in terms of life, both
individual and collective; whereas all the machinery of
state, public instruction, finance and industry ignores life
when indeed it does not destroy it. The only thing that
amazes me, therefore, as I look back over my experiences
is that I was not caught and hung many years ago.' What
lay at the very heart of all his work was his concentration
of 'life and that more abundantly', or, in his own words,
'the great need: Intenser Life' for men and women. This in
this period of intensest crises in all the main lines of life and
thought, social and individual alike, I have been seeking
life more abundantly. Seeking life first for self then for
others; but now more fully for others, beyond my ageing
self. Thinking and doing, seeking for others . . . now and
beyond.'

Truly from Geddes's earliest papers on *The Classification
of Statistics* to his latest chapters in the two-volume study
of *Life* which he wrote in collaboration with Professor J.
Arthur Thomson, Geddes was steadily interested in technics
and economics as elements in that synthesis of thought and
that doctrine of life and action for which he laid the
foundations. His published works do nothing like justice
to his genius. He had a profound distrust of what he used

F

to call the modern habit of 'verbalistic empaperment' and
in consequence it has to be said of him that like Thomas
Carlyle's hero in *Sartor Resartus* he left behind bags and
boxes of notes, mountains of diagrams, and a huge bundle
of correspondence all of which has still to be gathered,
deciphered, appraised by the generation which will one
day, I trust, hail him as its prophet.

Geddes's unpublished papers are now being collected
and edited at the Outlook Tower in Edinburgh: but as one
of his friends has once said: 'Much that was essential in
Geddes will be lost, even if these papers are fully mastered
and collated; but much that was significant will never be
lost even if every book and memorandum of his should
disappear, for it is already at work in the minds and hearts
of living men and women.'

'Posterity might leave Geddes's papers to moulder as
long as Leonardo's', it has also been said. 'That would be
a loss, but not irreparable. For what distinguishes Geddes's
thought, what sets it apart from the special researches he
has drawn on or swiftly anticipated is the total personality
behind it. Since men value the equanimity of Socrates or
the vision of Plato, they will come, I think, to treasure
likewise the life-insurgence of Patrick Geddes.

'Those who have encountered in some part of the world
this great wandering and creative Scot of the nineteenth
and twentieth centuries know something of his total
personality. Those who now can only read his works, or
books about him, may never fully sense the restless physical
energy, the boundless flow of ideas, the keen delight in
living, that set Geddes apart from less fortunate and less
developed mortals; but these readers will be able to understand the sum-total of his ideas far better than the contemporaries whose first-hand contacts whether short or
long, necessarily failed to give them any detached appreciation of the man. Any single talk with Geddes, or even a
series of talks, was like dropping in to hear one hour of a
lecture that had started long years before, and would not
end for years to come.'

As for the ceaseless folding and refolding of pieces of paper into squares in which he set key-words or algebraic symbols for different ideas or systems of ideas—and these pieces of paper became the main method of his mental life in his later years—these not only allowed him to outrun his own tireless rapidity as a brilliant conversationalist, but enabled him to compress into a few inches the equivalent of whole libraries of scientific tomes. Slower minds could make nothing of such a method however. Yet Geddes was not the first, and certainly will not be the last, to try to devise a means of simultaneous communication on a variety of levels and with reference to a whole complex of ideas.

Like Thomas Davidson, another great Scottish philosopher and educationalist, Geddes's constant effort was 'to help people to think for themselves, and to think round the whole circle, not in scraps and bits'. He knew that watertight compartments are useful only to a sinking ship, and traversed all the boundaries of separate subjects.

This did not commend him in academic and professional circles who depend for their livlihood on narrow specialisations. It has been said that this is 'the age of the common man', also that this is 'the age of mediocrity'.

Talent is at war against genius.

And men like Geddes and Davidson are defeated by their inferiors alike in academic preferment and popular recognition. It was for the same reason that Carlyle, Hume, and others failed to secure Chairs in Scottish universities and nonentities were appointed instead. This, too, was the reason why creative educationalists like Thomas Davidson and A. S. Neill were forced out of our schools and driven to continue their work in other countries. It is well to bear all this clearly in mind today when there is a long-overdue reaction against the 'freemasonry of mediocrity' and a technique for genius is being more and more urgently sought —and will almost certainly be found.

'After early and extensive biological studies', H. V. Lanchester wrote in his preface to *Patrick Geddes in India*,

'he diverged into a comprehensive philosophy aiming at
the co-ordination of man with his environment which he
described as "the new humanism". With this aim in view,
he became an amateur, in the best sense of the word, of all
the arts and sciences, and endeavoured to employ his knowledge in raising the standard of living for all with whom his
activities brought him in contact.'

A recent writer has said: 'This desire to utilise all extant
knowledge in an attempt to humanise scientific and tech-
nological advance is one that is shared by Hugh MacDiarmid, and one that has occupied him continually and
features strongly in his poetry, especially the huge epic
which is still in progress.'

Of Saurat, Sorabji, and Scott, each working in very
different fields, related to each other only by the fact that
each of them work on the same exceedingly high plane, I
have no doubt whatever that they are three of the finest
minds Great Britain has had in my lifetime and stand on
an altogether higher level than probably all the other men
I know or have known, except T. S. Eliot, whom I would
put along with them, antipathetic to me as much of his
writing is. It will no doubt seem incredible to many of my
readers that I who have known them both personally can
seriously contend that F. G. Scott is—but what is the
phrase to be?—a greater man, a finer artist, a more distinguished personality than, say, W. B. Yeats, or that Kaikhosru Sorabji is a greater musical genius than, say, Delius
or Elgar, or that Saurat is a greater philosopher and literary
critic (or rather critic of writers' ideas, of the philosophy
involved in their work) than anyone who is at all well known
or known at all to any considerable fraction of the British
reading public, either as a philosopher or literary critic
today. But my reply is simply that I am certain of these
propositions and the reason why these three men are
comparatively little known is precisely that which is given
by De Maeztu with regard to Orage, and by Collis with
regard to Havelock Ellis.

To F. G. Scott's position and work as a composer of

song-settings I devoted a long essay in my *Contemporary
Scottish Studies* (1926). He had an immense musical and
general background and if he had followed the customary
practice of brainy Scots and devoted himself to anything
but Scotland he would undoubtedly have won recognition
decades before he died (in November 1958 in his seventy-
ninth year). Happily he took the opposite course, and has
paid for it in being unable to 'get his work across' save to
an infinitesimal public, even in Scotland itself. And yet his
work is essentially popular and should take, or should have
taken, the Scottish public by storm. But as matters stand
the Scottish public has been so debauched and distorted by
English over-influence that the very qualities that have
been most typically Scottish all through the centuries, and
that characterise all the best work in our national cultural
heritage, now seem to them quite un-Scottish, and in one of
my poems on Glasgow I have to cry:

'Scott popular?—Scott, whose work is *di essenza popolare*,
This popular not meaning plebeian or poor in content
But sano, schietto, realistico
E religiosamente attinente al profondo spirito della razza!
Scott popular . . . in Glasgow?
What a place for bat-folding!'

It is impossible for so distinguished and dynamic an
artist to win the hearing he deserves in the infernal babble
of a country of whose people today it has been well said
that: 'Even the most striking of them are lacking, in a very
Scottish fashion, in any real originality. The fact is that
Scottish individualism about which we hear so much is not
so strong a trait as Scottish democratic feeling. (The
Scottish Churches, for example, had no use for hierarchy,
and the levelling down has been pretty thorough.) Self-
assertiveness has taken the place of individuality, and in
these days when the the problem is one of the free personality, every other little Scot is either a Liberal capitalist or
a state-obsessed Socialist with more Methodism than Marx-

ism in his make up.' Scott is the outstanding exception to this general state of affairs in recent Scotland.

'Scott', said James H. Whyte in the anthology, *Towards a New Scotland* (1935), 'was at work on his songs long before the War, and to his stimulus and encouragement—he is a splendid literary critic—more than to anyone else are directly and indirectly due most of the conscious endeavours to bring about a revival of the Scottish arts similar to the revival enjoyed in Ireland in modern times. In emulation of him, a whole group of Scottish artists are attempting to express themselves as Scots and as modern Scots, as opposed to the old-fashioned hacks who exploit a debilitated Scottishness that is their only pull on the Scottish masses.'

Apart from a host of part-songs, Scott's published work is contained in five volumes of *Scottish Lyrics Set to Music.* The choice of these shows the impact of a first-class critical mind on the whole corpus of available Scottish song, with the important exception of Gaelic song. It is true as Mr. Whyte says that 'there is a very rich folk-music in Scotland, and a musical literature bequeathed by composers for the bagpipe—a classical music more akin to Byzantine music than any contemporary European music, marvellously rich within certain narrow limits. Francis George Scott has mastered this old music, and subsumed it in a markedly modern idiom, in which he has set some of the finest of Scottish lyrics, old and new.' But the fact is that although he has made a thorough study of the music of the pibrochs (about which even among pipers little is known—and that mostly a mass of mis-conceptions), Scott found little to his purpose owing to the paucity of good translations of Scottish Gaelic poetry. Writing to me of his last (the fifth) book of song-settings, he said: 'I have, I think, managed "to sing a song at least"—in fact not only sung, but printed musical settings of some sixty Scottish poems. I'd say of this latest batch your own "*Watergaw*" and George Campbell Hay's "*Fisherman*" are the best, though not likely to be the most popular. Hay's poem has been treated in a pibroch-like fashion—very restrained, mystical, and with a voice like Paul Robeson's behind it, should be something of a knock-out.'

'I've always wanted and especially of recent years, to work along this contemplative, transcendental line, but unfortunately (owing to the rarity of the material) have only Jean Lang's *Brendan's Graveyard* in Book III and this Hay setting to show for it. It may be that what I'm after is intrinsically Gaelic in flavour and in a long conversation with Hay in Taynuilt we discussed this point and he promised to send along anything he can manage either of his own or in translation.'

A glance at the sources of Scott's settings in these five published collections is interesting; twenty-six are to Burns's words, four to Dunbar's, ten to mine, and William Drummond, John Imlah, Jean Lang, Mark Alexander Boyd, Patrick Birnie, Sir Walter Scott, William Creech, Allan Cunninghame, and George Campbell Hay account for one each. In addition to these there is his *Renaissance Overture*, rendered by the Scottish Orchestra, conducted by Issy Dobrowen, in January 1939 (it has not been published yet) and symphonic settings of Dunbar's *Seven Deadly Sins* (this has neither been published nor rendered in public). Of the former—the *Renaissance Overture*—I wrote at the time of the Scottish Orchestra performance:

'The crown of Scott's work—which is to say far and away the finest composition by any Scottish composer (for there is no comparison between Scott and any other composer Scotland has ever produced; he stands on a plane of his own, immeasurably removed from theirs), this great overture is a magnificent challenge to all the suppressed and latent potentialities capable of creating a distinctive culture in Scotland on a level in keeping with all the best traditions in the whole range of our national history and the relative status any true Scot must covet as Scotland's due.

'It is an immensely exciting work, dynamic to a degree, even dynamitic; a superb summation of all the vital elements in our national past, ordered in the most masterly fashion and projected vertically into the future by a single horn on its topmost note—symbolic of the passionate spirit of the composer himself, his relative position to all other contemporary Scottish composers and to the whole range of Scottish music to date, and of his rousing indomitable realisation of the unparalleled spiritual impetus which alone can redeem Scotland from its present woeful floundering in the Slough of Despond and encompass the supreme realisation of our undoubted potentialities. In its own field the evocative and challenging quality of his work is irresistible; one would fain hope that it might prove so in relation to Scottish life too and communicate in actual fact the superb impulse which is at once its theme and its nature—but will the fat ears of our people hear, or must Scott say too, "I have piped, but ye have not danced"?'

The reception of Scott's *Overture* by the newspaper critics was, of course, precisely as might have been predicted. It seems to have shocked most of them by its sheer din and ferocity. Some of the church mice tried to exonerate themselves by putting some of the blame on the conductor, Issy Dobrowen, for being too slap-dash in his methods, but Scott wasn't long in identifying himself with the conductor's reading—much to the annoyance of these precious gentry! The real trouble, of course, was just the hatred and fear of all dynamic which characterises these eunuchoid creatures. It was amusing to see how all of them sang dumb about the music's significance—not a word about its implications.

A Scottish renaissance is the last thing they want. Where would they be then, poor things? In the meantime they are doing all right—financially, which is the only way they are interested in or capable of conceiving anyone else being interested in. The level of Scottish criticism is the lowest in the world. No wonder a correspondent writes to me: 'We've had the contemporary art show (organised by the Saltire Society in Glasgow) and some damnable attempts at criticism in the newspapers—so bad that I've been tempted into saying that all art ought to be incomprehensible, after listening to other folks' ability to comprehend!

With the substitution of the word Scotland for Norway, the lines Henrik Ibsen addressed to the Norwegian composer, Edvard Grieg (who was partly of Scottish descent, and from earliest youth a zealous republican—in the battles in Norway over the union with Sweden he was always to be found on the extreme Left, and so it was one of the happiest days in his life when Norway won her independence in 1905), might well be addressed to Scott, viz.:

'Orpheus woke with crystal tones
Souls in brutes; struck fire from stones.

Stones there are in Scotland plenty;
Brutes far more than ten or twenty.

Play, so stones spark far and wide!
Play, to pierce the brutes' thick hide!'

Scott was a schoolteacher of mine at Langholm Academy when I was a boy of fourteen or fifteen. I lost touch with him completely from about 1906 to 1922, when he happened to see one of my early MacDiarmid lyrics in *The Scottish Chapbook* and wrote to me, not knowing, of course, that the pseudonym of 'Hugh MacDiarmid' covered an old Langholm pupil of his. We met, found that I had reached independently (for up to then I knew nothing of Scott's work as a composer, though he had already been setting Scottish songs when he was one of my teachers in Langholm) a position very close to his own with regard to Scottish Arts and Letters, and realised that we had a great deal more in common—a deep community of insight. We were both Border men—Scott belonging to Hawick, only twenty miles from Langholm. After that we became the closest of friends and there can be few cases of closer collaboration between a poet and a composer. Scott is one of the few men, perhaps the only man, I have known for whom I had an unqualified respect. Simply because he so clearly and completely understood that ability of any kind

depends upon self-respect and was incapable of losing his
on any account. I think the world of him and his work seems
to me of superlative importance to Scotland. I have said
that in the last few years my work has not been of a sort
that was suitable for his purposes. I have regretted this
very deeply indeed, and would have done anything I
possibly could to have met his requirements—if I could
have done anything at all. But these matters do not arrange
themselves in that fashion. It has at any rate been a weird
experience to have so many of my principal associates in
the Scottish Literary and Political Movement quite incapable of appreciating Scott—and, though my own standards
were much easier, of such a sort that Scott would not have
tolerated their company for a moment. The Scottish B.B.C.
all along treated Scott very shabbily, not because his
quality was not fully realised; on the contrary, because he
was clearly so infinitely better than the run of Scottish
contributors on whom the B.B.C. depends, and whom it
consequently could not afford to have put out of counten-
ance. Scott blew the gaff on all their pretensions too
conclusively.

> 'Out-Haydn'd, out-Gretry'd, out-Handel'd, out-Rossini'd
> By mannikins a million times pettier still
> Than any of these were to their hated betters.'

And I was forced to cry to him (thinking in particular of
Glasgow):

> 'Who knows in this infernal broth-like fog
> There may be greater artists yet by far than we,
> Unheard of, even by us, condemned to be invisible
> In this Tarnhelm of unconscionable ignorance
> Where "everybody is entitled to his own opinion"?'

Glasgow, which in another verse I have depicted as
follows:

'Where have I seen a human being looking
As Glasgow looks this gin-clear evening—with faces and
    fingers
A cadaverous blue, hand-clasp slimy and cold
As that of a corpse, fingernails grown immeasurably long
As they do in the grave, little white eyes, and hardly
Any face at all
Cold, lightning-like, unpleasant, light and blue,
Like having one's cold spots intoxicated with mescal,
Looking down a street the houses seem
Long pointed teeth like a ferret's over the slit
Of a crooked unspeakable smile, like the Thracian woman's
When Thales fell in the well; and the smell reminds me
Of the *odeur de souris* of Balzac's Cousin Pons,
Or Yankee adverts, about halitosis, and underarm odour.
All the strength seemed to leave my body as I looked.
It sucked the blood from my brain and heart like a vampire,
"A hag whose soul-gelding ugliness would chill
To eternal chastity a cantharidised satyr."
And a deadly grey weariness fell over my thoughts like dust,
A terrible shadow descended like dust over my thoughts,
Almost like reading a *Glasgow Herald* leader
Or any of our Scottish papers,
Smug class organs, standardised, superficial,
Unfair in the presentation of news, and worse than useless
As interpreters of the present scene or guides to the future,
Or like a dread darkness that descends on one
Who, as the result of an accident sustained
In the course of his favourite recreation, tricycling,
Suffers every now and then from loss of memory.'

It is in keeping with my general attitude—and with the
fact that my best friends are all the type of great artists
whose value is 'invisible to the mob'—that I should not
only denounce all 'witch-doctors, chiselers, lookers-under-
beds, local Solons, bourgeois bonzes, trained seals, and
back-street Bourbons', but that, on the occasion of the
International P.E.N. Congress in Scotland in 1934, I should

in a rhymed welcome to the foreign delegates, describe the
prominent Scots they would meet in the following lines:

'As when tempestuous Nature in a torment
Pours out her prodigies and Heaven is rent
With fearful glories, Scotland here emits,
In speedy sequence to your gaze her wits
(Nitwits!) and seers, lords, priests, and business-men . . .
Nonentities in everything but name.
And, above all, her potent *pisseurs d'encre*
Who, subs and copy-boys, rank on (more) rank,
Thunder in the cubby-holes . . .
Do not commit the pardonable mistake
Of slighting them, for, though you know them not,
Their backstairs powers must never be forgot.
Their weasel minds the least of them quintuple
By underhand intrigue and lack of scruple,
And like a weasel pack they always go
Wriggling like one though twenty form a row.'

One critic referred to this as an example of 'the famous
MacDiarmid invective and ability to make ridiculous a
humbug or lambast a time-server, for which we are eternally
grateful'.

But apart from the unscrupulous money-grabbers who
scoop the pool, and the solid phalanx of mediocrities in
Scotland in whom it is impossible to awaken any interest
or appreciation in Scott's work, the other great overriding
factor that seems to me to have far too narrowly restricted
Scott's output is his lack, due to his age and the very
different generation most formative of him, of that mental
resilience to which Sir Winston Churchill referred when he
said: 'It requires not only courage but mental resilience for
those whose youth lay in calmer and more slowly moving
times in order that they may adjust themselves to the giant
outlines and harsh structure of the twentieth century.'

In December 1945, I published the following article which
is in place here since the situation has not changed in the

interval except for the worse, and for a long time now Scott's work has been kept off the air, while singer after singer of Scottish songs has given programmes confined to worthless arrangements by Mansfield, Diack, Moffat, Stephen, Cedric Thorpe Davie, and others. Scotland is worse than any other country in the so-called civilised world in respect of that tyranny of the repetition complex of which Michael Tippett recently complained when he wrote: 'We all know that the big public is extremely conservative, and willing to ring the changes on a few beloved works till the end of time. So that our concert life, through the taste of this public, suffers from a kind of inertia of sensibility, that seems to want no musical experience whatever that it does not already know. When this taste is indeed the national taste, the art of the nation certainly dies. But the creative artist is passionately determined that it shall not die. In fact totalitarian societies, which are pathetically conformist and afraid of the new, have had to stamp him out. They are afraid; even of the struggling composer with his tiny public. And what are they afraid of? I think they are afraid of his passion, of his violence, of his unaccountability. For it is a fact of musical history (and this goes for the other arts as well) that during the last half-century, or even earlier, every major composer has at the outset found the taste of the big public and its consumer point of view unacceptable.' So it is true of Scott, as Mr. Tippett says it was of Bartok, that the big public 'instinctively hated his creative integrity, and no doubt he, for all his courage, was hurt and daunted by this hate. The dilemma is not a conspiracy but a fact. Why does the big public hate extreme artistic integrity? How can a great composer go forward at all in what looks like a voluntary cul-de-sac? Surely the matter is that the very big public masses together in a kind of dead passion of mediocrity, and that this blanket of mediocrity, whether communist or capitalist, is deeply offended by any living passion of the unusual, the rare, the rich, the exuberant, the heroic, and the aristocratic in art— the art of a poet like Yeats. While

it is clear from Yeats' life and writings that in this very
passion of defiance an artist can find both material for his
art, and vigour for his despised activity. But he may starve.'
The Edinburgh International Festival has done nothing to
remedy this state of affairs. Its promoters do not care if
every Scottish composer dies of starvation. The native contribution to the arts is almost wholly excluded from the
Festival programmes. The article I refer to is as follows:

'The mistake of preferring Barabbas is nowhere so
prevalent as in Scotland today; the injunction, "Seek ye
first the Kingdom of Heaven . . ." more universally neglected than in any other European country. A little country
like Finland can produce a man wholly dedicated to his art
like Sibelius. And not only so, but a sufficient number of
people to recognise the stand he has taken and the incomparable national importance of it—and, accordingly to
insist and ensure that he be given his proper place and that
whatever encouragement and facilitation, financially and
otherwise, lesser spirits can give him in his high task shall
be his.

'In Scotland alone there is no such incentive to, or
encouragement in, serious creative effort in any of the arts.
On the contrary! Even the St. Andrew's Night programme
of the Scottish B.B.C. was a shameful *exposé* of our national
atimy and amentality. It was a ludicrously undignified
melange of worthless "arrangements" by Sir Hugh S.
Roberton and Mr. Ian Whyte, crowned by the partici-
pation of the unspeakable buffoon, Mr. Will Fyfe. Nobody is
allowed to participate in these ceremonial displays of
Scottish bad taste and stupidity who has ever given any
evidence of any serious purpose except the snapping up of
whatever fees are going. But, you say, it is the kind of
entertainment the public likes. No doubt. The unfortunate
Scottish public has been thoroughly conditioned to like
nothing else. The fact that they like it all right does not
alter the fact that it is just as entertaining as Hell!

'And on top of that Edinburgh's Lord Provost and his

associates are going to have a great International Musical Festival in Edinburgh, and imagine that Edinburgh will as a result come to rival Salzburg! Timbuktoo or Kalgoorlie would have as much chance of doing anything of the kind. Every distinguished composer and executant might be attracted to the Festival; the more they came the more they would emphasise the absence of their peers in Scotland itself and the better the programmes the more ghastly would yawn the abyss between them and the utter inability of the Scottish people to assimilate and profit by anything of the sort, let alone be stimulated even to try to produce anything of comparable worth on their own part. None of these things is, of course, the aim of the Festival. It has commercial, not aesthetic, aims. All that is desired is (1) to get some useful publicity; (2) make money, and (3) jack up a little the general illusion that the Scots are really a cultivated people with an interest in the arts. In short it is just another lousy racket, typical enough of a so-called capital city whose principal daily paper is mean enough to refuse to notice an exhibition of the works of the principal sculptor resident in Scotland on the ground that to do so would partake of the nature of a free advertisement!

'That's all that interest in the arts amounts to in Edinburgh. But this Festival will, of course, allow the Lord Provosts and the Bailies and all the rest of the nitwits to strut about airing a lot of quasi-musical jargon just acquired *ad hoc*, and posing as cognoscenti, patrons of the arts, and what not, for the benefit of the dazzled citizenry, while anybody who really does know anything about music in Scotland, and above all, the very few who have done anything worth doing about it, will be kept well and truly in the outer darkness by their successful and self-satisfied inferiors, while the cream of Europe's music-makers are 'enjoying' an indescribable series of encounters with village idiots and strangers to the district.'

What the Festival has done to stimulate the creative arts in Scotland is considered in a later chapter of this book, but certainly what lies behind it all, the cause of its lamentable limitations, and the reasons why Lord Harewood and his assistant deputy director, Mr. Michael Whewell, were forced out of their positions by the Philistines is clearly expressed in what the Lord Provost of Glasgow, Sir Peter Meldrum, said at the opening of the Glasgow section of the Commonwealth Arts Festival (an utterance that certainly would not only have failed to surprise F. G. Scott, but could have been predicted by him), viz.: 'I would have preferred if this had been a Commonwealth Trades Festival. I have nothing against the Arts. But we all survive by trading with each other.'

If such people survive, the question is whether the Arts can.

I remember, as illustrating our deep community of insight, that when I wrote the *Drunk Man* working on my own I had got to the point when I had ceased to be able to see the forest for the trees. I found the necessary imaginative sympathy in F. G. Scott and handed over the whole mass of my manuscript to him. He was not long in seizing on the essentials and urging the ruthless discarding of the unessentials. I had no hesitation in taking his advice and in this way the significant shape was educed from the welter of stuff and the rest pruned away.

Drastic treatment of this kind is particularly necessary in literary work. Musicians and artists do not require it to the same degree, but in writing it is fatally easy in the absence of such consultative and co-operative correction to forget that the essence of art is presentation. I was, of course, particularly lucky in having at my elbow such a determined artist as Scott who in his own practice was wont to eliminate to the last degree and concentrate, at no matter what sacrifice of pet material, upon the highest ordering. . . . While Ezra Pound did something very similar to Eliot's *Waste Land,* what happened in my case has been widely misunderstood. All it amounted to was that Scott read the great mass of verse I'd written, advised me to scrap a good deal that he thought repetitive or inessential, and suggested a more effective placing in order of what remained.

I am not ashamed to make this confession, though it may be held to expose an inartistry on my part, since, if small things may be compared with great, I remember how even while working on the first allegro Beethoven still suspected so little what mighty significance the sonata was eventually to assume that he used one of the principal themes in a chorus for four voices sung at some trifling celebration in honour of the Archduke Rudolph. For that matter, after the work was completed, he still seems to have been in doubt as to the importance of the masterpiece he had created. He actually wrote to Ries asking the latter, if he chose, to suppress the largo, which forms a bridge between the adagio and the fugue and constitutes one of the most original pages he ever wrote. 'A new and startling witness', Romain Rolland, in that commanding addition to Beethoven literature, *Le Chant de la Résurrection,* calls this and similar facts, 'of the power and superior logic of the sub-conscious in Beethoven'. And Rolland makes the point that Beethoven himself repeatedly failed to realise (sometimes for a long period) that certain ideas belonged not to this or that work for which he had conceived them but quite somewhere else, and that in the course of time, by some mystic process, they found their proper path, and their musical association.

Apart from a host of part-songs, Scott's published work is contained in five volumes of *Scottish Lyrics Set To Music.* The choice of these shows the impact of a first-class critical mind on the whole corpus of available Scottish song, with the important exception of Gaelic song.

For several years prior to Scott's death we had in any case been driven apart. We would undoubtedly have done a great deal more together if it had not been for the fact that circumstances carried me first away to London and then located me in the remote Shetlands, and never

G

through all these years enabled us to be in each other's company for more than a few consecutive nights in any year. . . .

Scott became increasingly reactionary in the last decade of his life. One day I took Jankel Adler, the painter, to see him, and Scott immediately expressed himself of the most violent anti-semitic opinions. I signalled to Adler and we rose and left. I did not see much of Scott after that. I published a pamphlet about him, as a tribute on his seventy-fifth birthday, and members of his family told me afterwards that he was enormously pleased with it—but he never acknowledged the copies I sent him. I wired him my congratulations when Glasgow University gave him an honorary Ll.D. but he did not acknowledge this either, nor did he send me any congratulatory message when Edinburgh University did me a like honour. The rift between us was complete. I have said we had, for many years, a deep community of insight, and that I never knew a man for whom I had a greater respect. Were both these merely aspects of the 'illusion of friendship'? Was I wrong all along? Various friends of mine thought so. I do not know. But I fancy that one of the hidden reasons was that Scott was partly of Jewish blood, one of his grandmothers having been a Greenvelt, of a family who, coming to Scotland from Yorkshire, did a good deal to build up the Border textile industry. But I was not wrong about the incomparable quality of his song settings or the fact that he was the only Scottish composer who succeeded in doing what all of them should have at least tried to do.

One of the reasons, I think, for my instinctive avoidance of intimacy, my insistence on the maintenance of a 'certain distance' between my friends and myself, is probably the belief that if pressed beyond the point of simple social amiability, all of them, or almost all of them, would find themselves in the same position with regard to me as the Irish poet A.E. found himself. He put it thus: 'Here, I said to myself', on first encountering Hugh MacDiarmid's poems, 'is someone born under the same star. But I soon

found that the circle of our beings intersected only at that
one point, and, instead of the attraction of affinities, I
began to feel the attraction which opposites have for us.
I turned to other pages of *Sangschaw* and found the Mac-
Diarmid who grew into *The Drunk Man Looks at the
Thistle* or the poet of *To Circumjack Ceverastus*—a sardonic
rebel snarling at the orthodoxies with something like old
Carlyle's rasping, cantankerous, oracular utterance. It
was no spiritual kinsman of mine . . . I find hardly any
character in contemporary poetry so intellectually exciting.
I sit up and quarrel on almost every page but keep more
than I cast away. I do not think he cares much even if
his search brings him away from song or rather from those
who might listen to a voice nearer to themselves.'

My friend William Johnstone is a cousin of F. G. Scott's.
He was Principal of Camberwell School of Arts and Crafts
in London from 1938 to 1945, Principal of the Central
School of Arts and Crafts in London from 1946 to 1961,
and Director of the Summer School of Colorado Springs Fine
Art Centre, U.S.A., from 1949 to 1950. He has shown
between 1925 and 1958 in numerous group exhibitions in
Paris, Pittsburg, Brussels and elsewhere and has had one-
man exhibitions in London, Edinburgh, Colorado Springs,
Oxford, and Newcastle upon Tyne. Nevertheless, he is the
'bad boy' of Scottish painting, whose name mustn't be
mentioned in the hearing of any member of the Royal
Scottish Academy. Like Scott and myself, he belongs to
the Borders, and it is a great pity that the three of us could
not have been in close touch all these years. Alas, Johnstone
was in London, Scott in Glasgow, and myself in a small
island in the north-east of the Shetland Archipelago.

In many respects (above all, in the quality and particul-
larly the 'direction' of his work) William Johnstone is not
only the most important, but the only important, living
Scottish artist, and the only one of international significance. He has been just that for about thirty years. So
his name is hardly ever mentioned. I have pointed out that
modern Scotland has been consistently blind to its most

important creative individuals—intent either to ignore them or at least to cut them down to average size. It is only necessary to mention Aeneas Sweetman Dallas in the field of aesthetics and literary criticism, Cecil Gray in music criticism, Sir Patrick Geddes in town planning, sociology, and a host of other things, and Francis George Scott in song-setting.

To the number of these men Mr. Johnstone is a very important addition. You will look in vain for his name in almost all books about contemporary art, but his vital importance is an 'open secret' to all who really know, but are too busy stealing from him to acknowledge any debt. It is not surprising that the American poet, Ezra Pound, recognised this long ago, and was almost alone in doing so or at least in saying so. Mr. Pound has shown this rare percipience again and again in relation to all the arts and established in their due place—at least for the élite—many men misunderstood by the mob and derided by the busy little time-servers, most people naturally prefer to their betters. Hannah Arendt, in her book *The Human Condition*, has pointed out the inevitability of this in the present state of society. As she says: 'There is always the danger that, through a perverted form of "acting together"—by pull and pressure and the tricks of cliques—those are brought to the fore who know nothing and can do nothing.'

Emergent genius in Scotland, in the exceedingly rare cases when there is any, suffers especially from this state of affairs. What is today generally regarded as distinctively Scottish rules out not only every characteristic of any value Scottish psychological history has manifested but also anything of any present or future consequence, and thus makes Scotland 'safe for mediocrity'. This, of course, suits the English (or at least the London-controlled) book. Thirty years ago, when an exhibition of Scottish art was exhibited in Burlington House, Sir William Llewellyn, then President of the Royal Academy, confessed it had been an eye-opener to him; he had no idea that Scotland had had such a rich distinctive national school of painters. So Sir

William, and those who shared his experience on that occasion, promptly shut their eyes again. They did not want to see anything of the kind. Not that it matters. They were wrong anyway. What they so very briefly and belatedly thought they saw belonged to the past and had no contemporary consequence whatever. This is even truer of Eric Newton's more recent declaration that Scotland today has at least a dozen or twenty painters who compare favourably with any such number any other country possesses. None of them have any international significance, none of them exemplify any of the really vital developments in contemporary art. They are all, as I have said of their literary contemporaries, 'half glow-worms and half newts'. Of all of them it must simply be said, '*Ils n'existent pas, leur ambiance leur confert une existence*'.

If my assertion that William Johnstone is probably the only Scottish artist today who really matters is doubted, it is no use reeling off a host of names to me. Just answer these questions. In Scotland in the 1920's who but Johnstone had any concept of twentieth-century art? Who in London then had any concept of twentieth-century art and was practising it? Who in Britain like Malevich in Russia and Cizek in Vienna had any knowledge of any new approach to art teaching? When did the revival of interest in Anglo-Saxon and Celtic Art begin? Was it not Johnstone's book *Creative Art in England* that was responsible? On the researches of that book, stacks of nonentities have since based their petty claims. Hugh Gordon Porteous has rightly maintained that Johnstone anticipated five major movements in world painting and got credit for none and in Scotland least of any place. The Scots had to keep him out because they would *all* ('helot usurpers of the true kingdom of awareness', as I have called them) have had to get out if he got in. The English have been more cunning. They just used him but saw to it that he did not get any of the credit.

Mr. Pound has pointed out that in literature (but it applies equally well to painting, music, and other arts—

and *pace* Lord Snow to the sciences too) the values are
created by several clearly definable sorts of people, and by
a periphery of less determinate sorts (the latter includes
nearly all painters). They are (1) the inventors, discoverers
of a particular process or more than one mode and process;
(2) The masters. This is a very small class, and there are
very few real ones. The term is properly applied to inventors, who, apart from their own inventions, are able to
assimilate and co-ordinate a large number of preceding
inventions—i.e. who either start with a core of their own
and accumulate adjuncts, or digest a vast mass of subject-
matter, apply a number of known modes of expression,
and succeed in pervading the whole with some special
quality or some special character of their own, and bring the
whole to a state of homogeneous fulness.

These are the only two sorts that really matter. Below
them come the dilutors, who follow the inventors but
produce something of lower intensity, some flabbier variant,
some diffuseness or tumidity in the wake of the valid, then
those (and their number is legion) who do more or less good
work in the more or less good style of a period, and finally
the art-phoneys or charlatans, the starters of crazes, or
manipulators of 'gimmicks'. It will be seen that the first
two classes are more sharply defined; that the difficulty of
classification for lesser artists increases as one descends
through the list, save for the last class, which is again
fairly clear. The point is that if a man knows the facts
about the first two categories, he can evaluate almost any
work of art at first sight. He can form a just estimate of
its worth, and see how and where it belongs in this scheme.

It should be impossible viewing his paintings not to see
that William Johnstone belongs to one or other of the first
two categories and cannot for a moment be relegated to
any of the lower ones. As a recent writer has said: 'Imper-
sonal art practitioners ape alien discoveries—and it matters
very little whether they worship the vanishing point or the
drip-can. Contemporary conformists perform disguised as
devil-may-care explorers. Their apparent freedom is only

abject slavery. William Johnstone's courage is of another
brand. He does not repeat ready-made discoveries; he
moves beyond their last aesthetic milestone into unknown
zones which he alone must map.'

That is exactly the point. People should not look at his
paintings with any preconceived ideas and seek for
elements in them which can be labelled 'post-impressionist',
'pointillist', 'cubist', 'tachist', and the like. William Johnstone has lived through the whole history of the arts, all
the schools, and moves forward from them. Such an artist
(the only kind that finally matters) does not seek to assert,
argue, explain or advise. He supplies no hand-rails for
mental or spiritual cripples. He simply holds up pieces of
reality and says, See! He gives no commands, pronounces
no judgement, offers no consolation. He simply reveals.
We must not be obfuscated by all the so-called schools,
trends in art, fashions, and the jargon of the so-called
critics. That is all rubbish so far as the essence of the
matter is concerned. The Vision is essentially unchanging.
We must go back to Heraclitus here again and his image of
the Ever-Living Flame, as I have said in my chapter on
Sorabji.

Where Willie Johnstone's work is shown is perhaps the
only, certainly one of the very few, places in Britain today
where that basic revelation is ever clearly displayed. There
are none so blind as they who will not see.

4

Major Douglas and Social Credit;
John Maclean and the Clydesiders

MICHAEL COLLIE, writing about Laforgue's experiences in Germany in the 'eighties, says: 'The experience was exactly the same as that known by many Englishmen conscripted during peacetime and sent overseas: an exterior discipline of no evident value, a life of purposeless and often futile activity, hours of boredom, and for a good while a remoteness from local people likely to accentuate any feeling of dissatisfaction or personal uncertainty.' That certainly is how I would have to sum up my relationships with almost all the men I lived with in barracks in Sheffield and Aldershot in the First World War, then for two years in Salonika and subsequently in North Wales, and finally for nine months at Marseilles. The emptiness of their lives was quite incredible. They certainly had no intellectual interests of any kind and except on the merest trivia it was impossible to have any sort of conversation with them. I think I would have felt the same with any other mob of army associates, and indeed that is just how I feel if inadvertently I get mixed up with a group of other men anywhere. I have no use for their horse-play and resent any familiarity, even if it falls far short of back-slapping jocosity. No wonder I have always been an outsider except to a chosen few; I do not share any of the interests of the mass. Their unexamined lives do not seem to me worth having.

I am not interested in soccer or any other commericalised sport and would not dream of going to see any match. I would never be found with people lining a street to witness a royal procession, or to greet the Beatles or any other group of their kind, or for that matter some champion racing motorist or ace golfer or anybody or anything else likely to attract a big crowd except (and even this I regard as a weakness) a big political demonstration. I very seldom enter a pub that has TV or popular music or is crowded or flashily equipped, preferring quiet little pubs where one can hear oneself and whoever one is with talking. If I have to talk to or listen to most people I feel exactly as if I were looking at a dog in whose eyes I have the illusion of a perfect mutual understanding, an equality of life. These feelings are, I believe, fully reciprocated at least by the minority capable of thinking at all. I remember when I was standing at a bar one day becoming aware that a fellow a yard or so away was seeking to attract my attention. I did not wish to enter into conversation with him, so as I saw him finally make up his mind to address me and edging a foot or two nearer for the purpose I went downstairs to the lavatory. He followed me. 'Excuse me,' he said, 'but are you anybody special?' 'Certainly,' I said. He gave me one horrified look and bolted upstairs faster than I would have believed possible. I can recall few other such chance encounters of the slightest interest.

One of the men who profoundly interested me was Major Clifford Hugh Douglas, originator of the Social Credit Scheme. It was through the *New Age* I came into contact with him, as with probably most of my close friends. Douglas's death at his home at Fearnan, Perthshire, on 29th September 1952, removed from our midst one of the greatest Scotsmen of the past hundred years, and, in relation to his own subject, the greatest of all time. He was seventy-three years of age. I saw a good deal of him in the early 'thirties in his rooms in Figtree Court, in London, or in my own office in High Holborn where I was then one of the directors of the Unicorn Press. Douglas signed a transfer of the publishing rights in all his books to me, but it was never implemented because my partners were not interested in Social Credit and did not think books like Douglas's

Economic Democracy likely to prove a commercial success. However, I did publish one new book of his, namely *Warning Democracy*, and also several pamphlets on the subject.

I have read criticisms of Ezra Pound's *Cantos* to the effect that usury is not a suitable subject for poetry. I cannot agree and indeed delight in the Cantos in which he denounces it. When Christendom ceased to regard usury as a deadly sin the future of mankind, and every human decency, was foully and perhaps fatally betrayed. There are few things of which I am prouder than that I was the only man permitted by the B.B.C. to broadcast on the subject for a couple of decades after A. R. Orage's brilliant radio talk on the subject—the only other occasion in which the matter has been ventilated on the air. I did it from the Manchester studio of the B.B.C. and received a bumper mail, while my talk was also tape-recorded and played to meetings of Douglasite groups all over the country as well as being fully reported and commented on in the various Social Credit periodicals still appearing then.

Douglas's Social Credit system (or a partial form of it) was tried out by Alberta, Canada, in the inter-war years and was so successful that Social Credit Governments have not only continued to be returned there ever since but have consistently added to their majorities in the provincial legislature. Major Douglas was appointed chief reconstruction adviser to the Social Credit Government of Alberta in 1935, but he was never in favour of the precise steps taken to apply Social Credit there, regarding the limited powers of a provincial legislature as unfavourable to a proper 'try out' of his system, and he resigned the following year. Later British Columbia also adopted a modified form of Douglas Social Credit.

There are few men who, in their lifetime, acting simply and solely 'off their own bat' and not vested with Government power, see their ideas give rise to a world-wide movement. Douglas was one of these few. Although for many years the 'Powers that be' kept all mention of his name and discussion of his ideas out of every paper and periodical in the world except for a few little known organs of extremely limited circulation which existed for the specific purpose of promulgating Douglasism, his name won through in the 'thirties and led to the establishment of Social Credit Associations and study circles and active propagandist journals in all the continents.

Douglasism today is a live issue confronting every civilised Government; it is pushing its way ahead in the United States, in Australia, and in Canada. Look over history; how many times do you encounter a single man building up a movement against all the strongest vested interests in the world? It is ample proof of Major Douglas's genius that he showed an amazing power of adapting himself to all the complicated circumstances affecting and following the promulgation of his discovery and stuck to his point, undeflected, with cool understatement; despite one of the most vigorous and prolonged Press boycotts in the history of journalism, and, without compromising his position one iota, piloted the biggest revolutionary project in the history of humanity into a foremost place in the councils of every civilised country. For, make no mistake, however carefully the issue may be kept 'under the counter', it has been well enough recognised for the past thirty to forty years, at least by all the financial and political chiefs throughout the world. It has led to a vast literature.

Most people—especially bankers, bank clerks, and university professors and lecturers on economics—affect to pooh-pooh it as utter nonsense, hopelessly impracticable and not worth a moment's consideration by any sane person. But ask them questions about it and you will invariably find that they cannot tell you exactly what Douglas's proposals were. Then ask them to explain the existing financial system and you will find they cannot give you any intelligible account of it either. No wonder! For money is a mystery, and those in charge of the system have seen to it that it remains beyond understanding. They have had good reasons for wrapping up all their operations in secrecy.

Douglas was disappointed that his own country of Scotland was not the first to give his system a trial. He recognised, of course, that Scotland could not do so until it reacquired independence and a Parliament of its own. He was therefore one of the early members of the National Party of Scotland and published his *Plan for Scotland* to show how Scotland could adopt Social Credit as its economic policy. I was a member of a Committee that strongly recommended that it should do so. The National Party, however, missed this tremendous opportunity. Douglas himself was well enough aware of the debt he owed to previous Scottish thought on economic matters as well as to Scotland's traditional love of freedom and deep-seated radicalism. His system simply applied all these elements to contemporary purpose and carried them to fresh levels of achievement.

After all, as Ezra Pound has said, an earlier Scotsman had anticipated the realisation that lies at the root of Douglas's system. He expressed this in the phrase I italicise in the passage in which Pound says: 'The Bank of England, a felonious combination, or, more precisely, a gang of usurers taking sixty per cent interest, was founded in 1694. Paterson, the founder of the Bank, clearly stated the advantages of his scheme: "The bank hath the benefit of the interest on all moneys *which it creates out of nothing*".' It was on this basis that Major Douglas erected his charge that the issue and withdrawal of credit by the banking system does not reflect the physical realities of production and consumption, and that the theory of money so applied effects a continual and increasing—and unpayable—indebtedness of the community for the banks. One debt cannot be liquidated without incurring a greater one. That is the lever of the Monopoly of Credit. The 'Douglas Theorem' is that, owing to credit being treated as the property of the banks, a loan repayable on demand, instead of being administered as the money of the community held as a right, purchasing power is withdrawn from the public at a faster rate than it ceases to figure in the prices which the public has to meet if all its production is to be sold. That is to say, there enters into the costs of final products a fictitious element due entirely to the property conception of credit, an element which is fictitious in the sense that it does not represent the money equivalent of wealth consumed in making that product. In fact the amount of credit withheld from the community in this way is approximately the money value of the net difference between its total production (capital and ultimate goods) and its consumption (final products bought and depreciation of real capital).

This, it is claimed, is the irreducible cause of the inability to distribute the whole possible volume of consumable production, which increases as the proportion of power equipment to labour increases. Hence the defeat by money monopoly of any benefit which should accrue to humanity by the replacement of human energy by natural power in production. As the products of one set of processes cannot be sold by the purchasing power distributed in respect of these processes, industrialism has only survived at all because the unsaleable product of one period could be partly carried off by credit distributed for inaugurating further production.

But the day of reckoning, in the most literal sense of that word, has now come, and we are confronted with the logical but insane financial advice that the cure for an unsaleable surplus is more production or economy. This is the very crux of the money monopoly. However successful man is, in supplying his wants and saving his limbs, he must enjoy no relaxation of economic activity. In Major Douglas's words, as a mechanism for making work the financial system is as near perfect as possible; but as a means of distributing the products of what is now predominantly a natural-power productive plant, it fails completely. In fact that is not its objective.

Major Douglas was not, however, prepared to accept this 'philosophy' of economic activity as the chief end of man, and consequently made proposals for the return of credit to the people and the issue of National Dividends as each citizen's share in the benefit of natural power (i.e. labour saving and production-increasing) production. Major Douglas's proposals were in fact designed to answer the question which, with all their talk of freedom this and liberation that, the B.B.C. and all the press and politicians ignore; namely: *And the liberty of not getting into debt—how about that?* A nation that will not get itself into debt drives all the usurers to fury.

Mazzini, in his *Duties of Man*, recommended 'the establishment of public storehouses or depots from which the approximate value of the commodities deposited having been ascertained, the Associations would issue a document or bond, similar to a banknote, capable of circulating and being discounted, so that the Association would be able to continue its work without being thwarted by the need for quick sales'. Mazzini spoke, too, of a 'fund for the distribution of *credit*', thus anticipating Major Douglas's theories. 'The distribution of this *credit*,' Mazzini continues, 'should not be undertaken by the Government, nor by a National Central Bank, but, with a vigilant eye on the National Power, *by local banks administered by elective Local Councils.*'

Listen to what Douglas himself said in a passage that strikes the very keynote of his philosophy (and incidentally aligns him with all that is best in Scottish thought from the Declaration of Arbroath to the present day): 'There probably never was a time in which disinterested legislation was so rare, just as there probably never was a device which was so effective in silencing criticism of interested legislation as this idea that self-interest on a worldly plane must necessarily be wicked. I would therefore make the suggestion, in order to add to the gaiety of nations by creating a riot at once, that the first requisite of a satisfactory governmental system is that it shall divest itself of the idea that it has a mission to improve the morals or direct the philosophy of any of its constituent citizens. Sir Walter Fletcher said: "We can find safety and progress only in proportion as we bring our methods of statescraft under the guidance of biological truth." I think that this is one of those remarks which illuminate a subject much as the sky-line is illuminated upon a dark night by a flash of summer lightning. *We know little about ourselves, and less about our neighbour, and almost nothing at all about the nature of a healthy Society. Nor do we display any particular anxiety to increase our knowledge in these directions.*

'Yet there is, nowadays, none so poor that he is not prepared to produce at short notice the plans which will put every human being in his place, within the space of a few short weeks. Preferably with the aid of a few good machine-guns. It is no less than a tragedy that *the inductive method, for which in particular, the English temperament is specially suited*, is not in itself a reliable instrument in this emergency. The physical scientist, who wishes to obtain a sure foundation for the formulation of laws, begins by standardising his re-agents.

'Temperature would be meaningless if we had not something to call "zero". But in regard to biology we are in a difficulty. We do not even know how unhealthy we are, though we have a strong suspicion that we are very sick indeed. To those, then, who are anxious to make a definite contribution to the solving of a sick world, it may not be impertinent to suggest that the natural creative forces of the universe might plausibly be expected to produce at least as good results if left alone to work themselves out through the agency of the individual, as may be expected from planning which is undertaken without any conception of the relation of the plan to the constitution and temperament of those who are affected. If all history and all observation has not been misread, there is implanted in the individual *a primary desire for freedom and security, which rightly considered are forms of the same thing.* There is no such thing as a freedom and security which is held upon terms, whether these terms are dictated by the State, by a banking system, or by a World Government. Until it can be shown that, with the resources which science has placed at his disposal, the individual is incapable of making freedom and security for himself, this multiplication of organisations whose interference he cannot avoid will only make a world catastrophe more certain.'

The values to be safeguarded in the Douglas Commonwealth are liberty, leisure, and culture. The will-to-plenty of the individual is to be given satisfaction, and the whole business and industrial life of society relegated to a subordinate place, somehow as in the economy of the human body many biological processes proceed automatically or semi-automatically, leaving the psychology of the human being free to develop its interests.

Systems were made for men, not men for systems, declared Major Douglas in the first chapter of his first book, and the interest of man, which is self-development, takes precedence over all systems, economic, political, or theological. A ringing statement to come from an economist!

No wonder the newspapers gave him less obituary space than they accord to any film star or Yankee crooner. Douglas himself would not have been surprised at all. His entire propaganda was founded on the centuries-old recognition of the fact that *nescis, mi fili, quantilla prudentia mundus regatur* (you know, my son, with what a small stock of wisdom the world is governed). And he might well have exclaimed at any time during the twenty-odd years of our friendship as another friend of mine did: 'God knows what gets into all Governments, at certain stages of their existence. It's easy to understand why Arab princes surround themselves with incompetents, eunuchs, dolts and degenerates, for Arab princes consider themselves infallible; whatever they do must of necessity be right. Consequently they elevate childhood friends or toadying relatives to the most important posts in their kingdoms. But only God knows why such things happen perpetually in countries regarded as politically enlightened, like England, France, America, supposedly governed by patriotic men. Yet they always have happened, and with horrifying frequency; the pages of history are sprinkled with dolts, idiots, drunkards

Hugh MacDiarmid by Benno Schotz

Joan Muspratt

F. G. Scott   Kaikhosru Shapurji Sorabji

John MacLean

maintained in the highest offices—mediocrities whose stubbornness has sacrificed armies, whose blindness has destroyed navies, whose bad judgement has ruined their countries' prestige, starved helpless people by the million, wrecked cities, toppled arts and civilisation, learning and understanding in the dust—and most of these fools' names hold unsullied place in the lying annals of their respective nations!'

Major Douglas's name belongs to a different and extremely small list, not known at all to the newspapers, or the masses of mankind who are Bing Crosby's, or the Beatles', or the Duke of Edinburgh's, fans. Major Douglas was only a distinguished engineer whose blue-prints were all designed to bring about *the economic independence and complete freedom of the individual.*

The secret of much opposition to Social Credit may be the common idea that Douglas's *discovery* was the necessity of Credit Creation. Far from it—even Roosevelt, no official economist, saw the need for *that.* But Douglas, the engineer, constructed a machine that would work without creating and extending a Debt, now described as 'astrological'—but on every dollar of which *interest* has to be paid. The Douglas part of the new Economic System was simply a means by which, in Dividend and Just Price, Debt would be eliminated, and *the goods we can make* distributed. He was not allowed to state, before the Macmillan Commission, *why* his method *would not create inflation* as the 'New Deal' undoubtedly did.

I knew—and collaborated with—all those associated with the *New Age* and Major Douglas in the advocacy of Social Credit. There is now a vast literature on the subject in addition to Douglas's own books, but I think one of the best is *Human Ecology* by the late Dr. Thomas Robertson (brother of J. Fyfe Robertson, the well-known journalist and broadcaster). Dr. Robertson was a friend of mine in Glasgow in the 'forties and we discussed his book together while he was writing it. He does not deal with a point which has puzzled me a great deal. A friend said to me in

H

London when I was associated with Douglas, Orage, Mairet, Symons, Reckitt, Canon Demant, John Hargrave of the Green Shirt movement, Arthur Brenton, and other Douglasites: 'What are you doing among these people? Don't you realise they will all go religious-Fascist?' I did not realise anything of the kind, but they all did go religious-Fascist, and I still do not see why that should be so. It certainly has not happened in my own case.

Nicolas Berdyaev in *Slavery and Freedom* was right when he said: 'The bourgeois has an insurmountable tendency to create a world of fancy which enslaves man, and causes the disintegration of the world of true realities. The bourgeois' most fantastic creation, the most unreal, the most uncanny and horrible in its unreality, is the kingdom of money. And this kingdom of money in which all real substance disappears, possesses a terrible power, holds a terrible sway over human life, sets up governments and overthrows them, makes wars, enslaves the labouring masses, gives rise to unemployment and destitution, renders the life of people who are successful in this kingdom more and more fantastic. Leon Bloy was right. Money is a mystery; there is something mystic in the power of money. The kingdom of money, the extreme of impersonality, makes even property itself fictitious. Marx was right in saying that capitalism destroys personal property.'

I like to set alongside that quotation two other quotations from writings by men I have known personally. First of all, T. S. Eliot. 'About certain serious facts', he wrote, 'no one can dissent. The present system does not work properly, and more and more people are inclined to believe both that it never did and that it never can; and it is obviously neither scientific nor religious. It is imperfectly adapted to every purpose except that of making money; and even for money-making it does not work very well, for its rewards are neither conducive to social justice or even proportioned to intellectual ability. It is well adapted to speculation and usury, which are the lowest forms of mental activity; and it rewards well those who can cozen and corrupt the crowd.'

Sir Alfred Ewing's pessimistic Presidential Address to the British Association evoked the following reply: 'The existence of world-wide unemployment and poverty, the sinister shrinking of international trade, side by side with greater productive power, more abundant crops, and fuller control over nature, have suggested to many that the old objection of the manual worker to machinery is not without foundation. It is useless for the scientific worker to provide the greater productive powers or even more effective ways of protecting crops unless society has an economic and social organisation which provides the appropriate seeds, fertilisers, tools, etc., and cultivators capable of understanding their use. This presupposes some developed system of industry, transport, distribution, and education, in which the cultivator and the inventor can both be fostered. The immense complexity of modern pure and applied science requires a correspondingly complex social organisation. When, however, we turn from the sphere of production to that of commerce and distribution, we enter a world of crude empiricism, secrecy, and mystification into which scientific method or principles have yet to penetrate, and exact knowledge and its free interchange is almost totally absent. Our distributive and economic system remains on the basis of a pre-scientific era, wholly unadjusted to the change, and unable to bear the burdens placed upon it by this problem of new and almost incredible abundance. Adjustments are called for and can only be effective when the spirit and methods of science are freely applied in this sphere also, and it is recognised that the new powers involve, the release of the general human life from Nature's old exaction of drudgery for a mere pittance. The release into an enlarged and enriched leisure for all men for general human culture would appear to be the only alternative to chronic unemployment.'

The other quotation I wish to give is from the Irish writer Liam O'Flaherty, whom I met only once and with whom then I straightaway had a battle-royal on the floor of the pub so many of us—John Strachey, Tom Driberg,

'Peter Warlock', Catherine Carswell—used to frequent; the
Plough, in Museum Street, London. 'Capitalist finance',
writes O'Flaherty, 'has completed its enslavement of mankind, turning five-sixths of the earth into an internment
camp, where poor slaves starve in the midst of untold
wealth. It is no longer possible for a hungry slave to stow
himself away in a ship bound for the Argentine and eat a
cow from the countless herds that roam the pampas. If he
escapes imprisonment and reaches the cows, he will find
that he cannot eat the leanest steak from one of them. They
are all in pawn to some damned financier in Wall Street
or in the City of London; to fellows who would rather
slaughter them and leave their bodies to the vultures than
allow a hungry man to fill his belly with their flesh. There
is no longer any haven of respite on five-sixths of this mad
Earth for any poor creature who wishes to escape from the
horrors of capitalist civilisation. He must stand his ground
and fight it or go under. If he is barred by the collapse of
capitalist finance from being a wage slave, he must become
a brigand, or sell his talents in some whorish way, or die of
hunger where he stands. Men of my profession generally
take the choice of whoredom. While literature is still
regarded as a noble art, those who pursue it are in the main
a spineless horde, grovelling before some rump-fed boor,
who has made millions by selling trashy newspapers, or
else they are mouthpieces of the fantastic creeds that the
mediocre mob has invented in its war against the human
intellect. I have never been able to stomach any of these
creeds, to the degree of becoming abject before it and
writing to its bidding.

'On the other hand, I would rather rely on my vomit for
sustenance than attempt to cater for the rump-fed boors.
"Then I must run to earth," I cried, "like a hard-pressed
fox, until I have reorganised my strength, weave cunning
plots, throw by the board these vices that have placed me
at the mercy of my enemies, to appear once more with
shining eyes, a weasel to hypnotise the rabbits, who shall
be forced to give me bread for my dreams." I had at least

established the identity of the devil. That was half the battle. The other half lay in getting rid of the habits that had placed me at the devil's mercy. You must understand that the devil for a writer is a hankering after success and the fruits of success; luxury, social respectability and fame.'

If I had read that first I would never have come to blows with O'Flaherty, who remains, so far as I can recall, the only man with whom I have engaged in an actual physical fight.

Dr. Robertson gives the most succinct and comprehensive account of 'The Façade of Finance' and 'Behind the Financial Façade', as the relevant chapters in his book are entitled. He deals admirably with the psychological difficulty due to the notion 'that money is tangible, real, and substantial. Most people know that notes have no intrinsic value, but they nevertheless believe that somehow or other they represent gold and are in fact as good as gold. . . . The whole business of banking is in fact surrounded by a ritual and supported by a ceremonial in the face of which the stoutest might well shrink from criticism. It claims infallibility and believes it is man's only hope, and has its prophets, its exegesis, its dogmatics, and in fact the whole armamentarium of religion, which it is—the religion of mammon. . . . In the face of all this, is it to be wondered at that men's minds are locked and bolted against financial treason? Is it surprising that the ordinary man finds finance 'too difficult' and is content to 'leave it to the experts'.

As Maurice Colbourne said in *The Meaning of Social Credit*: 'The bulk of modern money is made, not of metal or paper, but of figures in bank ledgers. It is called financial credit, and is movable and divisible by the cheque system. It is interesting to note the immense amount of work which this intangible and intrinsically worthless medium of financial credit is called upon to perform for the community. For instance the value of cheque transactions in England and Wales which passed through the London Clearing House alone in 1930 is given in the Macmillan

Report as just under £64,641,000,000.' So, as Dr. Robertson insists, when we consider money it is clear we can for practical purposes discard the relatively paltry amount of coins made at the Royal Mint. Notes themselves are, moreover, of no intrinsic value and are mainly financial credit also since they are normally produced by the Bank of England on a part gold basis only. Reginald McKenna stated that in 1922 the notes and coin paid into city banks were less than 0.7 per cent of the total, which means, as he pointed out, that legal currency has been virtually superseded by cheques based on credit. Thus we stumble upon the astonishing fact that *money in practice means financial (bank) credit*, or 'bank deposit' money, not coinage, and only to a minor extent bank notes. Another surprising fact appears. Taking the rough figures quoted, we see that the then available currency in Great Britain amounted to £500 million, but bank deposits amounted to £2000 million. Assuming, which is not true, that bank notes had a 'real' value based on gold, we see that if all bank depositors tried to lift their 'money' it would only be possible in theory (not in practice) to pay a quarter of the sum due.

In *Monopoly of Credit* Major Douglas said: 'A Central Bank such as the Bank of England may be said to acquire gold for nothing . . . the institution concerned writes a draft upon itself for the sum involved, and the general public honours the draft by being willing to provide goods and services in exchange for it.'

As Hartley Withers says in *Meaning of Money*: 'Banking Deposits come into being to a small extent by cash paid into the banks across the counter; to a larger but still comparatively small extent by purchase of securities by banks, which create book credits, and chiefly by loans from banks, which also create book deposits.' In other words, *'the bulk of the deposits arise out of the action of the banks themselves'*.

The Cunliffe Report showed how the mechanism works. 'Suppose, for example, that in a given week the government requires £10,000,000 over and above receipts from taxation and loans from the public. They apply for an advance from the Bank of England, which by a book entry places the amount required to the credit of "Public Deposits" in the same way as any other banker credits the account of a customer when he grants his temporary accommodation. The amount is then paid out to contractors and other government creditors, and passes, when the cheques are cleared, to the credit of their bankers in the books of the Bank of England—in other words, it is transferred from Public to "Other Deposits", the effect of the whole transaction thus being to increase by £10,000,000 the purchasing power in the hands of the public in the form of deposits in the Joint Stock banks and the bankers' cash at the Bank of England by the same amount. Under the operation of these causes the total deposits in the banks of the United Kingdom (other than the Bank of England) increased from £1,070,681,000 on 31st December 1913 to £1,742,902,000 on 31st December, 1917.'

No wonder Mr. McKenna, in his *Post-War Banking Policy*, said: 'I am afraid the ordinary citizen will not like to be told that the banks or the Bank of England can create or destroy money.'

'We see beyond all doubt how banks create money', says Dr. Robertson. 'The next question then follows. If banks can create money as easily as this by ledger entry, why is there so little real purchasing power available? In other words, is there any limit to the capacity of banks to create money? Again the answer is clear—again from Mr. McKenna, in an address to the Midland Bank shareholders: '. . . variations in the quantity of money are due to variations in the total of the bank cash . . . the total of bank cash is determined solely by the action of the Bank of England.'

Dr. Robertson rams home these hidden (and to most people incredible and unacceptable) facts in the most convincing and indisputable way. As he says, the Bank of England 'has no government representatives on its board, nor joint stock bankers, but is chiefly a collection of private financiers belonging to the interlocked organisations of international finance (i.e. prior to the nationalisation of the Bank of England). Then there is another point of significance. The Bank of England is a secret organisation in respect that its shareholders and its reserves are unknown and it does not declare its policy. As far as its operations are concerned, these too are secret.'

The Macmillan Report said: 'The Bank of England is almost unique as a Central Bank in that it is a private institution practically independent of any legal control save in regard to its power of issuing bank notes and granting loans to the State.'

Nationalisation has in no way altered this.

The Communist parties are vehemently opposed to Social Credit. Why? They operate the orthodox financial system—basically the same as in the capitalist countries. Dr. Robertson deals conclusively with this point. I myself, though a member of the Communist Party, have always believed—and still believe—that Major Douglas's proposals should be applied in the transitional period before the achievement of integrated Communism.

Over thirty years ago I was in regular correspondence with leading Social Creditors in the United States. One of them, Gorham B. Munson, wrote a series of articles showing that Marxism and Social Credit were perfectly reconcilable. My other like-minded American correspondents then included Waldo Frank and Kenneth Burke.

To turn to another friend, I was more interested than I have been in any other Socialist speech or article for years when I read Alastair Sutherland's plea to save Socialism from the Labour Party, 'Regaining the Initiative', and Geoffrey Ostergaard's discussion of 'Labour and the Public Corporation', defining the latter (the consequence of the acceptance of Herbert Morrison's thesis which subverted British Labour Policy) as 'the Labour Party's chosen instrument to evade Socialism', both of which appeared in the *Oxford Clarion* of 5th May 1957. Lenin in a well-known letter singled out John Maclean along with Karl Liebknecht as a 'true Socialist' in contrast to men like Ramsay

MacDonald and Philip Snowden. Maclean is indeed the
man to whom to point as the chief opponent in Great
Britain to the disastrous trends with which Messrs. Sutherland and Ostergaard were concerned, those trends which in
R. H. S. Crossman's phrase may well, if allowed to develop
fully now, transform Britain within ten years into 'the
hierarchical, Managerial State of Burnham's nightmare'.
Nor were they alone in their arguments. Even *The Scotsman*
said: 'Mr. Attlee and his colleagues are probably too busy
healing the breaches in their party and clinging to power
to have much time for arduous thought. At one time the
Socialist movement could look confidently to the Fabian
Society to produce an impressive façade of polysyllabic
political philosophy, but the intellectuals seem to be as
perplexed as the rank and file.' A correspondence in *The
Times* on the bankruptcy of ideas in the Labour Party has
failed to evoke any evidence of new thinking on the Left.
In all seriousness, the secretary of the Fabian Society has
tried to demonstrate the intellectual vitality of Socialism
by pointing to the emergence of new ideas on the subject of
State control and centralisation. In effect, he says, the
power of the State has increased, is increasing, and ought
to be diminished. Socialists should actively turn their minds
to practical measures for distributing power instead of
concentrating it. It is satisfactory that Socialist intellectuals
should see the light, but they can hardly be congratulated
on the novelty of their ideas. Their new thought has been
expressed by the critics of nationalisation, *and especially in
Scotland* [my italics] for at least five years. The late G. D. H.
Cole was only too right when he said in the *New Statesman* that 'Labour politicians and trade union leaders have
shown no willingness to trust the common man; they have
conceived Socialisation as merely State business replacing
private business, without any change of spirit or status.'
John Maclean on the contrary was right in applying to
Scotland what Engels said in his preface to the Polish
translation of the Communist Manifesto (published in 1892),
viz. 'The Polish nobility was not able to maintain and has

not been able to re-establish the independence of Poland.
The bourgeoisie is becoming less and less interested in the
question. Polish independence can only be won by the
young proletariat of Poland. In their hands the fulfilment of
the hope will be safe.' James Connolly recalled, furthermore,
the words of another precursor of Marx and Engels: James
Hope, the weaver of Templepatrick, who was the son of a
Scottish immigrant and who helped to lead the United
Irishmen of Co. Antrim in 1798, namely 'so long as men of
rank and fortune lead a people, they will modify abuses,
reform to a certain extent, but they will never remove any
real grievances that weigh down a people'. That passage
became very topical for us in Scotland when the Duke of
Montrose's signature was first on the Covenant Association
followed by landed gentry, lawyers and divines.

'When we survey such people and remember the record
of many of these bourgeois nationalists of ours (and the fact
that Communists are debarred from membership of the
Covenant Association although Dr. MacCormick proclaimed
it above party politics and a new departure in democracy) we
can echo the words of Hope: " 'Patriots' may modify their
demands, but the people will have their wrongs eventually
and entirely redressed" (*vide* article by Andrew Boyd on
James Hope in the *Communist Review* for October 1948).
The Fabian Society has a reputation for making haste
slowly, with the ideas of political opponents. Under Fabian
guidance the Socialists have created a problem which they
now propose to solve. It looks uncommonly like the un-
ecomonic process of digging a hole and then filling it up.'

As John Maclean's right-hand man, the late James D.
MacDougall (also a friend of mine) said in an article in
The Camlachie Nationalist: 'When his trials and jail
sentences had made Maclean world-famous he was more in
demand than ever as a propagandist and his influence with
the ordinary Socialist worker was enormously enhanced.
The example of the action of Connolly and Larkin in their
association with the Irish National Struggle was not lost
upon him. More than ever he was now impressed with the

necessity of securing that his fame should not be manipu-
lated in the interests of corrupt London gangs. He correctly
sensed the coming of a Labour Government and in many
pieces of clever political argument foreshadowed its prob-
able course. How must his memory recur to those who in
the tribulations of the hour are enduring what he long ago
predicted would come. He had as a revolutionary always
opposed the Labour Party, and its policy of assuming
responsibility for capitalism. There were a number of
causes co-operating to the conviction to which Maclean's
last years were devoted, but one certainly of the most
powerful was Lenin's handling of the Nationalities question
in Russia. Lenin's view was that national emancipation
struggles were a necessary preliminary to the successful
waging of the class struggle within the freed nations. He
demanded for all the suppressed nations of Czarist Russia
the rights of separation and self determination. One of
Maclean's leading characteristics was his superb self-
confidence and hatred of trimmers and compromisers.
Always he went straight to the mark. Thousands of Scottish
people first saw their position in a true light when Maclean
enabled them to appreciate the financial and administrative
stranglehold that England exercised upon us. For the
Scottish bourgeoisie and their stuffy respectability, lack of
culture, and petty money-grubbing, he had nothing but
sovereign contempt as was shown in his many battles with
them over housing and work and maintenance for the unemployed. They cordially returned the hatred and through
their police machinery did him to death.'

Writing in *Conflict* for December 1948, Harry MacShane
said: 'Twenty-five years have elapsed since John Maclean
passed away. His name is revered by thousands of Scottish
workers many of whom have no clear idea of what he stood
for. They only know that he fought and suffered in the
interests of the working class. Why was he imprisoned?
Why was he made Russian consul for Glasgow? What was
the character of the educational work for which he was
famous? The answer to the last question partly answers

the other two. John Maclean started his Socialist activity early in the century, as a member of the Social Democratic Federation which claimed the allegiance of the majority of the adherents of Marx. He studied Marx and later became the most popular teacher of Marxist economics in the country. He was widely known, even before the First World War, because of the successful classes he organised. He went everywhere trying to interest people in Marxist theory. It was in order to further Marxist education that he founded the Scottish Labour College. Throughout the whole of his political life he attached the greatest importance to his educational work. But John was more than a theorist. He made use of his theoretical knowledge in the everyday work that seemed to him so necessary. He helped in every strike. He played a part in the Co-operative Movement and was engaged in every phase of work embarked upon by the general Labour Movement. Those who knew him before the First World War looked upon him as a reliable and trustworthy comrade and were not surprised in 1914 when he took the courageous stand that made him an international figure and brought him long terms of imprisonment. He was suspicious of many of the leading personalities in the Labour Movement. Time and again he had denounced Ramsay MacDonald. He had openly opposed the war mongering policy of certain leaders of the British Socialist Movement before the war, he denounced the Government for having led this country into war. Karl Liebknecht, who made a similar stand in Germany, was praised by John Maclean for his fearless fight. . . . The speech of John Maclean at his trial in 1918 reveals his fundamental principles. His appeal was to the workers. "The whole history of Society", he said, "has proved that Society moves forward as a consequence of an under-class overcoming the resistance of a class on top of them." '

Full support was given by Maclean to the Russian Revolution. 'Abnormal lines of action,' he said, 'must be taken and I urge abnormal lines of action to be taken such as our comrades in Russia took. The very circumstances of the war forced the Russian workers' committees and their National Soviet to take the line of action which they adopted, and the only way we could do it would be to adopt methods peculiar to the working class organisation in this country in the interests of the workers themselves.'

He was sentenced to five years' imprisonment. He had, in 1916, been sentenced to a term of three years' imprisonment but he did not complete his sentence. When the Bolsheviks came to power they made John Maclean an honorary member of the Petrograd Soviet. He was also appointed Russian Consul for Glasgow. This was recognition of the work he did on Clydeside. He made a bold effort to carry out the duties connected with his new post but he was not recognised by the British Government and in any case it was not long until he was arrested. John Maclean died on 30th November 1923. He was only forty-four.

His work before and during the War had been followed up, after the War, by intense activity on unemployment and in connection with the Irish fight for independence. This led to more imprisonment which took its toll. Whatever certain badly informed persons may think, John Maclean will always be regarded as an outstanding fighter for Revolutionary Socialism. He firmly believed in his Marxist principles and devoted his life to their realisation.

While it is undoubtedly true that Maclean was the greatest leader the working class of Scotland have yet had, and that all sorts of living currents in the movement today can be traced back to him, for the most part until very recently both the Communist Party of Great Britain and the Labour Party have been content to use his name while repudiating his policy. So great has been the conspiracy of silence that no collection of his writings has yet been published and no worthy biography. There have been pamphlets by Guy Aldred and Tom Anderson and a rather larger brochure by Tom Bell, but none of these do him anything like justice. A lot of letters, cuttings of Maclean's contributions to defunct papers, the typescript of Maxton's aborted beginning of a biography of Maclean, etc., had been entrusted to me and it was hoped I would fill the need of a biography of Maclean. Circumstances prevented my doing so, and finally I handed over all this material to my friend John Broom who has now brilliantly completed the long over-due task. It is to be hoped this may be published soon. I have had the privilege of writing a prefatory article to it.

In *Revolt on the Clyde* William Gallacher says: 'When Maclean died, the I.L.P.'s, with whom he had never associated when alive, took an active part, in organising a "Testimonial Fund". For the purposes of this fund, they persuaded Mrs. Maclean to hand over to them all Maclean's papers and records on the promise that this material would be used for publishing a life of Maclean, the proceeds of which would go to the fund. The material was handed over to Maxton. When I heard of this, many months later, I called on Maxton and offered my assistance. He told me the book was just about finished and that he would let me see it when it was completed. Since that time I have made several attempts to get the material as has also J. Figgins of the N.U.R. who was secretary of the Maclean Committee, but without avail. The I.L.P., which had no time for Maclean when he was alive, has succeeded in suppressing his biography since his death.' Probably the hardest—and truest—thing that has yet been said about the flock of Clydeside Labour M.P.'s who were the helot usurpers of John Maclean's title to Scottish working-class leadership was said in *Reynolds News*, 27th May 1951, when a veteran Glasgow I.L.P-er expressed the opinion that 'the important part London now plays in the Socialist Movement is very largely due to the work of the "reds from Clydeside" just after 1922, when the I.L.P. swung Scotland to the Left!'

As I pointed out to my friend Gallacher he was not correct. Maxton did attempt to write a biography of Maclean, but only managed to write about a couple of thousand words of an introductory chapter. The typescript of that small beginning was handed over to me, as were also many letters to Maclean, pamphlets by him, and typescripts of numerous articles he contributed to short-lived Socialist

papers. While I and my friends have found it impossible
to get a full biography published yet—largely owing to the
Second World War—we have succeeded in reviving a very
considerable interest in Maclean throughout Scotland,
published numerous articles about him in all sorts of
periodicals (the articles by James MacDougall and Harry
MacShane from which I have quoted are cases in point),
have organised huge public gatherings in commemoration
of him, and stimulated several of the significant poets in
Scotland today to write poems and songs in his honour. I
have no doubt that this trend will continue and that, to
quote the refrain of Hamish Henderson's splendid marching
song, 'Great John Maclean will come back to the Clyde'.

Another element that has militated very largely against
Maclean's memory is the idea that towards the end he
became mentally afflicted as a result of his prison experiences. But I have letters he wrote right up to the very end
and these are as clear and rational as ever. In my view what
finally broke him was less his admittedly great sufferings
in prison than his feeling that most of his friends had
repudiated his teachings and were committed to courses
which must prove disastrous—as indeed they have proved.
That sorry recession is coming to an end at last, however,
and the tide is beginning to flow in the right direction.
That so great a proportion of our people know nothing of
Maclean except his mere name—if that!—is not surprising
in Scotland where owing to the educational system scarcely
anything of any value in relation to our own literature,
history, national biography, or economic facts gets through
the filter. I bracket with Maclean's name the names of
John Murdoch (the crofters' leader—Maclean's agrarian
counterpart), Thomas Muir, and John Swinton (who aided
the Negroes in South Carolina before the Civil War, became
a friend of Walt Whitman, and knew Karl Marx, as (so I
have written elsewhere) examples of 'Scots who are
relatively far too little known and yet, in our opinion, of
far more consequence than most of those who figure prom-
inently either in our history books or in contemporary life.'

Towards most of the latter, indeed, we feel precisely as
Burns felt towards their equivalents in his lifetime of whom
he wrote: 'Few of the sore evils under the sun give me
more uneasiness than when, conscious that men are born
equal I meet with the self-sufficient stately stupidity of a
Squire Something or a Sir Somebody. How it mortifies me
to hear the fellow's shallow idiot attempts at wit applauded
—a fellow whose abilities would scarcely have made an
eightpenny tailor and whose heart is not worth three
farthings! . . . The noble Lord Glencairn showed so much
attention—engrossing attention—one day to a dunderpate
that I was within half a point of throwing down my gage in
contemptuous defiance.' It is an appalling commentary on
the condition of Scotland today that such 'famous fat-
heads' should be held in high public esteem and exercise
great influence, and that the ballyhoo of royal publicity—
all the disgusting publicisation of our Scottish Queen
Mother—should be almost as rampant in our midst as in
England, with no one apparently to re-echo what Burns
said in his 'Lines on Fergusson the Poet':

'O why should truest Worth and Genius pine
Beneath the iron grasp of Want and Woe,
While titled knaves and idiot-greatness shine
In all the splendour Fortune can bestow?'

Despite all that, however, and the conspiracy of silence
to which I have referred and the absence of any biography
or collection of his writings, one cannot go far in any
direction in Scotland without coming upon men who
'remember Maclean'.

William Gallacher gives the best pen-portrait of him in
Revolt on the Clyde when he writes of him as 'a driving
dynamo of energy, driving, always driving, towards his goal
. . . certainly the greatest revolutionary figure Scotland has
produced. . . . The work done by Maclean during the winter
of 1917–18 has never been equalled by anyone. His
educational work would have been sufficient for half a

Sir Patrick Geddes

(from *Pioneer of Sociology* by Philip Mairet, published by Lund Humphries)

George Davie

Poets in Peking
An address by
Hugh MacDiarmid
in honour of
William Blake and
Walt Whitman

1757–1827   1807–1882

dozen ordinary men, but on top of this he was carrying on
a truly terrific propaganda and agitational campaign.
Every minute of his time was devoted to the revolutionary
struggle, every ounce of his extraordinary energy was
thrown into the fight.'

No wonder I say of him in one of my poems:

'Scotland has had few men whose names
Matter—or should matter—to intelligent people,
But of these Maclean, next to Burns, was the greatest
But it should be of him, with every Scotsman and Scots-
    woman
To the end of time, as it was of Lenin in Russia.
When you might talk to a woman who had been
A young girl in 1917 and find that the name of Stalin lit
    no fires
But when you asked her if she had seen Lenin
Her eyes lighted up and her reply
Was the Russian word which means
Both beautiful and red,
Lenin, she said, was *"krassivy, krassivy"*.
John Maclean too was *krassivy, krassivy*
A description no other Scot has ever deserved.'

T. E. Nicholas, the Welsh poet, is a man of like quality.
A young Cornishman wrote me saying: 'Rolant Jones [a
prizewinner at many Eisteddfoddau] remembers having
'Nicholas Glais' to lunch one day and discovering for the
first time someone *scarlet*!' I found that out for myself
when I called on him at a time I had been addressing the
students at Aberystwyth.

I think the new, now rapidly extending, appreciation of
Maclean's significance dates back to the between-the-Wars
period when in the course of the developing Scottish
Renaissance Movement, it became clear to some of us that
most of the writers in question had been quite unable to
outgrow the distortions to which they were subjected in
their schooldays and at college, and that therefore, although
the portion of work done in connection with it that had

I

shown real progress was quite sufficient to justify the
Movement, it was nevertheless necessary to break with it—
to say good-bye to that Movement and go forward to
Scottish Workers' Republicanism *à la* John Maclean, and
that, as I tell in *Lucky Poet*, I did (carrying with me in so
doing all the other Scottish writers of my own age or—in
so far as I knew them—younger, of whose creative possibilities I still had any hope) in 1936 in a statement which
included the following paragraphs:

'Having regard to the future of civilisation and the
intensifying war and fascism menace of this phase of the
imminent collapse of capitalist society, and being passionately anxious to "pull our full weight" (as Scotland has
hitherto failed to do in the work of world revolution) in
our native country where these issues come closest to us
in an immediate practical sense, we are convinced that, just
as Connolly said that in Ireland the social revolution
would be incomplete without a national revolution too, so
in Scotland here it is clear that the objectives of the social
revolution can only be fully realised if it is accompanied by
autonomy on a Communist basis.

'In this we are adverting to Keir Hardie's admonition
that it had been a mistake to send Scottish Labour M.P.s
to Westminster and that a much greater impetus would have
been given to socialism if Scottish Socialists had given
priority in their programme to Scottish independence
concurrently with the Irish Independence issue, and taking
up again the great lead given by John Maclean which circumstances have so amply vindicated since, viz. (from his
Gorbals Election Address 1923): "Scotland's wisest policy
is to declare for a Republic in Scotland, so that the youth
of Scotland will not be forced out to die for England's
markets. I accordingly stand out as a Scottish Republican
candidate, feeling sure that if Scotland had to elect a
Parliament to sit in Scotland it would vote for a Working
Class Parliament."

'The Social Revolution is possible sooner in Scotland
than in England. The working-class policy ought to be to

break up the Empire to avert war and enable the workers to triumph in every country and colony. Scottish separation is part of the process of England's Imperial disintegration and is a help towards the ultimate triumph of the workers of the world. . . . Had the Labour men stayed in Glasgow and started a Scottish Parliament as did the genuine Irish in Dublin in 1918, England would have sat up and made concessions to Scotland just to keep her ramshackle Enpire intact to bluff other countries. . . . Ireland will only get her Republic when Scotland gets hers.

'Further evidence of the correctness and inescapable necessity of this line lies in the statistics of voting showing the persistent tremendous radicalism (leading more than once to all-over Socialist majorities) of the Scottish electorate vis-à-vis the English, and the extent to which the progressive will of the majority of the Scottish people has been stultified by the English connection.

'A return now to this separatist and anti-imperialist line (about which Scottish Socialism has always been so deplorably weak that these considerations have constituted a disastrous blind spot in the entire development of the working-class movement in Scotland) is in incontrovertible keeping with the present historical development in every other country.

'Along with this anti-Imperialist line of Scottish Separatist socialist republicanism invaluable impetus can be given to the social revolution in England, Ireland, Wales and elsewhere. As against the all-too-simple cry that the interests of the workers in Scotland and England are identical we have no hesitation in stressing that far more exact dialectical discrimination must be given to the alleged consequences of the identity of the interests of Scottish workers and English workers, since this in no wise conflicts with the question of Scottish independence, nor necessarily involves any incorporation Union of the two peoples, whose relationship signally illustrates the fact that, as Marx (and subsequently Lenin) insisted: "No nation that enslaves another can itself be free." The freeing of Scotland should be a foremost plank in the programme of the English workers themselves—in their own, no less than in Scotland's, interests.

'The line we advocate—in addition to greatly strengthening anti-imperialism vis-à-vis the great weakness of our Socialist M.P.s in this connection—will put an end to the sinister association in the Scottish cultural movement of abstract highbrowism and politics which have no concern with the cause of the workers, and greatly speed up the proletarianisation of Scottish Arts and Letters, i.e. the beginnings of self-education of the Scottish proletariat in their revolutionary tasks *with the aid of their own intelligentsia.*

'It is for this reason that we claim that we have, along this Red Scotland line, the end of Scottish Nationalism and the beginning of Workers' Republicanism. *Our line represents a complete break with recent Scottish cultural developments, and the realisation that further such developments must of necessity be revolutionary.* The Communist and Social Democratic neglect of and sidetracking of the Scottish Cause up to now has been responsible for the long confused and inefficient Scottish Nationalist groping, and the extent to which the whole thing has now played into Fascist hands. *No Scottish Socialist can read this exposition of the John Maclean line with any feeling other than shame at not having been engaged in pushing it all along.*

'In this connection we must point particularly to the glaring danger signal of the fact that while Fascism everywhere else in the world claims to be a unifying policy (e.g. phrases like *Hitler unifies Germany,* or in the Croix de Feu proclamation, *France is one*; there can be no question of disintegration—the Breton and Provençal movements must simply be disregarded—it is a question of maintaining the majority of *L'Esprit Latine* over *L'Esprit (Celtique)*. Similarly, British Finance Capitalism forced back to its last line of defence will cry: "*Britain über alles*" though for the moment, Socialism having neglected Scottish Nationalism, Sir Oswald Mosley did not hesitate to use it and cried in

Edinburgh (1936) amid loud Socialist disapproval, "No Scotsman wishes to be an Englishman". There is no gain-saying the sinister significance of this—it is the nemesis of communist and social democratic neglect of the Scottish question. In contradistinction the Red Scotland line we ad-vocate is in perfect keeping with the dicta of Marx, Engels, Lenin, and Stalin, and with the practice of the Soviet Union in regard to minority elements. We too in Scotland must have an autonomous republic and equal freedom and facilitation for our Scots Gaelic and Scots vernacular languages. Our minimal demand is to have Scotland on the same footing in all these respects as one of the autonomous republics of the U.S.S.R.

'I need only add to that the import of such later develop-ment as the repudiation by the Labour Government and despite their election pledges by the Scottish Labour M.P.s of the policy of Scottish Home Rule which had been one of the planks of the Labour Party ever since its formation, on the specious plea that "Scotland and England must be con-sidered a single economic unit" (i.e. in the teeth of all the facts!) and of the identity of this with the Tory Party's refusal to consider any political devolution (though some Scottish Tories favour administrative devolution) and with the ignominious assertions of the leaders of the reactionary Scottish Covenant Movement that they do not wish any separation from England but only, with all loyalty to the Throne and within the context of the British Commonwealth Home Rule, on the Northern Ireland model. I hope else-where to go on to consider the factors making for con-fusion with regard to the National Question in Scotland today and the way in which during the past twenty-five years Red Clydeside has been bleached a dull unvital grey (e.g. the association of nationalism with anachronistic "Lost Cause" movements, like latter-day Jacobitism, the narrow parochialism of the Scottish bourgeois nationalists them-selves, and the suspect and factitious pseudonationalism, doffed and donned as occasion demands, of politicians interested only in securing Scottish votes for their own

English controlled parties), and the reasons for the in-
sufficient analysis of the National Question in Scotland
among Scottish Marxists (e.g. the misgiving with which the
adherents of the John Maclean line of the early 'twenties
were viewed by the C.P.G.B., mistaken and erroneous
theoretical statements in such books as *John Maclean,
A Fighter For Freedom* by Tom Bell). A tendency to confuse
progressive nationalism with chauvinistic reactionary
nationalism, e.g. German nationalism after 1870 (ably disposed of in William Gallacher's article on 'A Parliament for
Scotland' in the *Daily Worker*, 16th December 1949), a
failure to study, or to recommend for study in this connection such famous Marxist texts as *The National and
Colonial Question* by Joseph Stalin; the controversy between
Lenin and Rosa Luxembourg on the National Question; *A
Socialist and War* by James Connolly, and the relevant
speeches and writings of John Maclean.'

The lack of attention devoted to the National Question
by the C.P.G.B. was indefensible. One hesitates to apply
the term Marxist to reasoning like that of Tom Bell when
he compared Maclean's 'error' on the national issue to the
error of the Bund in Czarist days. (The Bund was a Jewish
Socialist movement which attempted to rally all Jews
under its banner *irrespective of territory*.) The merest glance
will show that this is no parallel at all. Scotland possesses
that *unity of territory* postulated by Stalin in his definition
of a nation. It is interesting to recall in this connection a
passage from Krupskaya's *Memories of Lenin*. Krupskaya
is here referring to the period 1912–13: 'The under estimation of the right of nations for self-determination at
such a time filled Vladimir Ilyitch with indignation. Not
only had the "August bloc" failed to rise to the heights
demanded by the situation, not only did it fail to bring this
question out more sharply, but it even passed a resolution
to the effect that more cultural autonomy . . . was com-
patible with the point in the Party's programme which
demanded the right of nations to self-determination. This
was tantamount to surrendering the position on the national

question, and to restricting the whole struggle to the
struggle for culture—as if it were not obvious that culture
was bound by a thousand ties to the political system.'

It is equally relevant to recall the celebrated controversy
between Lenin and Rosa Luxembourg on the National
Question. This should indeed be regarded in Scotland as a
basic text for study in connection with the National
Question. Lenin combated Luxembourg's contention that
the 'right of self-determination is an empty abstraction'.
He asserted, on the contrary, that to deny the right of
nations to self-determination was tantamount in effect to
offering aid and comfort to the Imperialists against their
colonies, and generally against all nations struggling for
self-government. The following summary of this important
controversy is given by J. Winternitz in his pamphlet on
Marxism and Nationality, in the 'Marxism Today' Series:

'There were even true internationalists, devoted socialists,
who did not understand this bold high-principled policy
(i.e. of Lenin and Stalin on the National Question). Rosa
Luxembourg, the great leader of the revolutionary Left
Wing of the German working class movement, the uncom-
promising fighter against German Imperialism and Imper-
alist War, criticised the Bolshevik Policy on the National
Question, and held up the idea of the international unity of
the working-class against the principle of national self-
determination. Especially with regard to the Polish nation,
but also to the other nations oppressed by Czarist Russia,
she declared that the recognition of the right to national
independence would strengthen petty-bourgeois nationalist
tendencies, weaken the revolution, and lead to the disintegration of revolutionary Russia. But just the opposite
happened, as Lenin and Stalin had foreseen and predicted.
On the basis of voluntary decision, clearly recognising their
common interests with the great Russian Socialist Republic,
the Ukrainians, Byelo-Russians, Georgians, and other
peoples of the Caucasus, dozens of different nations, proclaimed their adherence to the Union of socialist Soviet
republics, this model of a free union of free nations, but if

the development in Poland was different and the most rabid, narrow-minded, anti-Russian bourgeois nationalism could win wide mass support, this was not only the responsibility of the Polish Socialist Party leadership who deserted the cause of international proletarian solidarity, but it was also the fault of the truly internationalist Social Democratic Party of Poland and Lithuania, founded by Rosa Luxembourg, because this party ignored the national aspirations of the Polish popular masses, and so isolated the working class movement from these masses.'

This last sentence is pregnant with meaning for us in Scotland today, and re-examination of the Scottish position in the light of these texts is an urgent necessity, although it has been largely met by the issue at the General Election of 1964 of the 'Communist Policy for Scotland' by the Scottish Committee of the Communist Party.

5

Maclean's significance today;
Willie Gallacher and Abe Moffat

I MUST say a good deal more about John Maclean because of the tremendous influence he has had on my own work for Scotland and my belief that it is only along Maclean's line that Scotland has any worthy future.

The consolidation of his great work called for the speedy and effective execution of his biography, so that although dead he might yet speak, and continue to be a great incitement and inspiration to the workers of Scotland, and to the workers of the world at large. Yet it is easily understandable to see why it has not as yet been published. As Guy Aldred said, it was the policy of the authorities during the First World War to denounce Ramsay MacDonald (destined for the highest political honours) as a dangerous man in order to hide the fact that John Maclean was really the dangerous man.

The sustained vindictiveness meted out by the Establishment to its opponents leads Philip Mairet in his book *Pioneer of Sociology; The Life and Letters of Patrick Geddes*, to say: 'The worst enmities were aroused by his achievements when he had failed to move men in a position to do what he proposed, and simply took action himself. Some of them privately hoped his schemes would miscarry, or even sought openly to obstruct them. If, nevertheless, a plan of his achieved conspicuous success, ill-wishers sometimes had to bear the reproach of being asked: "Why did not *you* do this before? You could have done it", and it was this that rankled. Years after, when such resentments might well have been forgotten, they were strong enough

to frustrate the efforts in Edinburgh, first by a professor
and later of the chancellor (Sir J. M. Barrie) to honour
Geddes with an Ll.D.'

This continued malevolence reminds me that a young
historian of my acquaintance, researching into the life and
activities of Thomas Muir, found the officials at the Register
House and at the National Library not only unhelpful;
they assured him there was nothing else in their keeping
beyond what was already known and used by such historians
as H. W. Meikle, George Pratt Insh and others. But he
persisted and found a lot of material casting new light on
the whole business in their repositories. He found boxes of
correspondence and other invaluable material in the
Kilmarnock Museum and elsewhere that had lain quite unknown to these historians. I am sure the same thing is true
of many issues in Scottish History. Material contrary to
the official assumptions has been—and still is—carefully
concealed. Maclean is still incomparably dangerous.
William Gallacher, in his Autobiography *Revolt on the Clyde*,
tells how in the autumn of 1922, 'while we were in London,
Kirkwood and I visited the Labour Party headquarters
and tried our utmost to get the official endorsement of
Maclean as the Labour candidate for Gorbals. Barnes had
refused to accept the decision of the Conference and was
still in the Government, and was, therefore, finished so far
as the Labour Party was concerned. But the leadership of
the Labour Party would not yield. "Anyone but Maclean",
they said. We told them there would be no other. It was
Maclean or nobody. The Local Labour Party was solidly
behind him; why should they withhold their endorsement?
Maclean wasn't suitable. Why wasn't he suitable? Oh, he
just wasn't suitable, and beyond this we could not get.'

There is the same opposition today to any attempt to
renew Maclean's influence and give the workers access to
the full facts of his career and—more important still—to
his writings. (In his autobiography Gallacher pays full
tribute to Maclean's tireless energy and his magnificent
anti-war work, but coupled with this recognition there was

not only a significant failure to treat Maclean's ideas seriously
or to tell the truth of the disgraceful way in which his work
to secure a Scottish Communist Party was undermined
when he was in jail, and the Communist Party of Great
Britain formed instead. Above all, Gallacher makes out
that Maclean was finally so broken by his prison experiences
as to be mentally irresponsible. Maclean's disgust with his
betrayers is misrepresented as a growing jealousy and
inability to work with others. Maclean's apprehensions with
regard to prison treatment are scoffed at as the delusions
of a man unbalanced by a persecution-complex (Gallacher
forgetting that his personal experiences as a short-term
prisoner have no relevance with regard to the treatment
accorded to a long-term prisoner). Harry MacShane followed Gallacher in all these insinuations as one sheep
follows another through a gap in a dyke. Having now had
the whole of the biographical material in my hands, and
having regard to the first-hand testimony of intimate
friends of Maclean, and to the unimpaired acuity of understanding and coherence of expression in Maclean's writings
at this very time when Gallacher and MacShane would
make out he was mentally diseased, I have no hesitation
whatever in dismissing this atrocious story. It was obviously
manufactured to discredit his advocacy at this time of
Scottish Workers' Republicanism, which is represented as a
typical distortion of an abberant mind.

This is no new expedient in politics, of course, nor is it
new in regard to Scottish Republicanism. Thomas Muir and
Fletcher of Saltoun have similarly had doubts cast on their
mental soundness, and one of the intentions in resorting to
this infamous expedient in respect of Maclean was, undoubtedly, an anxiety to represent his advocacy of Workers'
Republicanism as a new and unheralded departure and
hide the fact that, on the contrary, Maclean came at the
end of a long sequence of Scottish Radical and Republican
thinkers. That his doctrine is, as Rudolf Bringmann,
William Ferris and other writers on the Gaelic Commonwealth show, a doctrine profoundly related to our hidden

Gaelic traditions, and that in coming to it Maclean was not the victim of a mental disequilibrium nor (as MacShane suggested) merely imitative of the Irish Movement, but realising the deepest impulses of his whole nature in their final and highest form, and that so far from indicating any mental breakdown this development is in logical accord with the entire evolution of his political thought, and did not betray but crowned his career. Its relationship to all that had gone before, its consistency with his profound grasp of the whole situation in which Scotland was involved, and the forthrightness, courage and power with which he crowned his stand for Scotland being in themselves enough to dispose at once of the suggestion that Maclean's brain was in any way impaired.

The depth of his Marxian analysis forced John Maclean to stand for Scottish Autonomy and a Scottish Workers' Republic. The betrayal of Maclean's line by the Communist Party of Great Britain (only now so belatedly rectified) resulted in a loss to Scottish Socialism beyond all reckoning. Even Gallacher, who was largely responsible for it, admitted this in his autobiography. It was obvious that until the Communist Party abandoned its anti-Scottish line, and reverted to the lead given by John Maclean, it could never carry the masses of the Scottish people. A similar position was to be found in Catalonia—but there the Communist Party altered its line, and as a direct result, 'its membership went up by leaps and bounds'.

What I have said in the preceding paragraphs gives one of the reasons for the unconceivable delay in producing a biography of Maclean—to do so is to handle lightning. To have Maclean depicted to the life in an adequate biography might be to revive his unique and unprecedented influence with the Scottish workers. The working-class movement in Scotland today is full of people like Iglesias's Spanish followers—'Opium Poppies' (*adomideras*) as they were called, a lot of honest folk somewhat small-minded and devoted to the cult of the petty virtues, if possible non-drinkers and good fathers of their families, 'afraid above

all to go too far'. Striving not for social equality, but for
the betterment of the workers, their 'leaders' (saving the
mark) love the retail, the precedent, and the routine.
Punctilious administration is their main strength. Almost
all of them have been workers. They have, as Andrade puts
it, been educated 'not in the class struggle but in administrative patience'. They were, and remain, afraid of John
Maclean. So his career has been subjected to a general
conspiracy of silence, while fame as great Scotsmen has
been attributed to titled nonentities, party hacks, and all
manner of sycophants and swindlers 'whom the King has
been delighted to honour', in the country at large and in
the working class movement. There has been a failure in
all too many quarters to profit by the lessons of the tragic
fate of the great German and Austrian Social Democratic
organisations, and absence of concrete plans and a clear
theory, and a general prevalence of the weakness best
summed up in the Spanish word, *'Confusionismo'*.

Maclean has not been forgotten, of course, by the class
whose cause he so splendidly championed, though a great
deal has happened since, and it is not easy at this distance
to describe all the outs-and-ins and manifold bearings of
the positions he adopted, and show that not a single one
can be denounced as erroneous or misconceived from the
standpoint of a thorough grasp of dialectical materialism
no matter what changed positions in this respect or that
the Communist Party in Russia or elsewhere may have
adopted since. To show that would call for such a mastery
of Marxism as Maclean himself possessed—and apparently
no other Scot has yet attained. But the stumbling-block
is perhaps less the difficulty than the danger. Maclean's
was a great outgoing spirit with a fearless assurance of his
Socialist integrity informing everything that he said and
did, and this is in itself unpopular today in a country where
even them ajority of Communists are legalistic line-toers,
who seem to regard Communism as a 'guarded flame' that
must be sedulously shielded from the rude beasts that
encompass it, and move as if walking on eggs for fear any

inadvertent step or the next word they utter may land them in heresy and result in their expulsion from the Party, a state of alarm which, of course, is general today and by no means restricted to members of the Communist Party. The general feeling is that there are few quarters now in which it is not definitely far too dangerous to say boo to a goose. For, as a friend of mine wrote me, after a recent visit to Scotland: 'There is not the slightest doubt that at the moment fear is reigning supreme, and the dialectical process just now seems to be to huddle together. Anyway, there is a complete lack of individual assertion, and the man who does assert ever so slightly is to be crushed.'

Apart from this general condition of affairs, it is especially crude to be obviously Scottish; much better get any rude provincial difference of that sort polished away, and share the blessings of English civilisation, compared to which the Scottish tradition is mere barbarism, as a Fife litterateur, a typical 'superior person', has put it, unaware that during his last great trial Maclean, with his wonderful proleptic faculty, said, 'I should say the last place in which a revolution would take place would be Fife.' Assimilation to English standards, this literary gentleman tells us, is the criterion of good breeding. It is 'dreadfully immature to be irreconcilably opposed to English imperialism'. English culture is taken as synonymous with civilisation, nor does its present condition suggest that there should be inverted commas round the word, and any clinging to the broken tradition of Scots language and literature (let alone any 'damned Celtic romanticism') is dismissed as 'mere childishness' and the 'most nonsensical trash'. It behoves reasonable Scots today to recognise that the issue has already been finally decided against them, and to adjust themselves to English culture with all the grace and even gratitude they can muster. Yet this writer calls himself a Socialist! It is, of course, only the cultural snobbism of a renegade Scot and lickspittle of English Imperialism. For Fife, at the time he wrote, had become the centre of the Scottish Literary

Movement, subverted from the revolutionary programme of its initiators by fascising tendencies, and already hand in hand with the dangerous policy which had begun to fill Scotland with a proliferation of Fascistic Boards and Development Councils and offer a pseudo-satisfaction to Scottish Nationalism by transferring the Scottish Office to impressive new buildings in Edinburgh.

No wonder a blind eye is turned to John Maclean's place in Scottish History while all this is going on, for the essence of Maclean's whole position when he declared that he stood for a Scottish Workers' Autonomous Republic lay in a recognition of the fact that Capitalist Development is at a more advanced stage in Scotland than in England (therefore, too, Fascism is further developed) and that in addition to the Capitalist exploitation which the workers in Scotland suffer in common with the workers in England, Scotland is subject also to imperialist oppression from which England is free.

In Russia the rebellion of the suppressed Nationalities considerably aided the workers' revolution. In Spain it performed a similar function. It turns a great many middle-class people against the Central Government; the separatist fights for decentralisation; threatens the State with pulverisation, and, when successful, weakens the resistance the Central Government can put up against the revolutionary movement, and, despite Edwin Muir's supercilious contentions in his *Scott and Scotland*, the Scots language continues to be spoken by the lower classes, by 'illiterate peasants', and by 'the rabble of the town'. 'Nationalist movements are sound, justified, and usually irresistible.' The Scottish Movement will be no exception. The real trouble is that in Germany a combination of clever propaganda and of fierce and inhuman terror have managed to obsess the public mind with problems of foreign policy and caused an unfounded suspicion of all nationalisms as likely to lead to war and Nazi excesses. In England the astuteness of the ruling class, and the suicidal tendencies of the Parliamentary Opposition, have enforced this result and concentrated public attention, even within the Labour Movement, upon the questions of Imperial Policy to the exclusion of everything else. It is high time Scotland was completely taken up with the problems of internal policy instead. Every means will be taken by the Powers That Be to prevent anything of the sort happening. The Irish 'troubles' will be child's play in comparison with the bloody repression visited upon Scotland by the English Government should any such tendency develop. Yet we would win, as the Irish did, and with far less loss to the Scottish nation than for no good end we sustained in the two world wars.

Further evidence of the correctness of Maclean's line lies in the statistics of voting, showing the persistent tremendous radicalism vis-à-vis the English, culminating in actual Socialist majorities, of the Scottish electorate, and the extent to which the progressive will of the majority of the Scottish people has been stultified by the English connection. Along this anti-Imperialist line (Scottish social democracy has always been particularly weak in regard to anti-Imperialism) of Scottish separatism, invaluable impetus can be given for the social revolution in England, Ireland, Wales and elsewhere. As against the all-too-simple cry that the interests of the workers in Scotland and England are identical, there need be no hesitation in stressing that far more exact dialectical discrimination must be given to the alleged consequences of the identity of the interests of Scottish Workers and English Workers. The Communist and Social Democratic neglect of and side-trackings of the Scottish Cause up to now has been responsible for the long confused and inefficient Scottish Nationalist groping and the extent to which the whole thing has now played into Fascist hands. The general Fascist line is to stress its unifying power—'France is one. To hell with Breton nationalism', and 'Hitler unified Germany' and so on. This is the measure to which Socialist neglect of the Scottish Question has played, and is playing, into Fascist hands.

Scottish public life under English ascendancy is full of

sinister little Tory-Socialist alliances of all kinds. The
pretence that Maclean's ideas on the possibility of extreme
ill-treatment in prison were illusory and a product of mental
disease amounts to that. Gallacher should have realised
that the attitude of the authorities to Maclean, the really
dangerous man, and to Gallacher himself, who was relatively of no account, was a very different matter. There is
in any case no excuse for implying that the kind of treatment referred to is not meted out to political prisoners in
this country. Maclean's last pamphlet dealt in full and
incontrovertible detail with an appalling example of such
police brutality in Greenock. In any event the jealous
quickness to discount Maclean's statements and play into
the hands of his enemies is significant enough.

The Communist Party's change of line in regard to
Scotland does not absolve it of this crucial dishonesty. I
analysed the Communist Party's new Scottish policy (not
the one issued at the 1964 General Election but that issued
in the 'thirties) and showed that while its statement of
Scotland's problems was comprehensive and conclusive,
the proposals made to meet these problems were quite
inept. I argued the whole matter point by point in my
quarterly, *The Voice of Scotland*. The Communist Party did
not deign to reply to these criticisms. Communists in other
countries to whom I sent copies were convinced, and
indignant about the slipshod and inefficient way in which
the Scottish Secretariat of the C.P.G.B. had addressed
itself to a question of which it admitted the extreme
gravity, only to fob the matter off with totally inadequate
proposals. The whole thing appeared to be merely tactical.
I am aware that the change was dictated from London—
and took the Scottish Communists as a body completely
by surprise, and that a big proportion of the rank and file
(too long nourished on a false internationalism and quite
incapable of realising that Communism, like charity, should
begin at home) accepted the change with no good grace,
and later largely sabotaged it in practice. In these circumstances to blazon the great name of John Maclean, as was

K

done, was, seeing they had in fact repudiated Maclean as a lunatic, the very height of unscrupulous cynicism.

I have given some of the causes of the delay in publishing a Life of John Maclean. There are others—good reasons and bad; and among them the fact that ticklish personal questions were involved, so it was thought best 'to let sleeping dogs lie'. To write such a book would, it was clear, lead one to commit in the name of reality, many a sin against left utopianism, for one must report the ridiculous, the inefficient, and the reactionary in the Communist Movement, as well as its noble, delightful, intelligent, and moving aspects. The little men on the left have indulged in a form of utopianism which would have offended Marx even more deeply than that of his own day, for if lying rosily about the future seemed to him 'silly, stale, and basically reactionary', what would he have thought of romanticising the Communist Movement (as it existed at the time of Maclean's death and for forty years after that) in Scotland of all places?

It was—and in many quarters still is—in Scotland little better than it was in Spain before the Civil War. 'As regards the political education of the worker, the old reformist bureaucracy disapproves of theory. They are afraid that discussions and polemics might raise doubts in the minds of their members, and that the quietude of the party might be disturbed. They congratulate each other on their lack of theoretical interest, and are proud of "dealing with practical questions in a practical way". As one of them expressed it, they consider that "while poor in books and ideas, they are sure of their social function, conscious in their action, and scientific in their tactics". The younger generation, however, shows a very marked curiosity about political and theoretical questions. They have witnessed the distastes created by merely muddling along, and in the Spanish Socialist Party, as in the British Labour Party, a fierce struggle of the generations is going on. In recent months I have frequently been annoyed when, after making a speech which disturbed the older elements, one of them took me aside, tapped me on the shoulder, and said in a paternal way, "My boy, when you become older, etc." To my surprise I find that this situation is reproduced accurately in Spain. If one of the younger Socialists shows some revolutionary zeal, they take him aside, tap him on the shoulder, and say soothingly, "My boy, you must have read that in the books." And what is in the books naturally does not exist for people who are completely absorbed in their administrative routine. The older members of the Party just read their paper and nothing else.' (Edward Conze, *Spain Today*.)

Some Communist partisans no doubt may be offended by the elevation of an individual, whether it be John Maclean, or Lenin himself, who had the genius to evoke from the 'loose and sluggish plasm' of his countrymen 'all those triumphs to which life must rise and to which he thought himself the casual guidepost'. Yet it must be agreed that neither masses nor leader can function one without the other, and meanwhile Scotland itself offers the best example of the helplessness of masses waiting to be led, but without leaders possessed of that accuracy of insight and courage of judgement which Mr. Edmund Wilson (in his *Travels in Two Democracies*) celebrates in Lenin, and we, so far as Scotland is concerned, must yet do in John Maclean.

Whence, finally, came Maclean's great power—what was the secret of his unparalleled influence? Let me put it in more specific terms than the mere statement that it was due to the depth of his Marxian analysis of Scottish conditions. On what material did that analysis work? Maclean in himself united the diverse elements of Scottish life in an unique way—he was of Highland stock, his work lay in the great industrial belt of the Lowlands, and he married a Border woman. The unification of Scotland— Highland and Lowland, rural and urban—was complete in himself. It was from this that he derived his deep insight and great power. His basis lay far deeper than their conceptions go who take 'civilisation' for granted, un-

conscious of the alternatives to it that have been abandoned throughout nearly all the Western Hemisphere, and
of the fact that, as a German writer recently insisted,
Gaeldom, but for the English, gave good promise many
centuries ago of evolving an ideal 'people's state', and an
increasing number of anthropologists who have recently
written books on savage communities in Africa, Polynesia,
and elsewhere, stress the necessity of breaking the framework of so-called 'civilisation' altogether and returning
after a lapse of centuries to something like what these
savage communities have happily retained (in some
measure at least, despite the missionaries, Imperialists and
exploiters). It is a doctrine that especially appeals to the
Celt, since he stands outside the framework of European
civilisation altogether and his affinities are with the East
rather than the West—as were Lenin's.

It was the last Jacobite rebellion of the '45, when
Bonnie Prince Charlie led his feudal army of Scottish
Highlanders into a bourgeois society, and watched the
slower, less courageous and solid forces of a new order close
steadily upon him. At Culloden Moor the grey tombstones
of the MacDonalds, the MacIntoshes, and the rest mark the
final resting place of 'a form of government which had
ruled humanity for as far back as human history can go'.
The Hanoverian troop of the Duke of Cumberland (he
who became the 'Butcher' and 'Nolkejumskoi' in the eyes
of that complacent middle class for whom he had done
their work so thoroughly and well) were for twenty-five
minutes the agents of a power which was determined to
break this older order down, and to substitute for it a
form of society in which 'freedom' and 'individual liberty'
were to be heard more often than enjoyed.

Scottish Socialists—who want to understand the secret
of John Maclean's great appeal, or are puzzled by the
relative failure of every other Scottish working-class
leader, or are still in two minds about the question of
Scottish Independence—ought to reflect very carefully
indeed on the fact that Raymond Postgate and G. D. H.

Cole in their book *The British Common People, 1746–1938*
wisely seized upon this culminating incident as symbolic of
a demarcation in the history of British proletarianism. A
new dynasty, the present one, was now thoroughly secure.
Constitutional changes were fairly well solidified and a
Cabinet form of Government was established. A new
calendar cost the Puritanical and fatalistic working classes
eleven days of their lives, and that too may have been
symbolical of what the next two centuries were to hold.
Kay's flying shuttle and Huntsman's crucible steel process
heralded the beginning of an industrial revolution in coal,
iron, textile, and pottery works. An era of canal building
was about to begin. New laws were passed in London,
feudality as an instrument of economic and political power
was dead forever. Up to the cliffs of Caithness there was
no place anywhere that was not obedient to Whitehall.
The extinction of the older society made it possible for
England to become the workshop of the world for the
next century and more. This did not happen immediately,
yet the way had been prepared. Her successful withdrawal
from the Seven Years War with most of the spoils prepared
also for a new imperialistic policy, however subject to
change, and for colonial and commercial supremacy.
Enclosures increased and the old medieval cry 'Sheep
devour men' was heard again, resurrected from the
fifteenth-century proletarian revolt of Robert Kett and
the men of Norfolk.

The story of the 'common people' in the eighteenth and
early nineteenth century is largely a history of degradation.
In the second section of the book just named Mr. Postgate
presents an excellent condensation of *That Devil Wilkes*
and *The Rights of Man*. Nineteen chapters carry us through
the industrial revolution, the French wars, the Luddite
disturbances, and Peterloo, stories of half-hearted revolt
and whole-hearted repression.

The rise of trade unions, the activities of Owen, the
Co-operative Movement, the 'hungry 'forties', and Chart-
ism are not slighted. They hold the limelight for almost 200

pages more, until we come to the revival of Socialism. Here the present writer begins to disagree—as John Maclean would have disagreed. He does not think that the weakening and disappearance of revolutionary spirit in the 'eighties 'meant the emergency of a socialism of a distinctively British type', or that any 'narrow proletarianism spirit' was marked in Keir Hardie's 'non-doctrinaire movement for independent Labour representation'.

The part played by William Morris is largely ignored, when it is not misrepresented, while to claim that Robert Blatchford in *The Clarion* represented 'the same views' as those of the Fabians, Hardie, and Champion seems almost as unfounded as to claim that by 1891 'all was set fair, in appearance, for the inauguration of a united Socialist Constitutional party'. It is true that an untimely attempt was made and that a platform was composed, yet the attempt as well as the platform only served to emphasise the impossibility of agreement among so many diverse types. British socialism waned as far as native causes were concerned, when the workers, still largely too uneducated to distinguish between conflicting ideologies, rallied behind Hardie, Havelock Wilson, and John Burns. These were not the men to make Socialism strong in Britain, as subsequent events proved.

And events today are showing even more woefully to those who have eyes to see that the successors of these men in this process of regarding what is really the frittering away of the last remnants of the red radicalism, and the continued habit of regarding what is really a steady waning and degradation of British socialism as a series of progressive working-class victories, means that the lesson has not been learned and that so far as all these people are concerned John Maclean, who cut under and exposed all this process of pseudo-Socialism, which could only progressively betray those it purported to save, when he declared for Scottish Workers' Republicanism, has lived in vain and that they are living in a fool's paradise of mere 'keeping on hoping'.

The enormous following Maclean rallied to his call for a Scottish Workers' Republic shows how much the Socialist Movement in Scotland has lost by its indifference to the Scottish cause, for, as Gallacher admitted: 'In 1918 we had marched through Glasgow on 1st May 100,000 strong. On 1st May 1924 Harry MacShane and I led a demonstration through the streets—100 was our full muster.' That is the measure of what has been—and is still being—lost.

Maclean's attitude to the Scottish question and the unprecedented appeal he made to the Scottish workers were no accident. They derived both from the depth of his Marxian analysis of the social forces in Scotland and from the fact that, as Maxton said: 'Maclean was himself a Scot of the Scots—a synthesis of all that is healthiest and best in our stormy history—the honesty, the forthrightness, the perseverance, the deep humanity, the passion for education, the shrewd practicality, the undeluded materialism.' This is the reason why, writing about him, James Mac-Dougall and others have constantly to refer to Scottish History—to the Chartists, to the Covenanters, to this element and that in the evolution of our national character with its international reputation for hard-headed intelligence, the passion for independence, the fighting spirit, and all our kindred attributes. The role of Scotland in his work is an inseparable and crucial factor in any consideration of John Maclean, because it was in this that he was so sharply differentiated from most Scottish Socialists, with their mere lip-service to (or even opposition to) Scottish Home Rule. But Maclean was on sound and profound Leninist lines and was quite untainted by the Trotskyist exaltation of world revolution instead of getting on with the work immediately to hand.

And above all it ought to be remembered that Maclean's line was in keeping with Lenin's admonition that a revolution, however extreme, in an outlying colony—say India or Africa, to which our Socialists (or some of them) are so sympathetic—is as nothing in its importance for the working-class movement compared with a relatively mild revolution at the heart of an Empire. No wonder Lenin paid tributes to Maclean on several occasions and referred to him, along with Liebknecht, as among those who, in contradistinction to Ramsay MacDonald and the other British Socialists, had remained 'true to Socialism'.

The only other Scotsman prominent in politics who can be bracketed with John Maclean is William Gallacher. As I write these words I have just come from his funeral. There has probably never been a greater funeral cortège seen in Scotland. Working-class leaders from England and many other countries were there. It is estimated that 56,000 people lined the streets of Paisley as the procession passed on its way to the crematorium. I do not think I have ever met at one time so many friends of my own, normally living far apart—Judah Watten, the Australian novelist, and his wife; Hon. Ivor Montagu; John Gollan, General Secretary of the Communist Party of Great Britain; Abe Moffat, the Scottish Miners' leader; Emrys Hughes, M.P.; Lord and Lady Milverton (Wogan Phillips and his wife, Tamara); Palme Dutt; R. Page Arnot, the historian of the miners; John Platts Mills, Q.C.; Alec McCrindle and his wife, Honor Arundel; the veteran Bob Stewart; D. N. Pritt, Q.C., and scores of others—including Colin Wright of the Woodworkers, an octogenarian who died a few days later, and Georgi Frantser, editor of World Marxist Review, representing the Central Committee of the Soviet Communist Party, and other Communist leaders from France, Italy, Austria, Hungary, Bulgaria, Rumania, Cyprus, the Irish Republic, and Northern Ireland.

I have mentioned Bob Stewart, a veteran Communist, who has stood several times for a Dundee constituency. Once in the 'twenties I was Scottish Nationalist Candidate there, in opposition to Stewart, but though I campaigned and conducted meetings, I did not go forward to nomination. Later, when I joined the Communist Party, I had to be 'vetted', since I had a political past as a Scottish Nationalist and as a Socialist Town Councillor and magistrate. Bob Stewart was appointed to 'vet' me. After asking me various questions, he said, 'I don't know what to put you down as—how to describe your position.' 'Oh,' I replied, 'just put me down as a muddled intellectual.' 'Right,' he said, 'you're in.'

Well might the Provost of Paisley say in his short address at the crematorium, 'If only these vast crowds of his townspeople had followed him while he was alive!'

During the General Election I came down from Perth and Kinross, the constituency I was contesting against Sir Alec Douglas-Home, and went with my Election Agent, Alec Clark, to see Gallacher. When we went into his house he was lying back in a chair and we thought he was dead. It was a terrible shock. But in a few minutes he stirred and shortly was able to be propped up. He was very weak. The medicine he was taking had, as a side effect, made it almost impossible for him to eat anything. A still greater deprivation was that he could no longer enjoy his pipe. But soon he rallied and was as full of fun as ever. He was all right, he said—how could he be otherwise, when he had volumes of Lenin and Hugh MacDiarmid to hand! This quip reminded me of the happier occasion three years earlier when a huge gathering was held to mark his eightieth birthday. Asked by the Communist Party what he wanted as a present, he did me the enormous compliment of asking for Hugh MacDiarmid's poems. My *Collected Poems* had not yet been published, but several volumes of my verse were specially bound up in one book for him. And it was for that occasion I wrote the following poem in answer to a request by the Scottish Council of the Communist Party.

SCOTTISH UNIVERSAL[1]

Scottish Universal—but not Hugh Fraser's.
My theme's a better one in every way, sirs.

One of the few decent politicians in Britain today!

1. Scottish Universal, the combine headed by Sir Hugh Fraser, the millionaire draper.

That does not prevent a man having enemies.
On the contrary, the more unswervingly upright
The more powerful the hatred he arouses,
The deadlier the enmity combining against him.
So we have had it here—a man indefatigable
In his attention to affairs, serving his electors
With sustained ability and scrupulous devotion,
A genial man, exemplary citizen, and loving husband.
Not many men tested in the acrid fires
Of public life come through so intact and unsullied,
Pure gold thrice refined. I remember as a boy
Searching a wide Border moor, acres of purple heather,
Looking for white heather—and suddenly
I saw it, hundreds of yards away,
Unmistakable—so in the hosts of men I've known
Willie Gallacher shines out, single of purpose,
Lovely in his integrity, exemplifying.
All that is best in public service—distinct,
Clear-headed and clean-hearted,
A great humanist, true comrade and friend.
Without variableness or shadow of turning,
Eighty years young in his sterling spirit
And the immaculate courage of his convictions.

A sprig of white heather in the future's lapel,
A wave and cheerful handshake for all mankind!
But surely he has some fault? Yes, of course.
The worst of all, the unforgivable knack of being
                        always right.

Gallacher's death, at eighty-three, removed one of the best-known and best-loved leaders of the international working-class and Communist Movement, one of the founders of the C.P.G.B. and for many years (until 1963) its chairman and president.

Born of working-class parents, he began his industrial and political activity at an early age, and through the years developed as the unrelenting fighter for the Socialist cause and the national liberation of the peoples (and not least the Scottish people!). Embodied in his close on seven decades of political activity is the history of the working-class movement in Britain during the modern era. Propagandist for the Social Democratic Federation and British Socialist Party; leader of the Clyde shop stewards during the First World War; imprisoned, batoned, imprisoned again, he was the outstanding leader of the great mass movements of those days—rent strikes, munition strikes, and forty-hour strike, unemployed demonstrations.

He expressed not only the revolt on the Clyde, on which his famous book remains a permanent contribution to working-class history, but the revolt of the oppressed everywhere. First to welcome the Russian Socialist Revolution, he was a delegate from the shop-stewards' movement to the Second Congress of the Communist International, and a personal friend of Lenin. On the executive committee of the Communist Party from 1921 until his death, he took an active part in shaping its course throughout, and gave constant help and encouragement to the *Daily Worker*. Through all these stormy years he was always in the vanguard of the political struggle in Britain. As Communist M.P. for West Fife from 1935 to 1950, he demonstrated to the British political world, accustomed to the old traditions of betrayal or passivity, the true meaning of revolutionary Parliamentarianism. In the testing days of Munich his was the sole voice raised in Parliament against it at the time, while Churchill remained silent. No less outstanding was his demonstration of working-class internationalism. Fighter for Irish freedom; staunch ally of the national liberation struggles of the Chinese and Indian peoples and of the oppressed colonial peoples everywhere, his name became a banner of inspiration for peoples struggling against imperialism all over the world. He served many years on the executive committee of the Communist International. On the occasion of his eightieth birthday, the tributes in his honour flowed in from every country in the world. To the end, until his final illness immobilised him during the last few months, he continued and never spared himself in tireless activity. At the age of eighty-one this great Clyde mass leader of pre-1914 days went on the Aldermaston March. He was teacher and inspirer of generations of young people. In the words of John Gollan, Gallacher 'epitomised all that is best in our Communist Movement. A noble hatred of capitalism, a monumental irreverence for its institutions, class consciousness, devotion to principle, courage beyond compare and utter honesty and integrity.' I am proud to remember my friendship with him, and inseparably linked with that, the memory of my friendship with Jean Gallacher, his lifelong companion and indomitable fellow-fighter in the cause of Communism.

Thinking of Gallacher, I think of another great comrade alongside whom I stood as one of the guard of honour by Gallacher's coffin, before the funeral procession—Abe Moffat. He has told the story of his career splendidly in his autobiography, *My life with the Miners*. Abe Moffat retired from the Presidency of the Scottish mine-workers in 1961. Born in the Fife coalfield in 1896, he went down the pit at the age of fourteen and was continuously associated with the Scottish miners thereafter—as mine-worker, local Councillor, union official, and for nineteen years their President.

His memoirs tell a story of over fifty years' single-minded service to his fellow-workers. As a Communist Councillor in the early years, he had many a fight against the evictions of unemployed miners, while he himself was being victimised by the coalowners and ostracised by the right wing of his own union. He was one of the champions of the uniting of the separate miners' unions into a single organisation, and within a short time he progressed from unemployment and exclusion from the organisation to being President of the Scottish Mineworkers. In that capacity, and during seventeen years on the Executive of the National Union of Mineworkers, he played a leading part in the battles to raise the status of miners under

Nationalisation, and no less to bring their organised strength to bear in support of world peace and international amity. Not least will he be remembered for the great part he played in representing the miners in enquiries on pit disasters, and in fighting for pit safety and welfare. His incomparable staunchness has won the respect even of enemies and his memoirs contribute a notable chapter to the history of our times.

In his book Mr. Moffat says of the General Strike of 1926: 'Here was the greatest betrayal that ever took place in the history of the British Working class. For the first time in history the united struggle of the British trade union movement had brought it face to face with the power of the ruling class in this country. The ruling class had shown they were prepared to use the State machine and all kinds of repressive measures to compel the miners and other workers to accept wage reductions and increased working-hours. On the other hand, they also depended on the right-wing Labour leaders to undermine the united struggle of the British trade union movement, even if it meant the vanguard of the working class being sacrificed and compelled to work for starvation wages and worsened conditions. Collaboration with the ruling class in 1926, as always, led to heavy sacrifices on the part of the workers. Had the General Strike continued, there is no doubt the Government and the employing class would have been compelled to retreat and a great victory could have been won for the British working-class that would have changed the events of history. It was not the General Strike weapon that failed. It was the cowardly and treacherous policy of the right-wing Labour leaders that betrayed the working-class, as MacDonald, Thomas, and company proved later in 1931, when they deserted the movement and went right over to the side of the Tories and the ruling class.'

I agree with every word of that. I agree too that 'The initiative shown by the British working-class, Trade councils, uniting all sections of the Labour and Trade Union movement, becoming Councils of Action, granting permits for all kinds of transport, issuing bulletins, running feeding centres, were proof that the workers, with correct leadership, were capable of winning the struggle, and capable of running the country in an emergency, just as they could in normal times if economic and political power were in their hands.'

I was in the thick of the General Strike too. I was the only Socialist Town Councillor in Montrose and a Justice of the Peace for the county, and we had the whole area sewn up. One of my most poignant memories is of how, when the news of the great betrayal came through, I was in the act of addressing a packed meeting mainly of railwaymen. When I told them the terrible news most of them burst into tears—and I am not ashamed to say I did too.

There is one other particular issue on which I am wholly at one with Abe Moffat. That is the matter of Hungary. I too have visited Hungary and addressed student audiences at the universities of Budapest and Debrecen. I rejoined the Communist Party in 1956 when so many members left it on account of the Russian intervention in Hungary then. For several years now I have been President of the Scottish Council of the British Hungarian Friendship Society and have made many Hungarian friends. What Abe says is as follows—and I agree with every word of it:

'I never had any doubts in my life about where I stood politically.'

Q. What were your views when Russian troops moved into Hungary to suppress what seemed to be a spontaneous movement against Russia?

A. You have to understand that the Russians were invited by the Hungarian Government to go into Hungary, and that is not something new. As a matter of fact we (Britain) have walked into certain countries also, without being invited, but on this occasion the Russians were invited. I made my position perfectly clear at the time when the situation arose. I believe there were very serious mistakes made, but there would have been a more serious mistake if capitalism had been restored in Hungary. I have visited Hungary this year (1961) and could see with my own eyes the progress that had been made in that country.

Q. You have visited Russia on a number of occasions.

A. I have been three times in the Soviet Union.

Q. Would you say that you have been influenced or in any way directed by Russia while you have been a Communist leader?

A. I have never been directed by Russia or any other country in my life. I am quite capable of forming my own opinions without being directed from any source.

Q. But surely it is true there has been a carefully worked-out policy, determined very largely in Moscow for forty years, directing the Communists throughout the world?

A. It is not a statement of fact to say that the Russian Communists direct Communists in other countries. There is a common understanding because of a similar theory based on Marxism, and on that basis, therefore, we have a common understanding, but to say that the Russian Communists direct the British Communists or any other Communists is nonsense.

Q. But, in fact, the British Communists were so few in number that their delegations to Moscow, to International Communist Congresses, were inevitably very small and they would automatically have been dominated by the majority, who were Russians.

A. I do not think ever although you are in a minority that it is necessary to be dominated. I had the opportunity of attending the seventh World Communist Congress in 1935, and I do not know of anyone who dominated me. I had a say in that Congress in the same way as I had at miners' conferences or at the British Trade Union Congress in this country, and no one prevented me from doing that.

Q. Have you never felt there was a very real divergence between dictatorship, what the Russians, I think, call democratic centralism, and the radicalism, out of which you came in the Fife coalfield? Aren't these two different political movements?

A. It depends on what you mean by dictatorship, of course. I contend there is a dictatorship here, but dictatorship of what? Dictatorship of the ruling class. Whereas in the Soviet Union, while there is a dictatorship, it is a dictatorship of the working-class, a dictatorship of the people; whereas here it is a dictatorship of the minority.

(William Gallacher's *Last Memoirs* (Lawrence and Wishart) had not been published when this chapter was written.)

6

Sean O'Casey

It is fitting that a chapter dealing with John Maclean, Willie Gallacher, Abe Moffat, and other comrades should be followed by one devoted to the great Communist dramatist, Sean O'Casey. We were old friends and both vice-presidents of the British Peace Committee, and Sean dedicated *Sunset and Evening Star*, the sixth and last volume of his autobiography, to me and included in it a long chapter in appreciation of my poems. The last time I saw him he had come to Edinburgh to see the production of one of his plays at the King's Theatre. I did my utmost to have his presence in Scotland duly honoured and approached the Saltire Society and the Scottish Centre of the P.E.N. Club, but neither would move in the matter. Finally a party of friends arranged to meet in Norman McCaig's house and we entertained Sean and Eileen, his wife, there. Sean was very quiet and would not drink. After a while, however, Eileen gave him a signal, prearranged no doubt, and Sean had a glass of brandy. It was as if a blind had been pulled up to let the sunshine in. Sean was in great form and even sang us a song.

Writing in the *Daily Worker*, Jack Sutherland, the drama critic, said: 'I suppose it requires the nerve of a professor of dramatic literature at an American Univerity to write a book entitled *The Theatre of Revolt*, and to leave out any consideration of Sean O'Casey. The professor with the nerve is Robert Brustein. O'Casey, he says, "has always struck me as an extremely overrated writer with two or three competent naturalist plays to his credit, followed by a lot of

L

ideological bloat and embarrassing bombast". This is the
traditional bourgeois attack on O'Casey, though I have
never heard his masterpieces, *The Plough and the Stars* and
Juno and the Paycock, to which I presume he is referring,
described as "competent naturalist plays". Brustein's title
is of course highly misleading. The book is a collection of
studies of eight modern dramatists from Ibsen to Genet.
That they have all written plays which express doubt,
despair, hatred, or rebellion against aspects of bourgeois
society and life is unquestioned. But to lump them together under the heading of *The Theatre of Revolt* is absurd
—and an excuse for ignoring real rebels like O'Casey.'

Reviewing the sixth and final volume of Sean O'Casey's
memories recently, *The Times Literary Supplement* referred
to him as 'the most neglected of the famous dramatists of
the day', and as 'an old man in Devon', that is to say, an
exile from his own country, compelled by the bigoted
rancour and egregious clerical censorship of Ireland to live
in England for the past twenty years.

George Orwell once said: 'Considering the story of Anglo-
Irish relations, it isn't surprising that there should be
Irishmen whose life-work is abusing England; what does
call for remark is that they should be able to look for
support to the English people, and in some cases should
even, like Mr. O'Casey himself, prefer to live in the country
which is the object of their hatred.'

As O'Casey says, this was a very curious and revealing
cry from such a lover of freedom and all humanity. 'A
jingo snarl—and from Orwell; from the person who was
stridently, or pretended to be, out for universal freedom of
thought, the fellow who, it is said, fought against uniformity
in life; now bawling out a curse on the head of a writer
because he happened to be Irish.' O'Casey goes on to show
that Orwell knew very well that the support given to
O'Casey by the English was precious little. Two-thirds,
and more, of the support he got came from the United
States; half the other third from his own country, and the
rest from Britain, which included not only England but

also Scotland and Wales. O'Casey lived in England, but so far from living on her, he paid more in tax to her revenue than he received from two-thirds of the United Kingdom.

Even in replying to Orwell, however, Sean O'Casey shows an extraordinary lack of mere personal grievance and the deep understanding and constant fairmindedness that characterises him for, writing in the third person, he goes on to say in reply to Orwell's contention that 'England was the object of O'Casey's hatred', that 'To say simply that this remark is a lie is but to give it a good name; it is more, inasmuch as it throbs with malice, too; certainly O'Casey had no liking for the England that was Orwell and his like. But he had steeped himself in the culture and civilisation of the broad, the vital, the everlasting England, not through means provided by solicitous English Governments, but by desperate, never-ceasing efforts of his own; half a lifetime's work which shows, not a hatred, but a great and consuming love for England's culture.'

It is not only an English writer like Orwell who has vilified O'Casey in this way. The great Irish poet W. B. Yeats did it too. The Abbey Theatre in Dublin rejected O'Casey's play *The Silver Tassie* in 1928, although but for the success of previous O'Casey productions that theatre could never have kept its head above water. Yeats wrote: 'The play is all anti-war propaganda.' In a letter to another correspondent: 'We must keep propaganda out of our blood because three important persons know nothing of it —a man modelling a statue, a man playing a flute, a man in a woman's arms.' Yet Yeats did not keep Irish Nationalist propaganda out of his own poems, and many of his other poems were a plea for aristocracy and militarism. He had accused O'Casey of bitterness, but twenty years afterwards we find him writing: 'O'Casey has written me a friendly letter about my illness, and this has given me great pleasure.'

O'Casey came out clearly as the bigger man of the two. What was the root of the whole trouble? Why is O'Casey so neglected and so constantly vilified and belittled by men not fit to tie his shoe-laces? The reason emerges clearly from Sean O'Casey's reply to a lady who attempted to persuade him that Russian Communism was 'a false dream'. 'Lady,' said Sean softly, 'I have been a comrade to the Soviet Union for twenty-three years, and all she stands for in the way of Socialism, and I don't intend to break that bond for a few hasty remarks made by one who obviously hates the very bones of the Soviet people. And the more you shout, lady, the less I hear.'

'Of course,' Yeats acknowledged, 'if we had played his play, his fame is so great that we could have had full house, but we hoped to turn him into a different path.' Could political prejudice go further? Has any writer of genius ever attempted or hoped to thwart the admitted genius of another writer in so viciously arrogant and uncomprehending a way? Complaining that he himself had been denounced in the chief clerical newspaper, Yeats wrote: 'The educated Catholics, clerics or laymen, know we are fighting ignorance. They cannot openly support us.' But what was O'Casey fighting? Was it not an even greater ignorance, an ignorance Yeats shared to the full? Yet O'Casey continued to have great respect for Yeats *as a poet*. But Yeats was anti-democratic and implacably hostile to Communism. Whereas a Russian essayist has admirably summed up O'Casey's very different character in these words:

'An Irish worker who at an early age felt the full impact of wage slavery aggravated by national oppression, a militant fighter in the class battles of the Dublin proletariat, Sean O'Casey took an active part in the Easter Rising of 1916 and has long been associated with the Communist movement in Great Britain. Neither advanced age nor failing health (O'Casey is practically blind) have kept him out of the front ranks of the battle for peace. He is today one of the vice-presidents of the British Peace Committee and Chairman of the People's Press Limited which runs the *Daily Worker*.'

What apart from his political faith and the incessant impulse to express his genius to the best advantage, kept

Sean O'Casey going all these years, despite the wretchedly poor physique he acquired from his childhood and youth in a Dublin slum? Undoubtedly his happy home life. His wife, Eileen, gave him all the comfort and peace he needed and he was sustained throughout by his great love for her and their three children—two boys and a girl. While he could defend himself splendidly when attacked by Yeats or Orwell or any other reactionary and obscurantist, he could equally well express his admiration of fellow-fighters like Jim Larkin, the great Irish proletarian leader, and George Bernard Shaw, both of whom the present writer knew too. The latter has been abominably denigrated since his death. O'Casey compares Shaw and the Roman Catholic, G. K. Chesterton: 'Shaw was a member of an expanding universe. Chesterton of a narrowing one. Chesterton grew in childishness as Shaw grew in grace. Fear, ever behind Shaw, was ever in front of Chesterton.' He goes on to say: 'There is sense for everyone in Shaw's corner who hates the ulcerous misery of poverty. He was one of those who never hesitated to say into the ears of the man isolated by wealth, and into the ears of the multitude, that what are called man's petty and insignificant needs are related to the stars. "Men honoured Christ", he said, "so long as he remained a charming picture in a golden frame, or hung helpless on a varnished cross; but men begin to yell with alarm when the picture leaves the frame, or when the figure comes down from the cross to become a moving, terrible force in the world." The picture is out of the frame now, the figure is off the cross, and Christ now marches in the surge forward of the masse-men. Blok saw him march through Leningrad at the head of the Red Guards, and he has appeared in China amid cheers; today, too, his shadow falls on Africa. Lo, I am with you always —March! Left, left, left.'

Sean O'Casey, indeed, agreed whole-heartedly with the poem Francis Adams (the neglected Scottish poet I refer to elsewhere in this book) addressed 'To The Christians' over sixty years ago:

'Take then your paltry Christ,
    Your gentleman God,
We want the carpenter's son
    With his saw and hod.

We want the man who loved
    The poor and oppressed,
Who hated the Rich man and King,
    And the Scribe and Priest.

We want the Galilean
    Who knew cross and rod.
It's your "good taste" that prefers
    A bastard "God".'

That quotation is from the last of the six volumes of O'Casey's wonderful autobiography, carrying him to world fame from his youth over seventy years earlier in a horrible Dublin slum where he couldn't get a cheque for £15 cashed, the first money he had ever earned by writing, because he hadn't a banking account, and red tape prevented the publicans and shopkeepers he approached to cash it for him doing so, although he needed the money desperately in a last effort to save his mother's life. His account of that ghastly farce is inexpressibly moving. But so is much else in all these six books in which he uses all the armoury of feelings of a whole man—hatred, love, sorrow, laughter, inextricably mixed as they are in life itself. What a story of his pilgrimage from the early days when he was a builders' labourer, railway labourer, and general labourer. Seventy years' struggle.

Neither Yeats nor anybody else could ever turn such a man on to a 'different path'. Curiously enough Yeats had small, dark, lightless eyes. Sean O'Casey has small-pupilled eyes too, latterly nearly blind, yet this did not prevent him seizing unerringly on the salient detail of dress or posture or behaviour which could bring a character smack before us. He could grab a man out of the streets by his yellow muffler or his drooping moustache, and shake gorgeous comedy out of him, making every cut of his jib leap out of the rhythms of his speech, tagging a man to his navel by the way he spits or paws his face with his hand.

'Even in his early plays, *Juno and the Paycock*, *The Shadow of a Gunman*, *The Plough and the Stars*, O'Casey was definitely on the side of the common people, sharing their hardships and want, their fortitude and stamina in the struggle for Irish freedom. But these early works lacked the breadth of perspective, and a clean conception of the path that struggle must follow.' He acquired that understanding later, and, as has been said, 'not by closing his eyes to realities, but by discovering in these realities the potent forces that make for human progress'. The victory of Socialism in the Soviet Union was a source of optimism for O'Casey. Even when describing the bitterness of temporary reverses and sacrifices, of the oppression and poverty of the Irish worker O'Casey always inspires in his reader confidence in the strength of the working people and helps the reader clearly to visualise the successful outcome of the battle for freedom. Of his later plays it can truly be said that they are an antidote for doubts and dejection, for all the poison that is inculcated by the bourgeoisie and its agents. *The Star Turns Red* (1940) presents the drama of working-class solidarity against a Fascist reaction backed by the Vatican and the corrupt union bosses; *Red Roses For Me* (1942) shows the crimson hues of the setting sun momentarily transforming the discouraged faces of homeless unemployed and women beggars until they seem imbued with determination and resolve and the vision of a better city where the laughter of children and the happiness of youth may come into their own, and they sing the proud song:

'We swear to release thee from hunger and hardship,
From things that are ugly, and common and mean;
Thy people together shall build a brave city,
The fairest and finest that ever was seen.'

In the final volume of his reminiscences scene after scene springs to life as he writes: the scenes of the war-years, of blitzes and refugee children. Life as seen in all O'Casey's work and perhaps more markedly in this last volume, wears all its masks, gay, sad, ridiculous and terrible; but life, we are reminded, is young and has plenty of time to make good. The note left with the reader is one of courage and of wonder. No writer of our time has produced so searching an examination of himself and combined it with so vivid and memorable a picture of this strange, difficult, and remarkable world.

O'Casey venerated Shaw because he made the most of life. 'The earth was his home, and he loved it.' O'Casey shared that love and the great message of his books, and the key to their exuberant vitality and great courage and generosity of mind, is plain in passages such as this: 'How much time has been wasted during man's destiny in the struggle to decide what man's next world will be like! The keener the effort to find out, the less he knew about the present one he lived in. The one lovely world he knew, lived in, that gave him all he had, was, according to preacher and prelate, the one that ought to be least in his thoughts! He was recommended, ordered, from the day of his birth to bid good-bye to it. Oh, we have had enough of this abuse of this fair earth. It is no sad truth that this should be our home. Were it but to give us simple shelter, simple clothing, simple food, adding the lily and the rose, the apple and the pear, it would be a fit home for mortal or immortal men.'

'Odd spectacle of Ireland's only living dramatist with an international repute buried in one of the more arty-crafty corners of England (Torquay),' wrote a fellow-playwright. 'O'Casey looks a little out of place in these surroundings, and the housewives are inclined to stare after him as he walks by in his cap and jersey, with a Red Army badge displayed in his buttonhole. The better-informed ones know that it is just another inoffensive literary gent, and they pass the word along—that's Sean O'Casey.'

On 17th June 1950 during the Stockholm Signature Campaign, the *Daily Worker* published, together with statements of other writers, O'Casey's appeal for the banning of the atomic weapon. It ran as follows:

'We need a lot of things, we do that; but the first thing of all these things is our need for peace.

'May God damn the one who raises a voice for war against the Soviet Union.

'A war with the Soviet Union would but destroy a lot of the good things of the good earth, and we cannot afford to destroy any of them. We need them all.

'Neither old, young, nor little children want to get ready to die, here or in the Soviet Union.

'And we all want to live generously; we want to build, want to build rather than destroy.

'We refuse to destroy, unless it be to destroy all that is ugly, mean, and unhealthy that torments our life.

'We want our factories busy, we want the fields fruitful, we want the streets filled with vehicles carrying goods to all the people.

'Yes, and the sleeping babe nestling at the breast of its mother must sleep in peace.

'To do things, we must be sure of life. To be sure of life, we must first ban the atom bomb.

'You young mothers don't want to bear children to have them blown to pieces or to die in lonely places far from a comforting hand.

'We want life, and we are going to have life—life in honour and in peace.

'To hell with the atom bomb! On this decision we stand with our robust souls. Shove the skulkers aside! Peace for the whole world, for peace is our first need.'

7

Ezra Pound

I HAVE for many years been highly appreciative of, and in some ways greatly influenced by, Ezra Pound. One of the duties that fall to a person in my position every now and again is to pay commemorative tributes to the great dead or birthday tributes to writers who have just reached an advanced age. Recently, for instance, I had to write a poem on Shakespeare's 400th anniversary for the Arts Council, and a poem for a volume of essays and poems devoted to the centenary of W. B. Yeats's birth. Then lately I have had to write a couple of essays on the occasion of Pound's eightieth birthday. I was happy to do so. I well remember how pleased he was at a review I wrote of his book, *How to Read* (probably the only favourable notice it received in Great Britain), and how he sent me a copy of his translations of Cavalcanti. Since my own most recent publications have been extremely long poems, Pound's *Cantos* are pointers to a similar line of development, and the excellent case made out for them against their many critics, as also the defence of his translations against those who complain of Pound's egregious 'errors' and accuse him of inadequate scholarship and a very poor knowledge of the various languages with which he intromits, I am glad is by a Scottish writer and friend of mine, George S. Fraser, who has written what I think is the best of the many books and essays evoked by Pound's work—Mr. Fraser's book, *Ezra Pound* in the Writers and Critics series, published by Oliver and Boyd, Edinburgh—

to whom we owe the best justification of Pound on these counts.

Nearly forty years ago, in an essay on Charles Doughty's poetry, I wrote: 'Only in the U.S.S.R. (and other Socialist countries) today is the trend of poetic effort towards epic—in keeping with the great enterprise afoot in that country, and as a natural consequence of the linguistic experimentation in recent Russian Literature, the liberation and encouragement of minority languages and literatures, and the delatinisation and defrenchification of the Russian language. But the far greater enterprise of Charles Doughty has gone unrecognised or obstinately opposed. It is dismissed (in *The Times Literary Supplement*) as a "reversal of language"—which is on all fours with the fact that Wagner's *words* are generally dismissed as of no consequence. Yet Wagner was right when he spent years studying word-roots. He knew (as Charles Doughty knew) that we were coming to another of the quantitative—as against accentual—periods in culture. It is that lack of historical knowledge which disables no Marxist that is wrong with our mere impressionist commentators on such a phenomenon. (It is this question of quantity as against accent that distorts to most Scots the nature of our pibrochs (*piobaireachd*) of the great period. These knew no "Bar". They were *timeless* music—hence their affiliation with plainsong, with the *neuma*. Barred music—accented music—finds its ultimate form in symphony. Unbarred music—quantity music—expresses itself in pattern repetition; hence the idea that the Celt has no architectonic power, that his art is confined to niggling involutions and intricacies—yet the ultimate form here is not symphony; it is epic.) It is epic—and no lesser form—that equates with the classless society. Everything else—no matter how expressly it repudiates these in the mere logical meaning of what it *says* against what it *is*—belongs to the old order of bourgeois "values", to the nebulous entities described by terms like "spiritual" and "soul"; in short, it stands for the old romantic virtues, which is to say, pragmatically, for nothing. Doughty, as against, say, Auden and Day Lewis, is the only English poet who belongs to the New Order, to our own time. His significance today in this respect dwarfs all the other English poets since Elizabethan times, and the failure of contemporary English *literati* to recognise this is only another confirmation of the Communist diagnosis of the present phase of English literature (it is significant that ex-Prince D. S. Mirski had no difficulty in recognising the overtowering quality of Doughty) as being thoroughly in keeping with the imminent fatal collapse of a degenerate Capitalist society.'

The late Professor Laura Hofrichter's book on Heine shows how, after the great initial success of his early lyrics, Heine had to turn his back on them and seek some means of breaking the tonality of the lyric and introducing into his poems a variety of material. The chapters in Professor Hofrichter's book dealing with this crisis, and the years Heine took to solve the problem, as he ultimately did in his last poems (which, of course, not only never won the great popularity of the early lyrics but have been generally ignored or at least misunderstood and undervalued since) go to the root of the matter and should be carefully per-pended by those who fail even yet to see the full significance of Ezra Pound's great slogan: 'Make it new!'

The complaints against Pound's Cantos I generally hear are (1) against their alleged formlessness and heterogeneity of content; (2) their materialism; and (3) the topicality of a great deal of his references (since these references will rapidly date and cease to be of interest—or even intelligible —as if only the old established content of poetry was valid, and nothing radically new admissible!). So far as Pound's materialism—and by that most of the critics I have in mind mean only the vast amount of sheer fact upon which he draws—is concerned, it is necessary to remind readers that it is a fact that in actual aesthetic products materialist and sceptical writers have considerably surpassed religious ones. This is hardly true of ancient Greece, of course, where the greatest poets, Homer, Sappho, Aeschylus,

Sophocles, and Pindar, preceded the age of unbelief. One must remember, however, that it was far easier to be an aesthetic Pagan that it is to be an aesthetic Christian. Apollo, Hermes, and Aphrodite were really aesthetic beings, but one must have a marvellous eye for beauty if one can discover it in the Three Persons of the Godhead. Every Latin poet, without exception, was a materialist or sceptic. Catullus spoke for all when he said:

> 'Soles occidere et redire possunt;
> Nobis cum semel recidit brevis lux
> Nox est perpetua una dormienda.'

In Italy Dante was religious; but Petrarch, Politian, Ariosto, Machiavelli, Aretino, and all the Renaissance poets were sceptical. Tasso lived under the counter-Reformation and was one of the first pupils of the Jesuits, so he may be called religious. Spain must be conceded, I fear. Cervantes, Calderon, and Lope da Vega were not merely orthodox, but greatly approved the burning of heretics. In Germany, Schiller may have had a touch of religion, but Goethe was on the whole sceptical, and Lessing and Heine were the boldest of mockers. In France nearly all the writers since Voltaire, whether in prose or verse, until after the First World War, have been sceptics. To any doubter of my contention I give Verlaine—unless he objects to take him.

I will not go through the long history of English Literature, but in modern times Shelley, Fitzgerald, and Swinburne were sceptical enough, and where are there three religious poets to match them in aesthetic power? Tennyson alone can be named. It is a good deal to admit that the author of 'In Memoriam' was a believer, but I can afford to be generous.

In truth, it is ridiculous to call even the nominally believing poets religious. 'The Blessed Damozel' is a poem about heaven, but it is the very antithesis of a religious poem. The fact is that there has been, and remains, an

unbroken enmity between religion and art. The Greeks in
their best days were an exception, but even in Greece
Plato at least appeared with his purer religion, and desired
to expel poets and musicians from his republic. In Rome the
fight of religion against the theatre lasted almost till the
end of the Republic. To this day there are no bells in
Mahomedan churches because Mahomet thought music
wicked. In Italy beauty was worshipped by the bad
Popes, but abhorred by good ones. In the fifteenth century
the good Pope, Paul II, tortured and imprisoned poets, and
next century the good Popes of the counter-Reformation
waged implacable war against poetry and art. In England
the theatres were closed for many years, fiddlers were put
in the stocks, and poets had a narrow escape. In France
Molière could hardly get buried, and Lully was refused
absolution till he burnt an opera he had just composed.
Even in the eighteenth century the actress Le Couvreur
was refused Christian burial and had to be buried in a
field for cattle. To this day no priest may enter a theatre.
There is practically no form of art—neither music nor
poetry nor dancing nor the drama nor the novel—which
has not been persecuted for ages by every religion.

If we had not the recent deplorable cases of T. S. Eliot,
Edwin Muir, and W. H. Auden, it is interesting to find how
devitalising and injurious religion can be to a poet. D. G.
James in his *Scepticism and Poetry* says: 'When we consider
the tradition of English poetry since the Reformation, it is
obvious that it is not a Christian poetic tradition. None of
the major poets, with the exception of Milton, have written
as Christians. The case of Wordsworth therefore is of
enormous interest and importance to us. During the years
of his greatest poetic output he wrote as a man of passionately religious imagination, but not as a Christian. After
his acceptance of Christianity he wrote indeed much fine
poetry; but the fact of a decline of his poetic power is
undeniable. Keats and Shakespeare sought to evolve their
own mythologies; Wordsworth satisfied his imagination in
the contemplation of Christian dogma, which, considered

as a mythology, is absolute, where those of Shakespeare and Keats are halting and inexpressive. But a dogma is not merely poetry. It is a great deal more. In Wordsworth, the non-Christian tradition in English poetry once more adopted Christianity: but to its detriment. Wordsworth's later poetry is therefore the most perfect comment we have upon the present state of our civilisation; for Wordsworth who, when all is said and done, possessed one of the most powerful imaginations of our time, sought out Christianity and made it his own, only to impair, though by no means to destroy, the sources of his poetry. And we choose before the dogmatic poetry of the later Wordsworth the poetic failures of Keats and of Shakespeare.'

Mr. James is not the only scholar who has pointed out that the tradition of English poetry is essentially non-Christian. The French poet and philosopher, my friend the late Denis Saurat, went into the matter in far greater detail and in his book *Literature and Occult Tradition*, in which he reviews among other great figures Spenser, Milton, Blake, Goethe, Shelley, Hugo, Wagner, Whitman, and Nietzsche, contends that they have a certain common mental heritage and demonstrates with a wealth of learning how their thought is closely related to primitive conceptions which are embodied in mythology, and have lived on side by side with Christianity in the form of occult doctrines such as those of the Cabala and the theosophists. This view is illustrated by many extracts from the Zohar, one of the main (though almost inaccessible) repositories of Cabalistic doctrine. All the great European poets have derived much of their best poetry from these non-Christian —and largely anti-Christian—sources, without, of course, any recourse to, or indeed knowledge of, the originals. It is one of the great virtues of Ezra Pound in the Cantos that he has nothing to do with any of this pre-scientific material. That is one of the reasons why his work seems so strange to most poetry readers. It wholly lacks the stuff they find so much of in other great poets, and consequently afflicts them with an intolerable sense of unfamiliarity. Professor

Saurat implemented his book with a table listing all the leading ideas of traditional great poetry and showing in the columns just what percentage of these ideas was to be found in each of the great European poets. I am no statistician, but I think I am right in saying that not one of these ideas is to be found in Pound's Cantos. Incidentally, in the Soviet Union, in Yugoslavia, and elsewhere there has been, as I expected, a recrudescence of the very long poem, as long or longer than Pound's Cantos, and these have proved popular with the reading public in these countries, who manifest an appetite for poetry, a readiness to buy up hundreds of thousands of volumes of poetry immediately on publication, and an eagerness to stand in tens of thousands to hear poets reading their poems in the open air.

Again we read in Mr. James's book: 'As in science the formulation of a theorem must lead to further inquiry and research, so in poetry the enjoyment of poetic experience of any part of the world is fraught with the necessity of discovering a wider and more inclusive imaginative apprehension, in which more and more elements in experience are caught up and incorporated. The imagination of the great poet at least never rests from this momentous labour which endeavours to encompass the whole of life, and to achieve a comprehensive unity of imaginative pattern. In many minds, though by no means in all, such a labour, issuing in a failure to achieve such a unity and to perceive in experience such a harmony, leads on to an imaginative apprehension of life in which the world of our experience is seen as only fragmentary, and as a part of a wider reality which in its totality is susceptible only of the dimmest apprehension. Only in the light of that wider reality is this world seen as bodying forth a unity, a unity which in itself it does not possess. For some minds such an imagination of life comes to have a compulsive and controlling reality; an "unknown and no more" takes on an overwhelming significance for the whole of life. The imagination in its passion for unity and harmony is driven to the indulgence of this "dream", which, whether in reality it be "dream" or not, is "a presence which is not to be put by", and which conditions the whole of life.'

In other words, it is precisely the encompassment of the world by the imagination which is seen to be impossible; the essential labour of the imagination, its passion for unity and order, is defeated by experience; and whatsoever of unity and order life is seen to possess hangs on the sense of that which baffles the imagination.

In the preface to his anthology of longer poems Edwin Morgan says that 'whereas in a modern poem by Pound or Eliot the single narrative line has largely disappeared, being replaced by a surprising and significant juxtaposition of diverse material, the reader has to accustom himself to an effect which may be static in time (and therefore seem to lack movement) while being extremely active in space and intellectual scope'. And arguing against the idea that epic is impossible today, Mr. Morgan says: 'Yet when an older unity and an older kind of organisation are given up, perhaps a new unity can be created? By concentration and juxtaposition of disparate material, by hint and suggestion, by range of reference, by musical strategies of thematic development—perhaps by such means it would be possible to compress an epic intention into a few hundred lines?' But a poetry to encompass the whole problem of modern life? Hardly. Mr. Morgan is evidently attempting a compromise; he does not want really long poems—of, say, 30,000 to 60,000 lines—but only of a few hundred lines like *The Waste Land*. But in all the countries 'behind the Iron Curtain' monumental poems are being written—huge poems in keeping with the vastness of their subject-matter, or as I have said in one of my own poems:

'A speech, a poetry, to bring to bear upon Life
The concentrated strength of all our being
(Eloquent of victory in the stern struggle for self-
                                    conquest,

M

—Real freedom; life free, unhampered, unalloyed;
A deep religious impulse moving us, not that
Interpreted by others through systems of belief and
                                        practice
But the craving for the perfect synthesis of thought and
                                        action
Which alone can satisfy our test
Of ultimate truth, and conception of life's purpose)
And not like only the 8 per cent of the fuel
That does useful work in the motor car—the bare 2 per
                                        cent
The best incandescent lamp converts of the energy
                                        received
Into radiation visible to the human eye
—Against the glowworm's 96 per cent efficiency——'

And

' "A fineness and profundity of organisation
Which is the condition of a variety great enough
To express all the world's,
As subtle and complete and tight
As the integration of the thousands of brush strokes
In a Cézanne canvas . . . .
Of art as a vital principle in the process
Of devising forms to contain itself,
Of germinal forces directed
Not upon a void or an ego
But upon living materials, in a way
That becomes physically oppressive
To almost everybody,
Recalling the figure of Aschenbach, whose greatest
                                        works
Were heaped up to greatness in layer after layer—
In long days of work, out of hundreds
And hundreds of single inspirations. . . ." '

The grandeur of the time requires grand syntheses—not

only in fine arts or music, but also in literature, not only in prose but also in poetry. Mayakovsky's poems *Vladimir Ilyitch Lenin* and *Harasho* (*The Poem of October*) render in an impressive epic and lyrical synthesis the history of the preparation and carrying out of the first Socialist Revolution in the world. The Chilean Pablo Neruda celebrates the fight for national liberation waged by the peoples of Latin America in monumental cycles of poems, such as the well-known *Canto General* or the more recent *Canción de gesta*, devoted to revolutionary Cuba—not unlike the huge mural frescoes painted by the Mexican artists. Nazim Hikmet worked out a colossal poetical edifice planned in nine volumes, with more than 3000 heroes, suggestively entitled *Human Panorama*, or *History of the 20th Century*. After the epic *The Desert and Spring* Vladimir Lugovskoi wrote, in fourteen years, the great work of his life, *The Middle of the Century*, a book of poems which he called *The Century's Autobiography*, the result of profound lyrical and philosophical meditations on man, mankind, happiness, Communism. And my friend A. L. Lloyd, the folk-song expert, in a talk on the Third Programme reminds us: 'Not all epic songs are ancient. Eastern Europe abounds in long hero songs created within the last few centuries, dealing with resistance to invaders, struggles against authority, and even—in an epic composed by a Yugo-Slav shepherd—*The Stormy Years of the 20th Century*.'

The Christian religion can never recover from the appalling betrayal it perpetrated when it ceased to regard usury as a deadly sin. There is no computing how much of the gravest evil afflicting mankind today is due to that. All the time-servers, of course, sneer at Social Credit. We who think there is a very great deal to be said for Major C. H. Douglas's proposals are, of course, perfectly familiar with the 'psychological barrier' which prevents most people from finding them other than absurd, and, on the other hand, regarding the present money system as in the natural order of things and as unchangeable as the laws of the Medes and the Persians. But I think Pound is right in laying so much stress on this in his poetry. How otherwise could he have gone to the very root of our discontents? It is probably the most vital issue of all to deal with in relation to the nature, and present position and problems and future, of mankind. Is this not a theme for poetry? Is it a theme which any but a great poet dare tackle?

Long ago Gilbert Cannan wrote: 'Common-form religion in England now calls for no satire, unless the national god, Humbug, should suffer a sea-change and clothe himself in it once more. Turn the satiric vision upon English life, cut it open like a pigeon's crop, and you will find only two facts, money and sex, and those disguised. The ideas of all other facts have long since been thrown by the board, and these two, which are essential for the movement towards stagnation, have been coated over so that such movement may be as like stagnation as may be. Get the ideas of them clear, and at once other ideas, and the recognition of other facts, become necessary. That is work for satire to do, and it will be done as soon as the lively fellow of genius is squeezed out of the ferment which like mud underlies the stagnation. Until it has been done it is very certain that nothing else will—neither in art, nor in politics, nor in social reform, for English fathers will go on lying to their sons about money and sex so that they must either spend their lives in a hectic floundering reaction or subscribe to the current cant about those two all-important facts, and so come to a disastrous atrophy of all their faculties . . . It would be an excellent beginning of a really practical existence if there were clear ideas of money and sex to make way for the domination of mind over them. But nothing could be further from the case. Isolated facts are tyrannous, and these, meanly at war with each other, have pooled their differences and agreed to set up Humbug as their common representative . . . If the community be so far gone that its poetry is dithered with metaphysics, its tradition in the applied arts almost faded out of memory, its political institutions congealed into a mechanical routine, its drama sunk into cold fantasy, its satire diluted to a genial quipping of successful persons, its religion broken up into sectarianism, so that nothing can move men but money or sex, and these being unilluminated by poetry or art or statesmanship or drama or religion, then genius, which of its nature cannot despair, must take refuge and the offensive in laughter. . . . A modern poet could thus apply the logic of his genius to the idea of money or the idea of sex, if he could find either idea pure enough. Modern poets are out of luck, and they end in spleen, or rhetoric, or sentimentality, or metaphysics. A great poet will arise one day to apply his sturdy logic to the two impure ideas of money and sex, and he will arrive at satire, and his work will prove the release of ideas for the genius who comes after him. In a way he will be lucky, if it be luck to find your job lying to your hand and easy of performance, and easy this will be, because of all things genius is less bound by money and sex than any other, has no respect for them, can go for them without excess of hatred, and, as the ideas of them are easily indentifiable, will be able to pick them out of men's brains, wipe them clean, and replace them without any serious shock to the human constitution. When that operation has been performed, then money and sex will begin to exercise their natural function of gravitation towards all other facts, will establish connections with them again, and once more human energy will begin worthily to express itself, and, incidentally, English life will become dramatic instead of theatrical and hypocritical.'

Ezra Pound in the *Cantos* is, I think, the forerunner of that clarifying and rehumanising poet of genius. He has, of course, to suffer the fate of all pioneers, but he will be abundantly justified in the long run.

Until genius burns away all that rubbish, I will continue to be like the Scots-born Baroness Fiona von Thyssen, who, asked recently what she thought about Englishmen, said: 'I love England—but I *cannot*, repeat *cannot* take Englishmen. I think they're the most insensitive bunch of

punks that ever drew breath. They make absolutely no
attempt to try to understand the way a girl's mind works—
they're selfish and unsubtle and generally about as charming
as a rattlesnake. No, you can keep your Englishmen. I'd
go almost so far as to say that it's because of them I left
England.'

Scotland is in even a worse plight than England, of
course. The Scottish people do not want poetry of the kind
I've described—or, indeed, poetry of any kind; all they
want is sentimental, or, better still, jocose doggerel; and
as to long poems, it is natural that any attempt, like my
In Memoriam James Joyce, to provide anything of that
sort, should evoke, in our leading daily paper, the remarks
of a columnist, who, referring to the establishment in 1948
by Mme Jehane Grandjean and Maitre Hisayoshi Naga-
shima of the International School of Tanka and its organ
Revue du Tanka International said: 'The introduction of
Tanka into Western Literature is a reaction against poems
which are too long or lacking in clarity, but it will be above
all effective for spreading the spirit of poetry in all classes
of society. Tanka will develop in the child observation and
judgement and will help him to impart his feelings clearly.
His soul is generally speaking poetic; he loves the beautiful.
On his adventures he discovers a thousand magic things in
the bosom of nature: a sunset marvellous upon the misty
mountain: after a sudden shower burns gleaming like
diamonds in the returning sun, and the rainbow etching
itself upon the clouds, strike him with absolute delight.
But one must infer that a long philological essay like Mr.
MacDiarmid's will be a bit much for him. . . . Mr. Mac-
Diarmid himself has written that he is more concerned
with the East than the West, and the poetry he seeks must
be the work of one who has always known that the Tarim
Valley is more important than the Jordan or the Rhine
in world history. Since Mr. MacDiarmid's poem is, by and
large, in English, quite long, and provoking occasionally
something more than meditation, one may predict the
reaction of a Tanka-trained child, a sort of remote respect:

"Here is a poem
Written by Hugh MacDiarmid
    Mighty in its scope:
A vision of world language.
    The future will say Tanka" '

8

My life, especially recent years

I SERVED in the Royal Army Medical Corps in the First World War, rising to the rank of Quarter-Master-Sergeant. From 1916 to 1918 I was in Salonika with the 42nd General Hospital, which, located on the outskirts of the city towards Kalamaria, was established in the marble-floored premises of L'Orphenilat Grec. I was invalided home with malaria in 1918, but, after a period in a malaria concentration centre near Rhyl, was pronounced A1 again and fit for another spell of service overseas. After a brief stay near Dieppe, I was posted to the Sections Lahore Indian General Hospital stationed at the Château Mirabeau at Estaque near Marseilles. This hospital had been established to deal with Indian and other Asiatic soldiers who had broken down psychologically on the Western Front. We had always several hundred insane there and the death-rate was very high, culminating in the great Influenza Epidemic in 1918 when our patients had little or no power of resistance and died in great numbers. The officers of the hospital were all Indians, mostly Edinburgh-trained, and there were only, in addition to myself, four white N.C.O.s. I returned to Britain and was demobilised in 1920.

Shortly afterwards I became editor-reporter of *The Montrose Review*, and held that position until 1929. I threw myself whole-heartedly into the life of that community and became a Town Councillor, Parish Councillor, member of the School Management Committee and Justice of the Peace for the county. During these years too I published several volumes of Scots poetry, and literary essays, and was a regular contributor of special articles on Scottish subjects of all kinds to various newspapers and weekly and monthly periodicals. The nature of my articles in these quarters ensured that I was constantly involved in political and cultural controversies, and I was also in increasing demand all over Scotland as a public speaker. I took an active part in the formation of the National Party of Scotland and was one of the speakers at its inaugural public meeting in Glasgow in 1928, when I shared the platform with R. B. Cunninghame Graham, Compton Mackenzie, the Duke of Montrose, and others. Later a fusion was effected with the Scots National League under my friend, the Hon. Ruari Erskine of Marr. This was a more extreme body than the National Party of Scotland, and the consequence was that the cutting edge of the New Nationalist Movement was blunted and the control of the party fell more and more into the hands of mediocre demagogues whose first concern was to rid the movement of people like myself, Cunninghame Graham, Compton Mackenzie, and other writers and make it 'safe for mediocrity'. They wanted a Parliament in Edinburgh, but under such auspices that could only be a kind of glorified County Council. They had no real programme save to establish a smaller version of the Westminster Parliament in Edinburgh, while reserving finance, foreign affairs, and defence for the Imperial Parliament. I had nothing but contempt for such proposals and for the appalling commonplace characters who advanced them and spent no little of their time deciding which of them should hold this office or that in a Scottish Government. Bad as I considered the Powers-that-be in Scotland under the existing relationship with England, I thought things must be infinitely worse if men of this sort acquired power. They were themselves all anglicised Scots with little or no knowledge of or interest in Scottish languages, literature, and independent traditions of law and education. They had safeguarded themselves by securing a clause in the Constitution of the

Party, laying it down that no one could become a member who was a member of any of the English-controlled political parties, and in this way they managed within a few years to rid themselves of almost everyone of any distinction in the membership. The clique in control were, of course, themselves Tories or Liberals or Labour (though not Socialist)—if not members of these parties, but they had failed to realise that 'without a vision the people perish'—and they had no vision and hated those who had. I myself was expelled as a Communist, though as a matter of fact I was not a member of the Communist Party at that time.

In 1929 I left Montrose and went to London to become London editor of *Vox*, a radio critical journal which had been promoted by Compton (afterwards Sir Compton) Mackenzie and his brother-in-law, Christopher Stone, with offices in Soho Square shared by their very successful magazine, *The Gramophone*. Alas, *Vox* was under-capitalised and premature—radio was not sufficiently far developed to yield an adequate readership concerned with critical assessments of home and foreign programme material of all kinds; and very shortly the venture collapsed. I then spent a year in Liverpool as Publicity officer for the Liverpool Organisation, a civic publicity and trade development body supported by the Corporations of Liverpool, Bootle, Birkenhead and Wallasey. The Organisation was under the Chairmanship of Sir Frederick Marquis, afterwards Lord Woolton. I lost this post when the Liverpool Organisation merged with a similar body established in Manchester, and returned to London for a brief period.

My domestic affairs were in a bad way and I was divorced in 1931. Shortly afterwards I married again. I had, however, no money or income except for a few guineas now and again for free-lance contributions to periodicals, and we returned to Scotland, where I worked for some time on a little Scottish Nationalist and Douglasite weekly paper, *The Free Man*, edited by my friend Robin McKelvie Black, and from which I got a pittance. It was very difficult to keep our heads above water at this time, and I was not in good shape physically or psychologically. So it was a great relief when my friend Dr. David Orr, who was Medical Officer for the Northern Islands of the Shetland Archipelago, suggested we should join him on the island of Whalsay. How we survived virtually penniless I do not care to recall; but in many respects this Shetland sojourn, which lasted till after the outbreak of War in 1939, was an excellent experience. I got a lot of writing done, and advances on various books—*The Golden Treasury of Scottish Poetry, Lucky Poet, The Islands of Scotland*— served to keep the pot boiling.

After the Second World War began our position which had become increasingly precarious became quite untenable and I returned to Scotland to take a training course at a Government Establishment. I qualified as a precision fitter and obtained a job with a big general engineering firm, Mechans of Scotstoun. I was given charge of the Copper Shell Band Section, turning the bands off copper cups by a battery of power lathes, and then case-hardening them in an electric furnace. I enjoyed this work, but the hours involving compulsory overtime were long and I had to travel to work in the morning and return home at night all in the blackout conditions. So my health began to trouble me again. I had made a good recovery from a serious general break-down I had had in 1935, but the very rough conditions at Mechans and the fact that I suffered serious injuries when a stack of copper-cuttings fell on me and cut both of my legs very severely led me to seek a transfer to the Merchant Service. This was granted and I became first a deck hand—and then first engineer—on a Norwegian vessel, M.F.V. *Gurli*, chartered by the British Admiralty and engaged in servicing vessels of the British and American Navies in the waters of the Clyde Estuary. The other members of the crew were all Norwegians. They were excellent ship-mates, and I soon became an expert at making lobscouse, jam soup, and other specialities, doing the local purchasing, and helping with any necessary

secretarial work. With Anders Olsen as skipper and later
Arvid Carllson, I had a splendid time—all the more so
since we were based on Greenock and the Albert Harbour
there held the biggest small boat pool in Great Britain, with
French, Belgian, Dutch, Scandinavian and other vessels.
Greenock was as a consequence highly internationalised
then and each of its public houses a veritable Babel. My
wife was in Glasgow, but as I received 'seaman's rations'
(which were several times as much as ordinary civilian
rations) and she got these, since I ate on board ship, we
managed well enough.

With the end of the war, however, and the end of my
Merchant Service employment, things became difficult and
we had to subsist for a considerable time on the 'dole'.
Housing was a problem, but help came from an unexpectable quarter. At a meeting of the Saltire Society the Earl
of Selkirk praised my work for Scotland and the quality
of my lyrics, and a little later at his instance his brother,
the Duke of Hamilton, offered me a commodious house
adjacent to his Lanarkshire mansion of Dungavel, near
Strathaven. Standing in a fine wood, it is an ideal dwelling,
but unfortunately we had barely moved in and got ourselves settled when the National Coal Board bought over
the whole estate, to establish a School for Miners in the
mansion and in the adjoining lodges like ours houses for
the school staff. So we had to get out. It was a desperately
difficult business to find anywhere, but we managed to get
the present cottage on a hill-farm a few miles from Biggar.
It was in a derelict condition, not having been occupied
for several years, but it had the supreme advantage of
being rent-free, and my wife speedily made it not only
habitable but comfortable. We had no 'mod cons', and
were getting too old to put up with really primitive
conditions. In a year or two, however, some of the Edinburgh University students, members of the Young Communist League, and other friends came to the rescue and
did all the necessary digging, draining, etc., and we soon
found ourselves equipped with a kitchenette, bathroom,

hot and cold water, flush lavatory, and electric light and other gadgets. The long spell of hardship and near destitution was over and after about twenty years' tough struggle we were very comfortably ensconced in a house of our own with every likelihood that it would prove a permanency.

We could not have anticipated a few years earlier how completely things were about the change in our favour. I had gone with a delegation to the Soviet Union in 1950 and had had a comprehensive tour of the Ukraine and the Republic of Georgia, and it was when I returned from this I received a letter from the Prime Minister's office asking if I would accept a Civil List pension. This was a Gods end and put me on my feet at last.

It was in 1962, however, that the real break-through came. The occasion of my seventieth birthday was celebrated all over the world. There were scores of articles about my poetry in newspapers and periodicals in every so-called civilised country. I had hundreds of greetings telegrams and letters from many countries—so many that for several days round about 11th August, the actual date of my birthday, Biggar Post Office had to run what was virtually a shuttle-service several times a day to deliver the masses of mail. Barbara Niven was with us at the time and she took down a picture or two we had hanging on one of our walls and put up instead enough greetings telegrams to cover the entire wall. A most impressive sight!

Then the Communist Party branches in Glasgow and Edinburgh organised birthday parties for me, and a fund was raised by public subscription to give me a portrait of myself painted by a well-known Scottish portraitist, the late Peter Westwater, R.S.A. The Scottish Home Service of the B.B.C. had a programme about me, and both it and the Third Programme put on long broadcasts of my *A Drunk Man Looks At The Thistle* and *Impavidi Progrediamur*. The most astonishing thing was that on the morning of 11th August all the Scottish daily papers carried long laudatory articles on my work, photographs, etc. None of these papers would have given me any work when I needed it most sorely, and while they now paid tribute to my great services to Scotland and to the Scottish Renaissance Movement in Scottish Literature I had initiated and le*ct* what space they had for special articles on literary matters and for poems continued—and still for the most part continues—to be devoted to the sort of rubbish I had reacted against and to eschew contributions by myself or my leading associates. However, these eulogistic articles helped me in various ways, so long as one knew just what they were and took care to remember that in the *Kulturkampf* that was going on, their writers were really on the other side to mine and were not in any case of a calibre to make anything they said either for or against of any literary—as opposed to social—consequence.

It was otherwise, however, with the books that now began to appear—biographical and critical studies by Kenneth Buthlay, Duncan Glen, Ian Milner, Jessie Kocsmanova, and others, and, in a *Festschrift*, articles (of greater value than the newspaper outpourings) by Professor David Daiches, Edwin Morgan, Walter Keir, and others.

Altogether it was an astonishing outburst of national and international recognition—even (with, as many writers contended, inexplicable tardiness) in England in such organs as *The Times Literary Supplement*, the *New Statesman*, *The Spectator*, *The Listener*, *The Guardian*, etc. The most important mark of the occasion, however, was the publication on that memorable 11th August of my *Collected Poems*, published in America by the Macmillan Company, New York, with a subsidiary edition published by Oliver and Boyd, Edinburgh. This was speedily sold out—mainly in America, from which my greatest support has always come. Though I had at last been accorded a show in English cultural organs, when the Foyle Poetry Prize was presented to me at a big luncheon party in the Dorchester Hotel, not one of the dozen or so English poets there spoke to me at all, let alone congratulated me. Yet I had corresponded with some of them over the years and I was somewhat surprised at their holding aloof on such an

occasion. They had certainly no reason for envy or dis-
gruntlement, because most British literary prizes go to
writers who are safely in the English mainstream, and it
is impossible to imagine a Scottish poet becoming Poet
Laureate or receiving the Queen's Medal for Poetry.
However, I was glad enough to enjoy the company of that
great character W. A. Foyle, who had come up to town
especially for the occasion, despite his age and increasing
infirmity. Alas, he died not long after.

I was pleased also to meet Beryl Grey, the ballerina,
and it was a real thrill to hear Dame Sybil Thorndike read
poems of mine. Then I was whisked off to an upstairs room
to do an interview with Colm Brogan for the B.B.C., and
then to Lime Grove for a TV appearance with Robin Hall
and Jimmy McGregor under the chairmanship of Cliff
Michelmore. A hectic day, and another flood of newspaper
publicity, centring mainly round the story I told to
illustrate how tough a Scottish poet must be, when, during
the great snow-storm and blizzards of the previous winter,
when the drifts were piled up against our cottage right to
the top of the roof, my wife, lying in bed, was wakened by
an unusual noise. She concluded that it was me returning
from a Burns Supper, so, reassured, she turned over and
fell asleep again. The morning showed it had been caused
by a sheep which had walked right up the frozen surface
of one of the drifts and was standing on the roof.

While these English poets refrained from any association
with me, and I have in fact never had many friends among
the English *literati*, in the early days of the International
P.E.N. I was on friendly terms with John Galsworthy,
Hermon Ould, Mrs. Dawson Scott, and many others, in
particular H. W. Nevinson and Arthur Lynch. In the latter
case an additional attraction so far as I was concerned was
the fact that he had been sentenced to death for fighting on
the Boer side. When I knew him he was busy 'confuting'
Einstein's theory of relativity, but I am not in a position
to determine how far he succeeded in this. I have had the
pleasure of friendly association with others who, if not

actually sentenced to death, were unable to return to Britain lest they should be tried for high treason. One of these was the *Daily Worker* correspondent Alan Winnington whom I met in China, and subsequently in East Germany. I also knew several other international journalists, including Alexander Werth, Ralph Parker (who gave me the hospitality of his flat in Moscow), and the Australian Wilfred Burchett. Parker and Burchett I met last when they came into the bar of the hotel in which I was staying in Sofia and we celebrated the occasion with numerous glasses of *mastik*.

Outwith the P.E.N., the English writers I have known best are Lascelles Abercrombie (for whom I wrote my *First Hymn to Lenin*), T. Sturge Moore, W. W. Gibson, J. S. Collis, and Gordon Bottomley—in addition, of course, to the much more numerous tally of those I have known more recently and still know. These belong to a later phase when I was a frequenter of the Soho pubs. My recollections of W. W. Gibson go back to about 1908 when I met him and his sister in Edinburgh, and I was glad to write him towards the end of his life at the instance of the Yorkshire dialect poetess, Dorothy Una Ratcliffe (Mrs. McGrigor Phillips), who had told me that he was lonely, ill, and in very poor circumstances. He was very pleased to receive my letters.

Few and far between—and very limited in other respects —as my relations with English writers have been, the opposite is the case with Irish and Welsh writers. I owed a very great deal indeed to Dr. Oliver St. John Gogarty and to A.E. (George W. Russell). Gogarty took me round the pubs in Dublin he and Joyce used to frequent when they were medical students. I stayed when in Dublin at Gogarty's house in Ely Place, and through him met Walter Starkie, Eoin McNeill, and many others. I had independently established friendships with F. R. Higgins, Seumas O'Sullivan (James Starkie) and his wife Estelle (*née* Solomons). It was through Gogarty and A.E. that I met Yeats, at A.E.'s house. As a rule the sessions at A.E.'s

consisted of monologues by A.E. and Yeats, relieved with
occasional draughts of natural lemonade, but on one
occasion at any rate all the talking was done by Yeats and
myself. Yeats was eager for a thorough exposition of the
Social Credit proposals of Major C. H. Douglas and this I
tried to give him. I do not know whether I could call him
an apt pupil, but he listened very attentively and now
and again lured me into more detailed discussion of certain
aspects of the matter with apposite enough questions
though I felt that on the whole he was on very unfamiliar
ground, and that it would have been considerably easier to
set the matter before him if he had had a better knowledge
of orthodox economics to start with. However, I discharged
my duty to the best of my ability and advised him if he
wanted to pursue the matter further to get in touch with
P. J. Little, who was the leader of the small Social Credit
group in Dublin. At least Yeats and I got on all right
together and I will never forget the privilege and pleasure
I enjoyed as we walked back—he to Fitzwilliam Square and
I to Ely Place—in the 'wee sma' 'oors' of the following
morning.

As to Yeats's bias towards Fascism, I agree with my
friend C. Desmond Greaves, editor of *The Irish Democrat*,
who says of Dr. Conor Cruise O'Brien's brilliant essay on
Yeats's politics in the volume of tributes edited by Professor A. Norman Jeffares: ' "How can a good poet be a
reactionary?", he asks just as Marx asked about Balzac.
Marx replied that Balzac as a truthful artist displayed the
life of his time, while having a false consciousness of it.
So did Yeats.' Mr. Greaves questions this—and so do I.
Apart from hesitating to endorse this too easy get-out, Mr.
Greaves goes on to say—and I would second him—'Dr.
O'Brien shows how at every point Yeats's reaction to
political events was that of the "Protestant middle-class
of merchants and professional people", albeit with aristocratic pretension. Thus sometimes he took the workers'
side, as in the 1913 Dublin lock-out, and wryly applauded
the 1916 Rising, after it was over. But later he accepted

N

the imposed partition settlement and (as Dr. O'Brien proves) more than dabbled in Fascism in the 1930's, when indeed, the class he belonged to was busy dabbling in it.

I was very pleased a year or two later to know that he had my poem 'O Who's Been Here Afore Me, Lass?' off by heart and was in the way of muttering it to himself as he went about his occasions. He did me the honour of including it in his very debatable *Oxford Book of Modern Verse*, and in his preface to that book made the cryptic remark that 'There are certain poets I have left aside because they stand between two or more schools and might have confused the story', naming as among these poets Richard Hughes, Robert Nichols, and myself. Altogether then, it seemed that my seventieth birthday would have seen me properly established as the Grand Old Man of Scottish Letters if it had not been that I constantly failed for alcoholic or other reasons of behaviour to be generally acceptable as anything of the sort and had a disconcerting way of breaking out in unexpected and highly controversial ways. Many of my 'friends' thought I had finally put paid to my account when I announced my membership of the Communist Party and began to play an increasingly active role in that connection. Nearly all those who have published books or pamphlets about me express the view that this accounts in great measure for my failure to acquire far more widespread recognition earlier. There was no little surprise and consternation in 1957 when Edinburgh University gave me the honorary degree of LL.D., and in the citation pronounced at the laureation said: 'The blood of the Border reivers flows in his veins. In days of old he would have ridden forth to harry the English; in these degenerate days he has to content himself with assaulting them with his pen. His pseudonym of Hugh MacDiarmid is well-known, and the bitterness of his controversy can be seen in his many writings, for he is a regular contributor to many British and foreign newspapers and periodicals. He is one of the founders of the Scottish Nationalist Party, the founder of the Scottish Centre of the P.E.N. Club, and the editor of *The Voice of Scotland.* It was in 1925 that there appeared a volume of lyrical poems under the name of Hugh Mac-Diarmid. The intelligent reader was not slow to appreciate that in these poems accomplishment and intensity were balanced as they were not in any Scots poet since Burns. A second volume of verse in the following year confirmed the first impression. Then came something rarer and more formidable—*A Drunk Man Looks At The Thistle*, a poem of serious intellectual import on a large scale of which there are not many such in Scots verse. The student might recall at intervals Dunbar and Burns and John Davidson but all this poetry—lyrical and discursive alike—was also individual and energetic, and, like all good poetry, formidably technical. His work has not failed to provoke criticisms for its techniques, its ideas, its scope, yet nobody ever accepted every word of George Buchanan or David Hume or Thomas Carlyle, and it is with such Scotsmen that he must be ranged as a major figure and not merely an accomplished entertainer whose very antagonisms have their value. Every man will choose from his work what he likes, and there is a body of poems that no man can decry and that Scotland will keep for its inheritance. In all these there is that invaluable spring of energy that so notably infected others. Hugh MacDiarmid will be remembered as a poet and as a leader of poets who would not be what they are without him.'

I have a photograph which I value of the group of honorary graduands on that occasion. I am to be seen at the extreme right and his Grace the Most Reverend Michael Ramsay, Archbishop of Canterbury, at the extreme left. A very remarkable apposition, I think.

It is the custom on these occasions for the honorary graduates in their robes to walk in procession to St. Giles, and the preacher on this occasion was the Very Reverend Dr. George MacLeod. I was in the front row of the pews our party were occupying, when Dr. MacLeod and attendant clergy came up the aisle. I may be wrong but I have a

distinct impression that as he noticed me there Dr. MacLeod
gave a very pronounced wink.

Many of my British—and still more of my Continental—
comrades had thought when I received the Civil list pension
that this was an attempt to wean me away from Communism, and the conferment of the doctorate reinforced
this feeling. If there had been any such intention it was
certainly a complete failure. Some time before I had word
of Edinburgh's desire to honour me in this way, there was
some word of Glasgow University contemplating a similar
move, and I said then that I would not accept it. But a
Dunoon restaurateur, an old Communist, came to me and
said I would have no right to refuse it—for the Party's
sake, if not for my own. I had for that reason no hesitation
in accepting Edinburgh University's offer.

I foreknew that acceptance must add greatly in certain
ways to my responsibilities—and certainly from then
onwards I have been bombarded by requests for lectures
and addresses by all manner of organisations, and these I
have done—and continue to do—my best to fulfil. I became
an Old Age Retirement Pensioner when I was sixty-five,
and the eight years since then have been among the busiest
in my life. Now my wife and others frequently urge me to
call a halt, but I cannot. Those instrumental in securing
the Civil List pension for me were, I believe, Dr. O. H.
Mavor ('James Bridie'), George Bernard Shaw, the Right
Hon. Walter Elliot, Sir John Boyd, and Dr. Douglas
Young: and certainly I feel I owe it to them to make all
that can be made of the distinction by way of service to
the causes I hold dearest, and in particular I recall G.B.S.'s
admonition to spend oneself to the full and have as little
as possible left to swell the scrap-heap at the end.

In addition to all these speaking engagements in Great
Britain, I have been so fortunate as to have frequent
invitations from foreign governments, and acceptance of
these in the last fifteen years has led me several times to
the Soviet Union, several times to Czechoslovakia, once to
Hungary and Rumania, twice to Bulgaria, and most

recently to the German Democratic Republic. On the last-named occasion I attended an international writers' conference there—in Berlin, Weimar, and Dresden—and at Buchenwald, of all places, I had the joy of meeting again after over thirty years my friend the Indian novelist Mulk Raj Anand. We embraced in these terrible surroundings on the terrace above the long line of flaming pyres—one for each nation whose people had been murdered by the Nazis.

At that conference there was a big contingent of Australian writers, and my friend, Ian Milner, of the English Seminar at the Charles University in Prague, had written me to say that many of them were friends of his and he was sure I would enjoy meeting them. I did. They included Frank Hardy, author of *Power Without Glory*, a copy of which I had bought in Peking; Judah Watten, the novelist; Clem Christensen, editor of *Meanjin Quarterly*; Flexmore Hudson, the poet; Geoffrey Dutton; Max Harris; Dorothy Hewitt; the indomitable so-badly crippled Alan Marshall; John Morrison; F. B. Vickers; Bill Wannen; and another old friend I was delighted to meet again after many years, John Manifold. Amongst the Americans were Walter Lowenfels, William Saroyan, Julian Mayfield, and Harry Carlisle, and our party from Britain comprised Anna and John Berger, Sid Chaplin, Margot Heinemann-Bernal, Jakob Lind, Christopher Middleton, and James Aldridge, while among our hosts were Ludwig Renn and Anna Seghers. Others among the writers present from fifty-two countries included Henry Alleg, noted for his writing about the Algerian liberation movement; Marcos Ana, who spent twenty-three years in Franco's jails in Spain; and Tibor Dery, who was imprisoned during the 1956 events in Hungary. I also attended a reception given by the Berliner Ensemble and had the pleasure of conversing with Helene Weigall. I attended a meeting of the editorial board of *Sinn und Form* and was invited to speak. I refused at first but triggered off by someone making a chance reference to Burns—of what W. E. Henley would have called a 'common Burnsite' character, showing no sense of what is really valuable in Burns's work and what the position of Scots Literature is today—I finally agreed. Margot Heinemann (Professor J. D. Bernal's wife) had offered to translate for me, but I forgot all about that and instead of speaking in short paragraphs which she could translate immediately I had spoken them, I rattled on in great style for twenty minutes or so. Margot was faced with a tremendous task, but she acquitted herself splendidly and managed to reproduce in her memory, and translate and deliver, almost all I had said quite accurately, though the subject-matter was new to her. It was a remarkable feat.

While I like Czechoslovakia and have many good friends there, in many ways my five weeks in China was my most interesting experience. The delegation was a small one and included the Earl and Countess of Huntingdon (the Earl sits in the House of Lords as Lord Hastings and the Countess is well known as Margaret Lane, the novelist); Graham Greene; Professor Laureys of the Chair of Comparative Education in London University; Basil Grey of the Far Eastern section of the British Museum; Lord Chorley, the lawyer and President of the British Alpine Club, whom I raced up and down the Great Wall of China, and beat—an achievement he attributed to my Border blood and experience in running and jumping among banks of heather bushes and peat bogs; and Beryl de Zoete, the authority on Balinese and Indian dancing. China is, of course, an enormous country, but we managed to see most of it, since there are abundant internal air services, and though many of the planes are old and rattle like 'tin lizzies' as they go over the mountains in a way that may well daunt any but the very stoutest heart, nevertheless they switched us from area to area in the most expeditious and effective fashion.

Graham Greene came into my room in the hotel one evening and said as he was leaving in the morning for Canton, whereas I and others were going back to Moscow, there was something he wished to leave with me. It was a small stoneware jar of *Moh Tih*, or, as it is called, 'white Wuchang wine'. He said he daren't take it with him as it was liable to explode and wreck the plane, and he enjoined me to be extremely careful too. 'Well,' I said, 'I can't imagine it can do any harm to a confirmed whisky drinker.' So I uncorked it there and then, and drank it. It tasted like a mixture of petrol and vodka, but I suffered no ill-effects beyond the initial 'grue' at its taste.

My travels have most recently included a trip to Canada to see my daughter Christine, her husband Dr. Alistair McIntosh, and their four children. They live at Georgetown, twenty-five miles from Toronto. I did not wish to deliver any lectures but simply to have a holiday, but I consented to speak on Scottish poetry and read some of my poems at Queen's University College. One of my best friends is Professor Emeritus Barker Fairley, formerly of the Chair of German in Manchester University, and author of some of the best studies of Goethe and of Heine in English. I found that his successor as German Professor at Queen's, Professor Humphrey Milnes, had long been an ardent collector of my books and had lectured on and given readings of my poems—incidentally contriving a wonderfully good pronunciation of the Scots. They were enthusiastic about this lecture, and when we arrived there the hall was packed. Unsuspected addicts of my poetry had come from as far afield as Vancouver. The affair was a great success, and after it I met among many others Professor 'Bill' Knox, who had for years given lectures on my work in Canada and in American universities.

There are a surprising number of such friends of mine all over Canada and the United States, and I was sorry I had not agreed to lecture at other Canadian universities. But I hope to go again. On this occasion I preferred to go up to the Muskoka Lakes, where my son-in-law has a summer chalet, and a motor-boat; and we had a wonderful time there. The only other public function I fulfilled was to read poems in the Peace House, again for a packed audience. I read amongst others a poem in which I give

full vent to my dislike of Edinburgh and immediately I
had done so a little fellow sitting on the wooden stairs
(for the affair was held in a big cellar) shouted in an unmistakable accent, 'Whit aboot Glesca?' 'Oh, very well,' I
said. 'I have a Glasgow poem too—but it is worse, I warn
you, than the Edinburgh one.' So I read it too, and several
other Communist and anti-war poems, and had animated
discussions with the young people in the audience.

Another satisfactory feature of my Toronto visit was to
meet several of the editorial board of *The Marxist Quarterly*
published there—Margaret Fairley (Barker Fairley's wife,
and herself the authoress of a number of historical and
political books on Canadian matters), Stanley Ryerson,
James Endicott of the World Peace Council (whose brother
Norman Endicott is the Secretary of Queen's College),
and others. We also met Anna Atenas (now married in
Toronto to an artist whose unpronounceable name I cannot
recall) whom my wife and I had known in Bulgaria; and
the artist Aba Bayevsky, who painted a splendid portrait
of me one day while at the same time I recorded the whole
of *A Drunk Man Looks At The Thistle* for Professor
Humphrey Milnes—a terrible achievement which left me
with a thirst I never expect to be able to allay.

Where am I going to go next if health and harness hold?
I have no idea. The Poetry Center in New York recently
asked me over—but my wife was opposed to my going.
She was afraid I'd 'do a Dylan Thomas' on her. Certainly
I'd be likely to take full advantage of American hospitality,
but as a Communist poet I might have too exciting a time
altogether. We'll see. I'd certainly like to go. Nearly every
other contemporary poet I've ever heard about seems to
have been there. It will be a pity if my name does not
appear on that wonderful list.

9

My election contest with
Sir Alec Douglas-Home

IN THIS chapter and the next I wish for the sake of the
record to set out two matters which I am sure will come up
in any recollection of me in the future. The first of these
deals with the question of my Communism. Many writers in
newspapers and elsewhere have doubted that I am really a
Communist and have preferred to regard me as an oddity, a
maverick. It has been useless to show that I am—and have
been for many years—a card-carrying member of the
Communist Party in good standing, or to point out that I
would scarcely have been chosen as Communist candidate
against Sir Alec Douglas-Home in the 1964 General
Election if there had been any question of my political
competence and reliability. It would have been equally
useless if I had taken the trouble to point to the tributes
paid to my services to the Communist Party of Great
Britain and to International Communism by the Executive
of the British Party on the one hand and by the Russian
Communist Party on the other, or to draw attention to
the long appreciative articles devoted to my work in the
French *Humanité* and the Italian *L'Unita* on the occasion
of my seventieth birthday. The latter—headed '*Ha 70
anni il maggior poeta scozzese del secolo*' and in bigger type
'*Con MacDiarmid in un "pub" di Edinburgo*'—tells how:
'*Era dunque ovvio che io cercassi MacDiarmid in un bar.
Nel suo settantesimo anno, il suo gusto per la bevanda
nazionale é vivo come sempre, e la nostra conversazione ba
proceduto assieme con L'ingestione di una stupefacente
quantitá di whisky.*' The ferocity of that, and other

references to the boozy atmosphere of the occasion, might well be taken to guarantee the truth of the rest of the article were it not for the overkindness (due, no doubt, to the bland influence of the malt whisky that was drunk) of such a testimony as the following: '*Personalmente MacDiarmid é un uomo extremamente simpatico, universalmente popolare in Edinburgo e in tutta la Scozia.*' I would indeed be a very peculiar Communist indeed if that were so. As a matter of fact, however, most of the critics who have written about my acceptance as a poet hold that my Communism has lost me the interest of many readers and some have even contended that it has turned many former and countless would-be friends against me and has militated greatly against my literary influence. So I reproduce here an interview I gave to two Scottish *Daily Express* journalists during the Election in October 1964, which should serve to settle any doubts as to my political position.

Q. Dr. Grieve, you are contesting this election as a Communist. What kind of Communist are you? A Marxist-Leninist theorist? Or is your Communism simply a protest against British bourgeois society?

A. I am a Marxist-Leninist theorist Communist. I am a member of the Communist Party of Great Britain. All sorts of people try to discriminate between various kinds of Communist. There is only one, a man is either a Communist or he's not a Communist. I'm a Communist.

Q. Some years ago you were a Scottish Nationalist?
A. I still am.

Q. You still are?
A. Very much so.

Q. Do you feel you will get more votes as a Communist in Kinross and West Perth than you got as a Nationalist in Kelvingrove in 1950?

A. I didn't expect many votes in Kelvingrove because I was standing on a very extreme ticket—as a Republican Scottish Nationalist with Communist overtones. In West Perthshire, of course, the Scottish Nationalist (Mr. Arthur Donaldson) has stood before, while this is the first time a Communist has stood in the constituency.

Q. This must surely, though, be only a demonstration against the Prime Minister? You can't be hoping, as Communists in some other constituencies may, to come anywhere near the head of the poll? In Fife, for example.

A. Yes, I think they have a chance in Fife. I don't think we have a similar chance in this constituency, but you've got to begin somewhere, you know. I think it is high time that the thin end of the Marxist wedge was inserted firmly into this constituency.

Q. So you selected it because you think it is a stronghold of feudalism and not just because of the Prime Minister?

A. It was largely for both reasons. It was essential to oppose the Prime Minister, as a Communist and as a Scotsman.

Q. You attacked the Prime Minister recently as a big landowner. Do you direct the same sort of attack against the constituency generally? It has a good many landowners in it.

A. I direct the same sort of attack against millionaire landowners, land monopolists actually.

Q. By standing here you are splitting the anti-Government vote. Would it not have been better from your point of view to avoid splitting left-wing support?—And incidentally dividing the Nationalist vote.

A. I don't think either of these things will happen as a matter of fact.

Q. What do you think will happen, then? Where are you getting your support from?

A. We are getting a certain measure of support, though I am not guessing how little or how big it will be. We have been encouraged by our meetings so far and by personal contacts. I put it like this when I became Communist candidate. There are 32,000 voters in this constituency. The great majority are working-class people. It is only a minority who are big landlords or business men. So with the great majority there must be some common ground, and I am trying to find that. I think my campaign will bear fruit in the future, if not immediately.

Q. Had you no difficulty in getting signatories for your nomination papers?

A. None. Quite surprising. We got them very quickly and very easily.

Q. Were all the people who signed really Communists or did they just sympathise with your broad ideals?

A. I can't say. But I should think that most, if not all, of them were certainly Communists.

Q. Why did you break with the Scottish Nationalists? Some of the things you have been saying seem to accord very closely with Nationalist ideas and the National Party has been making some recent headway in Scotland.

A. I think the Scottish policy of the Communist Party is a very much better practical programme for securing the things we require in Scotland. At the time when I broke away from the S.N.P. its policy was that defence, foreign affairs, and finance should be reserved to the Imperial Parliament. They have modified this to some extent, but so far as I can see from recent statements they have issued the first clause in their constitution still pledges loyalty to the Throne. Then they go on to indicate that they believe that the presence of the Queen in Holyrood Palace for two or three months per annum would in some way relieve Scottish political and economic problems. I don't agree with that at all. I think it is perfectly inept.

Q. On the economy, I see from your manifesto that you are utterly against closures of any kind. Surely, in the coal industry, with some pits worked right out, it is inevitable that there should be some closures.

A. Well, there are some outworked seams, of course. What I am really protesting about is the idea, current for some time among writers on economic affairs, that we have too many eggs in the one basket, that there must be a greater diversification of Scottish industry. I think that is bad economic doctrine. If we allow our basic industries to be drawn away from us, or become extinct or less profitable, then we are going to have to depend more and more upon light industries. That is to say, upon the periphery of an economic situation. If we lose the substance of the economic situation and depend upon peripheral developments, I know of no country that has succeeded in having industrial prosperity along such lines.

Q. Do you then agree with Harold Wilson that cars, refrigerators, and that kind of thing can become frivolous?

A. I think that we in Scotland must move with the times and have new industries—electronics and other science-based industries. But the American practice of over-producing certain things and overselling them is a short-term policy that may give an appearance of prosperity but is bound in the long run to land us in greater and greater crises as has happened in America.

Q. Do you think that, economically, Scotland is still a badly neglected nation?

A. Undoubtedly.

Q. In spite of the advances in new industries and projects like Hunterston?

A. All the advances you speak of have not made the slightest difference to Scotland's basic economic problem—unemployment. It is still double that of the worst hit areas in the South. Our emigration drain is unparalleled. Our rural depopulation is continuing. We have had big advances in the tourist industry and in winter sports, but the big landowners who own so much of Scotland are more and more hampering that development, introducing restrictions that hinder access to the land.

Q. Do you not agree that there is bound to be some kind of rationalisation, in, for example, shipbuilding, as there has already been in coal-mining?

A. There may require to be a certain rationalisation. The thing is, we are on the verge of new developments, new techniques. If we are not in a position to ensure that we shall get a fair share of these developments then we will lose out again. The real trouble with Scotland, since the Union, is that we have not had a say in policy-making. We have always been a small minority in the House of Commons. Even on purely Scottish issues, our views could be over-ridden by an English majority who had no knowledge of or interest in us—indeed, whose interests were often opposed to ours. I think that will continue.

Q. This plan you have for meetings of Scottish M.P.s in Edinburgh four times a year, what difference will it make, when the national Parliament will still have supreme control? What is the purpose of these meetings?

A. I think it serves a better purpose than the parliamentary committees dealing with Scottish Bills at the present time. They do not consist entirely of Scottish M.P.s. There is room for intervention by English M.P.s whose interests are opposed to the Bill in question. By bringing the Scottish members together to thrash out Scottish problems I think we make a real gain. There has been far too little research into Scottish problems and discussion of them.

Q. Do you feel the Scottish Grand Committee is a waste of time?

A. Very largely, I think.

Q. If you were returned to Parliament, what would be your role in the Commons? Primarily as an agitator?

A. Yes. I think it would be a live—a very different—House of Commons if a few Communist M.P.s got in, or even only one. I think Willie Gallacher, for example, was one of the finest M.P.s I have known in my lifetime.

Q. You complain in your manifesto about the lack of university places. We have the four old universities plus Dundee, Stirling, Strathclyde, and Heriot-Watt. Do you want more?

A. Yes. We had four universities in Scotland before England had any. You must remember that England has had more than thirty new universities. Furthermore we have a dual culture. I certainly think we should also have a largely Gaelic University, probably in Inverness.

Q. The Scottish Nationalists produced a Budget this week in which they claimed we were subsidising the English to the extent of, I think, £143 million a year.

A. Yes. I saw that. That is money that goes direct to the Exchequer without coming back to Scotland in any way.

Q. Have you any view on how this anomaly, if it does exist, should be put right?

A. It can only be put right by the establishment of an independent Scottish Parliament.

Q. Which is not a part of your current platform?

A. No, we have not gone into that particular point.

Q. Are you yourself working within the Communist

Party for strengthening of its policy on Scottish independence?

A. Oh, yes, undoubtedly.

Q. There are nine Communist candidates in Scotland. How do you rate their chances? What measure of success can they look for?

A. One man sure to gain a good place in the poll is the West Fife candidate. There are others who may not do so well. I am not a prophet nor the son of a prophet, so I am not prepared to prophesy. We will simply do our best. But we are satisfied that the whole campaign in the nine constituencies is well worthwhile. It has its propaganda value, and we are making new friends and members for the Party.

Q. Would you like to predict your own chances?

A. No. This is a first shot, a first time of asking. In a constituency with this particular composition it is perhaps more difficult to make much headway at first than in a more industrialised constituency.

Q. Would you be satisfied to save your deposit?

A. It would be an undoubted achievement to save our deposit. But as you know one of our reasons for fighting this seat is on the issue of political broadcasts and telecasts. I think we've won our point there—for next time.

Q. Have you noticed that the Tory candidate in West Fife is an engine driver and strong trade unionist? Does this not convince you of Tory democracy?

A. I thought that Tory democracy and Tory democrats were as extinct as the coelacanth or the Loch Ness monster. I'm surprised to know that any still survive and occasionally surface.

Q. One final point. You have it in for the big landowners. How would you deal with them? Abolish them?

A. We are going to nationalise the land, except owner-occupied land.

Q. And compensation?

A. Well, that's a matter for consideration. Personally I would be against it.

10

Evidence in the election court

THE second matter I think it useful to set out here in full is the evidence I gave in my action against Sir Alec Douglas-Home in the Scottish Election Court in Parliament House in Edinburgh on 21st December 1964. The raising of this action, and the proceedings before the Court, attracted world-wide attention, and although I lost the case the great majority of the Press at home and abroad thought I ought to have won it, and in fact political broadcasting and telecasting time has now been granted to two of the smaller parties—the Scottish Nationalists and the Welsh Nationalists; but not, of course, to the Communists.[1]

Summing up the case for me that first day of the hearing, Mr. A. J. Mackenzie Stuart, Q.C., said that a General Election was no more than a panoply of individual elections. The question was not whether any party political broadcasts were fair to the Conservative, Liberal, and Labour parties, but to all four men standing in the Kinross and West Perthshire constituency at the General Election. Dr. Grieve was asking the Court to declare the election of Sir Alec Douglas-Home as M.P. for Kinross and West Perthshire void.

Before the first witness was called to give evidence before the two Court of Session judges, Lords Migdale and Kilbrandon, Mr. Mackenzie Stuart submitted that at least

1. Despite the Election Court's finding, it should be noted that time for political broadcasts and telecasts was given to the Scottish and Welsh and Communist Parties in connection with the General Election (1966).

at this stage the B.B.C. and I.T.A., who were represented by counsel, had no office in the proceedings.

The Hon. H. S. Keith, Q.C., explained that Sir Hugh Carleton Green and Sir Robert Fraser were present on behalf of the B.B.C. and I.T.A. organisations which were indirectly being accused of a corrupt practice in the petition.

In the witness box Dr. Grieve said that in August this year (1964) he was invited by the B.B.C. to take part in a centenary programme on the subject of Charles Murray, the Aberdeenshire poet. He prepared a script which was approved by the features producer. On 7th September he received a letter from the features producer telling him that as he had been adopted as a Parliamentary candidate, his contribution had to be excluded from the programme because it would be broadcast in the period of the election. Dr. Grieve said he replied stating: 'I did not know that a Parliamentary candidature affected a purely literary, non-political broadcast.'

Mr. Mackenzie Stuart said it appeared while he was not allowed to broadcast on a non-controversial subject he was going to be paid for it.

Dr. Grieve: Yes, but I have not been. (Laughter.)

On 23rd September he was one of a delegation who met officials of the B.B.C. in Glasgow. The purpose was to find out, if they could, under what rule or enactment the B.B.C. restricted political broadcasts or telecasts to representatives of certain parties and denied the same facilities to others; also, the purpose of the delegation was to find out if that rule could be altered for this particular General Election to enable the smaller parties to have a certain amount of political broadcasts and telecasts.

In the course of the interview he challenged the legality of the attitude taken up by the B.B.C. Later he wrote to both the Director-General of the B.B.C. and the Chairman of I.T.A. on the subject of broadcasting facilities. From the B.B.C. he received a reply stating: 'The agreed series of party election broadcasts in which Sir Alec Douglas-Home

takes part as leader of the Conservative Party makes no
provision for broadcasts other than those arranged with the
main political parties, and no change is contemplated in
the arrangements already announced for this series of
broadcasts.'

He received a reply from Sir Robert Fraser of the I.T.A.
stating: 'This broadcast in which Sir Alec took part as the
Leader of the Conservative Party was one of a series of
party election broadcasts of which the arrangements were
agreed some while ago. This series will not contain broadcasts other than those arranged with the main political
parties.'

Cross-examined by Mr. Keith, Dr. Grieve said that over
a period the Communist Party had been in touch with the
the B.B.C. about broadcasts. Repeatedly he had tried to
find out, and had found out, that there was nothing doing
as far as the minor parties were concerned. 'I was not able
to elicit any information about how that rule was come
by.'

Mr. Keith: Were you never told that a party that put
up at least fifty candidates at the General Election would
be given a broadcast?'

A. No. They seemed to vary that figure. He had never
seen an official announcement to that effect. He did not
consider that it was reasonable policy by the B.B.C. to
make provision for broadcasts by parties with a minimum
number of fifty candidates.

Asked if he considered if every party should have a
chance of broadcasting even though they only had one
candidate, he replied: 'Why not?'

Mr. Keith: Would you have had any complaint if the
B.B.C. had allowed any party with twenty candidates to
broadcast?—No, for the time being.

Q. Would you have thought that was all right?
A. Yes.

Dr. Grieve said it was questionable whether he would
have raised the petition if the B.B.C. had set the figure at
twenty, but there were other factors. In his petition he

was complaining about five Conservative Party political broadcasts.

Mr. Keith: Do you believe that the B.B.C. put out these broadcasts with the intention of promoting Sir Alec's election at Kinross and West Perthshire?

Mr. Mackenzie Stuart intervened to tell the witness not to answer the question, which was a matter for the court.

Lord Migdale said the court would allow the question, and Dr. Grieve replied: 'I believe the B.B.C. were cognisant of the fact that this would be the effect of permitting those broadcasts.'

Mr. Keith: So you believe that putting out these broadcasts did promote Sir Alec's election.

A. Undoubtedly.

Q. Do you believe that if these broadcasts had not been put out he would not have been elected?

A. No. I don't say that.

Asked if he believed that the broadcasts made any difference about whether Sir Alec was going to be returned or not, Dr. Grieve replied: 'They were a valuable asset to him. I think the opposition candidates might have had much bigger polls if they had had equal facilities.'

Mr. Keith: Are you referring to the Labour candidate?

A. Not necessarily. I was rather thinking of myself. I think if I had been allowed to broadcast and put the Communist case I would have got more votes.

Mr. Keith: I take it you do not maintain that the B.B.C. had any intention to display any partiality as regards the Election?

A. Yes, undoubtedly. The B.B.C. is part of the Establishment and is keyed in to the requirements of the Establishment.

Mr. Keith: Do you believe that the B.B.C. deliberately intended to hamper the activities and prospects of minor parties?

A. Yes. I think so.

Q. Do you not agree that there are limits in the amount

to which the B.B.C. should provide facilities for all minor parties?

A. Yes, there are limits.

Q. Do you accept there are limits by which the B.B.C. can cater for all parties, however small.

A. Not all parties, however small. They are in favour of climbing down in regard to small parties, but not the Communist Party. Re-examined by Mr. Mackenzie Stuart, Dr. Grieve said it was correct to say that Sir Alec was allowed to broadcast in the interest of the party he led while he (Dr. Grieve) was not allowed to broadcast on a literary matter.

As I have already said I lost the case, but I, and the Communist Party, were greatly comforted by the general expressions in the Press and elsewhere that we ought to have won, and that the political broadcasts and telecasts arrangements would have to be altered in the way we wished. We were satisfied too with the enormous publicity throughout the world the matter received, and with our thus having been able to so effectively expose a piece of characteristic anti-Democratic trickery.

In my petition I accused Sir Alec or his agent of 'corrupt and illegal practices' under the Representation of the People Act, 1949.

I alleged that Sir Alec or the agent acting on his behalf and with his consent or connivance aided, abetted, counselled or procured the B.B.C. and the Independent Television Authority to incur expense with a view to promoting or procuring his election on account of presenting to the electors Sir Alec or his views or the extent or nature of his backing or disparaging another candidate by party political broadcasts on television and radio on 24th September and 13th October 1964.

I also alleged expenses were incurred by similar broadcasts on 26th and 30th September and 6th and 9th October.

I also accused Sir Alec or his agent of procuring the television companies to refrain from making any return or

declaration of such expenses, contrary to Section 63 of the
Act. Alternatively Sir Alec, I alleged, had paid or ought
to have paid a sum to the B.B.C. and I.T.A. for such
expenses, and in my opinion any such expense, together
with the sums permitted to be expended under the Act,
would have exceeded the authorised sum.

I also claimed that in Sir Alec's return of election
expenses no expenses were included as authorised or incurred by or on his account of television or radio programmes. Such expense ought to have been included in
the return, and Sir Alec's declaration under the Act was
accordingly false.

I therefore asked the court to determine that Sir Alec
was not duly elected or returned and that the election was
void.

Mr. Mackenzie Stuart, reading from a joint minute,
said the combined cost to the B.B.C. and I.T.A. in connection with the five Conservative-Unionist broadcasts was
not less than £4600. The maximum expenditure allowed by
any candidate in Kinross was £724 8s. 6d. and Sir Alec's
total expenses amounted to £717 4s. 1d.

One thing amused me very much when I went to Broadcasting House in Glasgow with the Communist Party
delegation mentioned above. In the reception chamber
there was in a wall niche a gilded bust of myself by Benno
Schotz, R.S.A., with a light above it, and when we went up
to the conference room there was another bust of me,
this time in terra-cotta.

I do not think a similar honour is ever likely to be paid
to Sir Alec Douglas Home.

11

Lewis Grassic Gibbon, William Soutar, Sidney Goodsir Smith, Norman McCaig and others

BEN HECHT quotes Maxwell Bodenheim somewhere as having said of H. L. Mencken: 'Mr. Mencken, who is constantly informing his readers of his libations, is a total fraud. He drinks beer, a habit no more bacchanalian than taking enemas.'

Dylan Thomas was a beer drinker and in the pubs I frequented with him in Glasgow, London, and Oxford I never saw him drink anything but beer and I never saw him really under the influence of drink. I do not doubt that American hospitality was far too much for him and especially that he should have avoided 'the hard stuff' and kept to beer.

A dreadful lot of rubbish has been written about him; the bottom reached by those whose views were summarised by Philip Toynbee in *The Observer* Weekend Review of 17th October 1965: 'not only a sponge but a sponger, too; a drunken bum and layabout, rude, ungrateful and dirty; a self-pitying grown-up baby; a liar, a lecher, a coward, a thief and a poseur; a bad husband and a worse father'.

But two things must be said in reply. Those who knew Dylan were always ready to overlook any of his defects —his company was worth it. And all those who have denounced the dead poet in this way must be reminded that, no matter what truth may be in their charges, Dylan was a far bigger man than all of them put together.

I knew Brendan Behan, too, and enjoyed his company, though he was a little too rumbustious for my taste. I preferred his brother Dominic, to whom Brendan was wont to refer as 'that skinny bastard'. His obituarists have, on the whole, done justice to Brendan. Dylan, on the other hand, has been, I think, grossly overpraised as a poet. I believe he realised that his poetic vein had been worked out or was about to be exhausted and that that was a large part of his trouble. True, he was breaking out in other directions and especially seemed likely to find an outlet in drama. Altogether, however, he knew he did not deserve the role for which he had been cast and could not maintain it. I do not say this 'behind his back'. He knew that was how I felt. But he was a generous soul and at his best splendid company, and I am proud to have known him and ranked as one of his friends. He liked my poetry better than I liked his, and went out of his way at the height of his celebrity to try to help me.

For a long time I was a regular habitué of certain Soho pubs—the Wheatsheaf, the Fitzroy, the Marquis of Granby, and others, and clubs including David Tennant's Gargoyle. Among my boon companions were Betty May ('the cat woman'), Nina Hammett, W. S. Graham, Julian Hanchant, the wild Scottish artists Colquhoun and MacBride, Tambimutti, Elisabeth Lutyens the composer, John Heath Stubbs, and many others. Most of us were 'sponges and (at times) spongers'. Long absence from London and then only brief visits few and far between showed me that things had changed. The kind of people I liked to meet—writers and artists—had probably migrated to other pubs, those of them who were still alive. One of the last of my associates in this way was Louis McNeice, who reminded me very much in his physique and temper and cultural background (both classical scholars) of my friend and fellow poet in Edinburgh, Norman McCaig. Another was James Burns Singer, poet, marine biologist, and literary critic. I had known him in Glasgow and had seldom, I think, met a more extensively read man. He had

a bad family background. His father went insane; his
mother committed suicide. James, I thought, had immense
potentialities if the defects of his temperament and
physique permitted him to 'bring his pigs to market'. They
did not. He died at the early age of thirty-six in September
1964. As *The Times* obituary said: 'His poetry has appeared
in all the leading periodicals and been included in several
anthologies and his poems and descriptive prose have also
been broadcast on the B.B.C. Third Programme. In 1960,
in collaboration with Jerzy Peterkiewicz, he published a
volume of translations of Polish poetry, *Five Centuries of
Polish Poetry*. G. S. Fraser said: 'James Burns Singer's
books *Still and All* (volume of poems) and *Living Silver*, a
prose book about the British Fishing industry, both
published in 1957, had great originality and distinction
but did not convey the full range of his promise. He was a
brilliant reviewer and wrote what is probably the best
critical essay on the Scottish poet he most admired, Hugh
MacDiarmid.'

I agree about this. It appeared in *Encounter*, but I
thought the title 'Scarlet Eminence' absurd. Fraser also
gave a splendid pen picture of our friend: 'Pale, fey, slim,
and elfin-looking, he had a Carlylean fierceness in denounc-
ing what struck him as the shams of London literary life,
but this was combined with a gentleness and affection that
made it easy to forgive his most sardonic diatribes. He will
be remembered by all his friends for his troubling sincerity,
his electric vitality, and a certain quality of childlike
innocence. He had known much of poverty and the harsh-
ness of life in his early years, but latterly he had known
much comfort and happiness in his marriage to his wife
Marie, a distinguished coloured American psychologist,
who survives him.'

I do not know whether Scottish Literature has suffered
more than most by the premature deaths of promising
young writers, but quite a number on whom I and others
had pinned high hopes have died on the very threshold of
their work—not, of course, counting those of 'the lost

generation', the young men (including most of my contemporaries and best friends) in the first decade of the
century. But one of the greatest losses was unquestionably
sustained by the death of James Leslie Mitchell (Lewis
Grassic Gibbon) in his early thirties. That was indeed a
major loss. Despite his youth, he had accomplished a great
deal. He had published sixteen books in categories ranging
from novels and short stories to the future of exploration,
biography, politics, and archaeology. He was only becoming
known to the literary world. The trilogy of novels entitled
Scots Quair was his greatest achievement, quite different
from his other novels (published not over his pseudonym
but over his real name), and evidently drawn from a much
deeper source of his nature than these others, which, like
most novels by Scottish writers were of the usual run of
English novels. There are only a handful of such non-
English novels but they constitute at least the foundation
for a tradition of Scottish novel-writing that is quite
separate and owes nothing whatever to the English novel.
This quality of sheer Scottishness in literature has naturally
had a chequered course—not least at the instance of the
de-Scoticised Scots who form the majority of our reading
public. It reflects a great part of the Scottish Life which
underlies superficial assimilation to English standards, and
only occasionally forces its way to the surface.

Another critic, J. D. Scott, writing in *Horizon*, pointed
out that after 1832 'the national inspiration failed altogether. For more than sixty years, sixty years that saw the
publication of *Les Fleurs du Mal*, and *L'Education Senti-
mentale*, of *Middlemarch* and *Erewhon*, of *On the Eve* and
The Mint, of *Leaves of Grass* and *Daisy Miller*, and of the
Origin of Species and *Das Kapital*, no Scottish writer
attempted to "forge in the smithy of his soul the uncreated
conscience of his race". The country of Dunbar and Burns
was silent. It was not until the end of the century that the
silence was broken. Stevenson's *Weir of Hermiston* came in
1893; eight years later George Douglas Brown's *The House
with the Green Shutters*; J. MacDougall Hay's *Gillespie* in

1914' and finally Lewis Grassic Gibbon's *A Scots Quair*
from 1932 to 1934. We may add to that tiny tally some
Tobias Smollett and the best of Eric Linklater. Fionn
MacColla's *The Albannaich*, belonging, however, to Gaelic
Scotland, also deserves mention alongside these, and so,
more conspicuously, does Sydney Goodsir Smith's *Carotid
Cornucopius*. They all in some measure link up with the
best of the Makars and of Fergusson and Burns and with
Sir Thomas Urquhart's translation of Rabelais.

Edwin Muir pointed out that Sir Walter Scott 'was the
first writer of really great powers to bow his knee unquestionably to gentility and abrogate his responsibility. . . .
There were not many genteel writers before Scott; there
have not been many ungenteel ones since.' There is nothing
genteel about *A Scots Quair*. It is a major contribution to
the line of succession I have indicated. As Dr. Kurt Wittig
points out in *The Scottish Tradition in Literature*, it is 'the
most ambitious single effort in Scottish fiction. The story
moves on three distinct levels: personal, social, and
mythical. . . . If a *A Scots Quair* succeeds on this mytho-
logical plane (and many will probably agree with me that
it does) that is largely because the whole story is told
subjectively. Unlike most other novelists, Mitchell does not
present an "objective" picture of outer reality; instead, we
are given the picture of reality as created in the mind of
his characters. This, however, has nothing to do with the
parole interieure of the modern European or American
novel. For we do not consistently view reality through the
mind of one character, but are constantly flitting in and
out of different minds . . . the total effect of this is a reality
that is *both* subjective and communal. This is the culmination of the inherently dramatic character of Scots, for all
the time somebody is imagined to be speaking—or letting
his thinking become audible—though his identity may not
be specified. One consequence of this dramatisation of the
ego and its mind is the peculiar fact—which we have seen,
for instance, in Hogg or Galt or Neil Munro—that a man
can view himself as "you"; another is the intense animism

or demonism that colours the resultant subjective vision of reality. Different images are flashed together, "dead" things are animated ("snow stroked the window with quiet soft fingers") and the whole landscape, the whole environs, becomes a living impersonation, an active force. *Scots Quair* was perhaps the first major Scottish work of fiction in which any kind of Scots was used throughout for narrative as well as dialogue—that is to say, as a first-order language. And it is by far the most promising attempt that has yet been made towards the creation of a modern Scots prose.'

That is its great significance—this volcanic emergence of the Scots genius at its most veridical when the general view was that Scots was dead and incapable of becoming the medium of a modern literature. It naturally created an upheaval, as *The House with the Green Shutters* did when it appeared, and, in a different category, as did George Malcolm Thomson's *Caledonia*. All three were denounced as muck-raking, as abhorrently ungenteel. But Gibbon's rhythmic prose (not really indebted to James Joyce at all, any more than Joyce himself was to Tobias Smollett) was the only medium in which he could have effected his great purpose. The French writer Pinget has said that prose has now taken over the functions that used to be performed by verse, that fiction is now the place where poetry is most likely to be found—and it is certainly to be found in far greater measure in *A Scots Quair* than in the whole corpus of Scots poetry since the fifteenth- and sixteenth-century Makars, with the exception of the best in Fergusson and Burns. J. M. Cohen in *A History of Western Literature* points out that 'the novel is only the youngest of artisitc forms, and it is easy to imagine that even its commercial varieties may decay in the next fifty years, destroyed by the competition of television and the televised film. . . . In poetry, therefore, remains the hope for literature's survival; and since poetry is at present only read by small numbers, it may well remain for some time, as it is now, private in its form and language. *Avant-garde* poetry, however, with its deliberate defiances of the Philistine, its unrelated images, its neglect of syntax, and of the rules of typography, probably shot its bolt between the wars. It is plainly absurd for the poet to challenge a society which does not read him rather than accommodate himself to the few who may; and poetry since Baudelaire has clearly failed to increase its readership by provocative methods. That there is some new poetry, concerned on the whole with the serious subject of man's isolation, with his need of a myth by which to understand the universe, and of some willed change in his own states of mind, is the most hopeful sign at this mid-century.'

Poetry of this kind in Scotland is mostly to be found not in volumes of verse but in novels, and in Gibbon's *Scots Quair* it is abundant and expresses fully the three concerns Mr. Cohen indicates in the above passage. To those who come without preconceptions and without pretended difficulties with the language or a dislike or lack of interest in anything Scottish, Gibbon's sweeping canvas carrying the reader right from peasant life on the small farms of Kincardine and the Mearns to a modern industrial city, and surcharged throughout, thanks to the sheer magic of the writer's art, with the smells of the earth, the wind on the hills, and the tang of the sea, must come as a revelation, the discovery of a new country. A heart of vehement passion and trustfulness, responsive to all the grief and pain of his people, is revealed in this trilogy in all its grandeur. The chief secret of its success lies in Gibbon's great passionate soul. His rich talents happily combined a soaring lyricism with a passionate love of Nature as embodied in his native landscapes, a robust vernacular idiom and humour, profound and clear-etched characterisation, scrupulous fidelity to life, monumental qualities of epic appropriate to his wide-ranging theme, and a forward-lookingness natural to his wholesome love of life and his instinct to equip himself as thoroughly as he possibly could on every level pertinent to such a comprehensive delineation of past, present and future as he might encompass

with his magnificent memory, total recall, and faith in the
ultimate triumph of humanity.

'Would the years have brought the philosophic mind?'
asks another writer, and answers: 'He had a painfully
hurried life—four years as a reporter, eight in the Services
(which he used to study archaeology) and seven years of
feverish writing. On the verge of material success when
he died, he might have found time to sit back and take
stock of himself. . . . Years and leisure were needed to
mature his great gifts. He got neither and the loss is ours.'

Yes, but the achievement in *Scots Quair*, in *Spartacus*,
in some of the short stories, is magnificent; the years withheld might have produced other things—but these are
splendid in and for themselves, and it may be hoped that
others will build on the foundations he laid and carry to
fresh levels of achievement his unparalleled service to
Scotland. In the meantime, let us be grateful for what he
has given us, and from Ian S. Munro's biography of
Gibbon learn to know what manner of man this was who,
literally at the eleventh hour, showed so conclusively that
the veritable Scots Muse is far from dead, and may well
have a great future before her now, despite all the defeatists.

Writing in *The Scottish Educational Journal*, Ian J.
Simpson put the matter in a nutshell when he said: 'There
used to be a type of Scot, particularly in the north-east,
who asked, and got, little from life beyond the right to
drive himself to death. Such were Shon Campbell, the
legendary student, the farmers whose monuments are the
"consumption" dykes of Aberdeenshire—and J. Leslie
Mitchell. During the last seven years of his short life there
came from him, under his own name or that of Lewis
Grassic Gibbon, what may seem to be a heterogeneous out-
pouring of Scotland, the Middle East, exploration, Central
American archaeology, the revolt of Spartacus—sixteen
books in all. Yet however disparate his subjects appear,
they have all the same burden—"Man is born free and is
everywhere in chains". Like Rousseau and Shelley, he was
obsessed with the belief that A Golden Age in the morning

of the world had been brought to an end by the encroachments of civilisation. Prometheus had been free, is bound,
and must be unbound. The monuments of the Maya, the
monoliths of the Picts, are mute reminders of a happier era
before enslavement by conquerors from Asia, and Spain; or
by lairds, the Kirk, and a cold grudging soil.'

I did not share his belief in such a Golden Age; any
Golden Age humanity might have lies in the future and
must be fought for. I only knew Gibbon personally for a
year or two. We met in London and I visited him at
Welwyn Garden City where he had established his home.
His widow still lives there. Their two children are now
married and have families of their own. I found Gibbon
desperately busy, up to his eyebrows in manuscripts and
proofs and newspaper cuttings, and full of projects for
books. He was just getting into easier circumstances when
he took ill. He felt he had no time to be ill and waved
aside suggestions that he should see a doctor. He felt it was
just a temporary upset. But he quickly got worse. He had
delayed too long, however, and died of peritonitis. He and I
had collaborated in a book of essays, poems, and miscel-
lanea entitled *Scottish Scene* which is still in demand, and I
had expected to collaborate with him on other books. We
devised plans for a comprehensive series of small books on
Scottish subjects and this was taken up by Messrs. George
Routledge and a considerable number of books were
published—not Gibbon's, however (he was too busy with
other books), nor mine (for political reasons), but Edwin
Muir, Willa Muir, Morton Shand, and other Scottish
writers figured in the series. It was ironical that neither
Gibbon nor I who had suggested the series, and were its
joint editors, appeared in it. Gibbon owed much to the
friendship and encouragement of H. G. Wells. He had at
first little sympathy with the project of a Scottish Renaissance Movement but he came round. In politics too he
gravitated to Communism and became an out-and-out
Republican.

William Soutar died at forty-five. Shortly after he

The Scotsman

The Company I've Kept (Hugh Mac-Diarmid, Sydney Goodsir Smith, David Orr, Neil MacCallum, and Norman McCaig at the inaugural meeting of the 200 Burns Club)

Trafalgar Square, with lion

Michael Peto

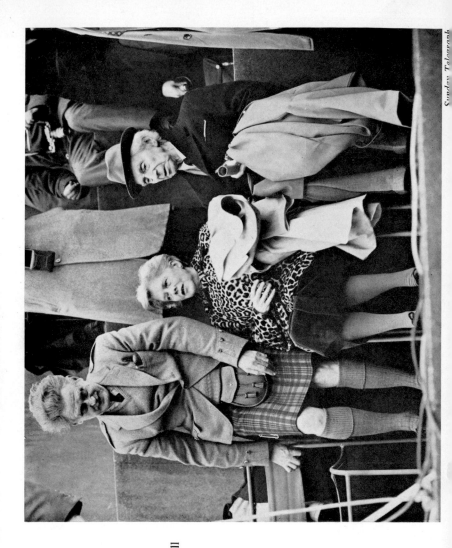

Trafalgar Square,
with Lord and Lady Russell

graduated at Edinburgh University he was stricken down
by an illness diagnosed as 'a form of spondylitis', which
crippled him increasingly, and for more than thirteen
years, until his death on 15th October 1943, he was confined to his parents' house in Perth. I edited his *Collected
Poems* but did not know that his papers included a great
many poems which I had not seen. So the edition was
sadly defective. A selection of his *Poems in Scots and
English* has been admirably edited by Dr. William R.
Aitken, who says in his Introduction: 'Soutar endured his
long illness with heroic fortitude, living out the definition
of heroism he had jotted down as a young man in the
Navy: "What we call heroism, the great deed of the
moment, is the synthesis of a life and character; and
character is what you have been doing and thinking all
your life." There was no self-pity in his attitude nor
morbidity in his outlook. If there is perhaps a hint of his
pilgrim's progress in the titles of his ensuing books of
poetry in English: *Conflict* (1931) and *The Solitary Way*
(1934), with its two sections "Search" and "Solitariness",
if he was, inevitably, a detached observer, in his own
words "set aside from the thoroughfare of life", he was
none the less always alert in his interest and active in his
sympathy. Although his room was his world, he remained
"involved in Mankind".'

His parents' household was a very religious one, and
this atmosphere—and his subsequent friendship with John
Middleton Murry—was, I feel, an inappropriate one for
the development of his best potentialities. These are
briefly glimpsed from time to time in his poems, but for the
most part there is far too much moralising. As I wrote in
my introduction to his *Collected Poems*, 'his work is generally
too pedestrian. It takes all his skill in minor variation to
prevent the weight of repetitiveness in it, and the un-
exciting jog-trot of his verse, from drowning out the vivid
details and turns and twists of whimsicality with which he
offsets that sameness.' Elsewhere I have said that he
thought he was following the ballad tradition when in

P

fact he was only following the tradition of our hymns. However, as his friend Severn said of Keats, it could be said of Soutar, that 'nothing seemed to escape him, the song of a bird and the undernote of response from covert or hedge, the rustle of some animal, the changing of the green and brown lights and furtive shadows'. Soutar was a voluminous writer. Besides his poetry (and he made himself write several poems a day!) he left a long sequence of diaries, journals covering a period of ten years, and a record of his dreams over more than twenty years. An admirable study of Soutar's life and work by Alexander Scott has been published under the poignantly appropriate title, *Still Life*. 'Soutar's work', as I have said, 'is almost equally divided between poems in English and poems in Scots. Many critics have pointed out in relation to modern Scottish poets writing in both languages that Scots invariably proves their happier medium and that, through it, they were able to liberate faculties of their personalities for which their English work afforded no outlet. This general rule was as applicable to Soutar as to all the others: but he applied himself to Scots verse far more systematically than almost any of his predecessors, and, indeed, his output in Scots, and the extent of the Scots vocabulary he used, were greater than are to be found in any other Scots poet since Burns, except for two or three poets still living.'

I also said—and it is worth insisting upon again—'his *Seeds in the Wind* (poems in Scots for children) is not poetry on the same high level as some of his other Scots poems, but it met a felt need, not only among Scots children themselves and among their parents and teachers, fills a unique place, and is likely to be increasingly used in our schools; in short, *The Times Literary Supplement* was right in declaring on its appearance: "In its own country the book should assuredly become at once a minor classic." Alas, that is not the way things happen in Scotland. Recognition is slow. Soutar got little encouragement during his lifetime. *Seeds in the Wind* is winning appreciation slowly but surely. I have no doubt that it *is* a minor classic

of our literature, that the reality of the Scottish Literary
Renaissance Movement can hardly be better exemplified
than just by the difference between these poems for Scots
children and the previous sentimental trash designed for
this purpose from the days of the *Whistle Binkie* school to
our own time, and that it will yet win due esteem as such;
but "at once"—or even "soon"—is not to be looked for in
our all-too-grudging and graceless land.

'A minor classic! The adjective "minor" must be stressed.
I think that the lack of longer poems in Soutar's work, the
extent to which he devoted himself to extremely short
poems, and to trifling oddments like his riddles and epi-
grams, was—consequence of his bedridden state—that, and
the disabling doubt expressed in a letter to myself (June
1934) when he says: "Do you think it is possible to write
great poetry today? I very much doubt it when the whole
world is rotten and going to bits. Isn't it very possible that
your present sense of frustration is the most natural
condition for a poet of my magnitude; and nothing more
(though disturbing enough to the individual) than an
indication that there are many things which poetry cannot
do today until the social life is reorganised." Even more
serious—and due, I think, to the same causes—was his
inability to take "the mad leap into the symbol" and the
infrequency with which his muse takes wing. He was a
whimsical and reflective poet—very Scottish in his insight
into our national psychology and in his humour—and
idiomatically authentic in his use of Scots, but the movement of his verse is almost always too tame—the Scots
Muse has a wilder music and a far more complicated and
unexpectable movement. And nearly all Scots poets
(unlike the English poets) have been song-writers. It is
strange that so genuine a Scots poet as Soutar should sing
so seldom.'

Soutar and I, though friends for many years, by no means
saw eye to eye about the use of Scots, the possible future of
Scottish literature, or politics or religion. But I was glad to
remark that his latest work showed an increasing pre-

occupation with Marxism and Left Wing politics. 'The fact
of the matter is that his thought was evolving—he entertained changing ideas, but was very worried about the
War and about political problems. Only one thing is
certain. His heart was always in the right place. It will
always be true of his poetry—and his place in relation to
Scotland—as he himself sings in "Birthday":

> 'There cam a flaucht o' levin
> That brocht nae thunner ca'
> But left ahint a lanely lowe
> That wadna gang awa'.'

In addition to Soutar, my Scots-writing poet friends have
been Sydney Goodsir Smith, Alexander Scott, T. S. Law,
Albert Mackie, Douglas Young, Helen B. Cruickshank,
Robert Garrioch Sutherland, Tom Scott, Alistair Mackie,
and J. K. Annand. Between them, on a rigorous selection,
they have done a sufficient amount of excellent work to
justify the claim that the last forty-five years have witnessed not only a revival of Scots poetry, but constitute one
of the richest periods in our literary history. Most of those
I have named are still actively writing. Douglas Young is a
fine scholar and has written much in various forms. His
best work includes first-rate translations into Scots of the
plays of Aristophanes; and he also produced a splendid
translation of Paul Valéry's *Cimetière Marin*. But all our
modern Scottish poets have been internationalists and have
translated poems and other works from many languages.

Sydney Goodsir Smith and I have been friends ever since
he began writing—thirty years ago. His work as a poet is
very varied (not in language though—he has stuck to
Scots more consistently than most of us). I think his best
work appeared in the collection entitled *Under the Eildon
Tree* and particularly in a section where he gave full freedom
to his Rabelaisan propensities. I do not know that it is
really a recommendation to mention the fact that Dame
Edith Sitwell thought very highly of his lyrics and praised

them most extravagantly. She included four of them in her big *Atlantic Book of British and American Poetry*. I do not share her opinion of the poems in question, but prefer some of those he wrote on commission for the B.B.C. and his translations of Blok and Tristan Corbière. However, his output has been very considerable and there is ample room to 'distinguish and divide'. And he is not limited to poetry. He had the distinction of having his play *Wallace* produced at the Edinburgh International Festival and has written several other plays. *Wallace* should have ended with the entire cast singing *Scots Wha Ha'e*, but the English producer unfortunately wouldn't have this and insisted on the National Anthem instead, which made a farcical finale. Smith has done excellent critical work, too, in his *Brief Introduction to Scottish Literature* and in his editions of Robert Fergusson and Gavin Douglas. He is also an artist and is art critic of *The Scotsman*.

His best editorial service was when conjointly with the late James Barke and Professor de Launcey Ferguson he issued Burns's *Merry Muses*. This came at a most opportune time, when all the bigots in Scotland were protesting against the relaxation of moral standards and the prevalence of 'dirt, doubt, and disbelief' in our literature, theatre, radio and TV programmes. Reviewing it in *New Statesman* I said: 'Edinburgh has been quite a bit in the news this last year or two owing to the revival of censoriousness on the part of a vociferous minority. The naked lady "Happening" at a Drama Conference at the time of the penultimate (1963) Festival led to portentous official denunciations and a spate of letters in the local papers. These not only deplored the incident and protested vehemently against any relaxation of moral standards, but also objected to the introduction of experimental *avant-garde* elements to the programmes. Fortunately internal evidence showed that most of these protests emanated from a small group of members of the Moral Rearmament movement who in many cases wrote letters over various names to give the impression that the indignation was more widespread among the citizenry than it actually was. The same citizens and the "Holy Willie" element amongst them have at least refrained from inveighing against the annual celebrations of Burns's anniversary. Few, if any, of these Calvinistic worthies have ever dared to go as far as the English writer who protested that an end should be put to the annual laudation of "one of the lewdest, most drunken, and most dissolute libertines who ever stained human records. In all the long erratic history of hero worship there is probably not such another example where a reprobate, a deliberate boasting defaulter from ordinary human decency, has carried his excesses to such repulsive extremes." '

Those who feel this to any degree may well be appalled by *The Merry Muses of Caledonia* by Robert Burns. Burns has been so whitewashed and made safe for public adulation that only a tiny percentage of his admirers can up to now have read the poems in it. It was published a few years ago in an expensive limited edition for subscribers only by the Auk Society, an *ad hoc* club formed for the purpose. Whether the present commercial edition will escape in a city which has recently prosecuted a bookseller for selling a copy of the *Kama Sutra*, obtainable with impunity in bookshops all over Britain and on loan from the public libraries, remains to be seen. Those responsible for its appearance should be congratulated. Outside Scotland itself, alas, too many readers are most likely to be reinforced in the view expressed by Kenneth Hopkins in *English Poetry*, where, despite frequent admissions that Scottish poetry is a different matter altogether and outside his scope, he says:

'The final word on Burns must always be that he is the least rewarding of his country's major exports, neither so nourishing as porridge, or stimulating as whisky nor so relaxing as golf.'

The world has long thought (or said it thought) otherwise. Burns's bicentenary showed no diminishment of his world-wide acclaim. Though ninety-nine per cent of these

enthusiasts can only know the official sedulously respect-
abilised Burns, and of his works little but "Auld Lang
Syne" and a few of his hackneyed love-songs, those
qualified to judge agree with Walt Whitman who said of
these same *Merry Muses of Caledonia*:

'I find his most characteristic Nature's masterly touch
and luxuriant life-blood, colour and heat not in *Tam
O'Shanter, The Cottar's Saturday Night, Scots Wha Ha'e,
Highland Mary, The Twa Dogs*, and the like, but in *The
Jolly Beggars, Rigs o' Barley, Scotch Drink, The Epistle to
John Rankine*, and *Holy Willie's Prayer* (to say nothing of
a certain cluster, known still to a small inner circle in
Scotland, but, for good reasons, not published anywhere).
You may see and feel the man indirectly in his other verses,
all of them, with more or less lifelikeness—but these I
have named last call out pronouncedly in his own voice,
"I, Rob, am here!" '

It is typical of the stupidity, confusion and unscrupu-
lousness of far too many Burnsians that even when Dr.
Duncan NcNaught issued, in supposed vindication of
Burns and on behalf of the Burns Federation of which he
was President, his privately circulated 1911 reprint of the
first edition of *The Merry Muses*, he could not resist the old
game of editorial falsification. Sydney Goodsir Smith,
collaborating with Professor J. de Launcey Ferguson and
and James Barke in preparing the present book, found that
McNaught had garbled, bowdlerised, and partly rewritten
the text, although his proclaimed purpose was to rescue
Burns from the distortions of previous editors. Scotland is
naturally rich in bawdy poetry. I remember Yeats remark-
ing of one piece attributed to Burns, which contains the
lines:

> 'I put my hand atweesh her feet
> And felt her wee bit mawkin'

that it was the best bawdy poem he had ever heard—a
judgement heartily endorsed by Gogarty, a connoisseur in
such matters.

There is nothing here to equal Dunbar's superb satire,
'The Twa Maryit Wemen and the Wedo', one of the most
flaying things in all literature, and nothing so devastatingly
Rabelaisian as the unpublished (and probably unpublish-
able) 'Ball of Kirriemuir'! It is, as Mr. Barke says,
'typical of the Scots that when the Highland Division
entered Tripoli after the success of the North African
campaign, they paraded before Winston Churchill singing
verses from "The Ball of Kirriemuir" in their lustiest voice.
It is reported that, at first, Churchill was slightly puzzled
by the song, but soon broke into a broad grin. This, indeed,
is the great leaven that breaks through all Scottish bawdry.
It is never sneering or sly or prurient or sexy or titillating.
It is lusty like a good broad bare female buttock.'

Caledonia *stern* and wild, in very truth. Admirably put
together, with excellent introductory essays, this volume
will make it impossible for hypocritical Burnsites to claim
that most of *The Merry Muses* is apocryphal. Burns has at
last been set securely on his authentic feet of clay. As
Yeats wrote:

> 'Love has pitched his mansion in
> The place of excrement.'

Burns simply agreed with God that was the right place
for it.

The Lord Provost of Edinburgh, the Convener of the
Church of Scotland's Church and National Committee, the
members of the Edinburgh International Festival Committee, and all the hosts of 'blue noses' and bigots in our
midst, may, under the cloak of religion, think otherwise.
But these people should not be allowed any say in relation
to literature and the Arts. They have already gone far to
ruin the Edinburgh Festival and caused the resignation of
the Earl of Harewood and his deputy director, Michael
Whewell, and have viciously attacked by far the best
theatrical venture in our midst, the Traverse Theatre

Club, and its gallant impresario, Jim Haynes. The leopards do not change their spots, and just as Dr. McNaught falsified his material so most of these people had no hesitation in attacking plays they had never seen. One of Edinburgh's M.P.s, Mr. Stoddart, was in this lamentable category.

There has been a certain Scottish literary renaissance in the last forty years and the best work produced in it has been aligned with the few novels I have named as in the authentic independent Scots tradition—and has had little or nothing to do with 'polite literature'. And unlike the novels in question, some of the very best of it has been concerned with Edinburgh—not the conventionally accepted Edinburgh, but the real Edinburgh. The poetry of Sydney Goodsir Smith and of Robert Garrioch, for example. Best of all, however—and to my mind the best thing that has ever been written about Edinburgh, and the truest bodying-forth of all that is most distinctive of the city—is Sydney Goodsir Smith's *Carotid Cornucopius*. It carries to the furthest extreme the elements that characterise that handful of veridical novels, and unlike them it is not historical but of today—tremendous break-through of the old wild spirit, and—what is even more noteworthy— clearly *au courant* with the developments of European prose in our time. Here, in *Carotid*, the awareness of James Joyce and most other *avant-garde* writers, and above all of Jarry's *Ubu Roi*, has clearly been superadded to the recaptured spirit of Dunbar, Sir Thomas Urquhart, and Burns. One may not meet Carotid, the Caird o' the Cannon Gait, even in the Rose Street pubs of Edinburgh today, but in most of them you will continually hear and see bits and pieces of him: they are the salt of Scottish life. Goodsir Smith gives us, as it were, a composite of the fun and games—the 'feast of reason (or unreason) and flow of soul'—which even today crop up in gatherings of Scottish people, and especially on their social occasions. Blue noses are in the great majority, of course, but the modern equivalents of 'rantin', roarin' Willie' are encountered every

now and again and outbursts of the spirit Dunbar expressed
when he wrote:

> 'Now all this tyme lat us be merry
> And sett nocht by this warld a cherry;
> Now, quhile thair is gude wyne to sell
> He that does on dry breid wirry
> I gif him to the Devill of Hell.'

Under the ballyhoo of which ninety-nine per cent of all
that has hitherto been written of Edinburgh consists, this
veracious account of the 'splores, cantraip, wisdoms, hough-
magandies, peribibulations, and all kinna abstrapulous
junketings and ongoings about the High Toon of Edinburgh, Capital of Boney Scotland', this tremendous
synthetic embodiment of all the uproarious, scandalous,
drunken life of the city, *Carotid Cornucopius* is the genuine
article; it is Edinburgh put into words as incredibly
jumbled and spatch-cocked as its own totality of architecture, and as full as Edinburgh itself is, and is always
likely to be, of what John Wilkes called in Gertrude
Corradini's case 'the divine gift of lewdness'.

I do not suppose the book sold well. How could it in a
country where the columnist in the chief daily paper can
say (in all earnestness): 'Dundee doesn't disdain fiction.
The late Annie S. Swan, who wrote about the relationship
between the sexes more imaginatively and adventurously
in our opinion than D. H. Lawrence, owed much to the
city. Dixon Hawke, the detective, and his assistant Tommy
Burke, were true Dundonians.'

No doubt so far as the last sentence goes, but the only
possible retort to the preceding one is a five-letter word.

I believe in always being where extremes meet. Norman
McCaig is extremely different from Sydney Goodsir Smith
or myself, yet all three of us are close friends and fellow-
frequenters of the Rose Street pubs. There is nothing uproarious about Norman, yet he is the best of boon companions. He is not only that but he is almost the only

fellow-writer I know now in Scotland with whom I can
have a really serious discussion on literary, and other
intellectual and artistic, matters. But he is apolitical or
anti-political. He has published about ten books of verse
and is in my opinion the best Scottish poet writing in
English at the present time. He seems to have influenced
to a considerable degree a whole group of younger Scottish
poets writing in English—Iain Crichton Smith, Stewart
Conn, Robin Fulton, and others; but Norman is clearly
maître d'école.

His subject-matter is for the most part Highland or
Hebridean and he rings the changes on his themes with
great ingenuity and the most dexterous play of words.
He has to a wonderful degree the gift of the memorable
phrase. Not only is he a precisian, but he has made a name
for himself as a very just and penetrating book-reviewer and
as a broadcaster. His flat in Edinburgh, where he and his
wife, Isabel, are the most generous of hosts, is a rendezvous
for congenial spirits from far and near. One of his essential
differences from Sydney Goodsir Smith and myself is that
his background is Gaelic Scotland—ours the Lowlands.
Norman is a schoolteacher and one with a real vocation.
He is now a deputy headmaster, but he ought to have been
a headmaster long ago—and would have been if it had not
been for the fact that he was a conscientous objector and
served a term of imprisonment on that account. Every
time for years the list of names for headmasterships was
put forward, an ecclesiastical member of the Education
Authority put a spoke in Norman's wheel on that account
with that peculiar and unrelenting viciousness characteristic
of many clergymen in relation to public affairs. There is no
wittier and more delightful author in Scotland today and
if he seems somewhat reserved and, as someone said of
MacNeice, a 'dispassionate poet', so far as his company is
concerned (though it may have the effect of narrowing the
content and appeal of his poetry) that is all to the good,
where there is such a general absence of standards of
conduct and conversation as in Scotland today. A certain

fastidiousness is highly desirable, and Norman at least is
not given to that tendency to slop over that afflicts the
majority of our countrymen who do not know they are
doing it, and would not care if they did know, but simply
have no sense of continence whatever. Norman, Sydney,
and I may not resemble the Three Musketeers in the least,
but we make an excellent trio—all the more so probably
because our work is so utterly different from each other's.

12

George Davie and the Democratic intellect

Scotland's geography is difficult. It makes it virtually impossible to have sustained and frequent intercourse with the people with whom we wish to, or should, associate. I am sure F. G. Scott and I could have done a great deal more together if we had been able to reside nearer each other. That is the case too with Lewis Grassic Gibbon and I. Glasgow and Edinburgh, to say nothing of Dundee and Aberdeen, might as well for many purposes be on different planets. There can be little coming and going. That is why I saw so little of James Bridie. I was unable even to see productions of most of his plays. I have since read all his published work and my appreciation has mounted. It is far from absurd to call him the Scottish George Bernard Shaw. He was unquestionably the greatest playwright— the only really great one even—Scotland has yet had.

Robert Maclellan has written fine plays in the Scots he knew as a boy in Lanarkshire, but they have all dealt with historical subjects and not with live contemporary issues, which is a great pity. And he lives away on the island of Arran and comes infrequently to the mainland, so that a year or more may elapse between meetings with him. Sorley Maclean, the Gaelic poet, is away up at Plockton in the far North-West, and hardly ever comes to town. There is no doubt that he is one of the greatest poets Scottish Gaeldom has had, but his experiences during the Second World War in North Africa silenced him. So far as I know he has written little or nothing since. The other leading Gaelic poet of our time—and also one of the

greatest for a couple of centuries—George Campbell Hay
has been sequestrated owing to mental illness for twenty
years and it is very doubtful whether he will be able to
add to his poetic output. This is a great tragedy.

A brilliant young historian on whom high hopes were
pinned, James Bremner Allan Dow, died tragically in
Glasgow only two weeks after his marriage. He was
accidentally electrocuted. Dr. Annie Dunlop wrote: 'The
news of his tragic death broke upon me when I was in the
company of his historical friends in Edinburgh and St.
Andrews. A sense of desolation and dismay fell upon us all.
There seemed no redeeming feature about the extraordinary accident that had shattered so many fair hopes. In
the memorial address his Professor described him as "one
of the new generation of historians of Scotland, who
wished to consider human experience over many generations and understand the world of his own day, especially
as it was reflected in the lives of the men and women who
did not rule Scotland but composed it".' A lecturer in
Scottish Economic History at Glasgow University, Dow was
only twenty-seven. I had known and admired him for
several years. Glasgow University appointed him a Ross
Fellow in 1961, charged with investigating the primary
sources available for the study of relations between
Scotland and Sweden. 'Self-trained both linguistically and
in archival work, searching very difficult material, his
reports to the Trust were models of clarity and compre-
hensiveness. But James Dow was not the man to stop at
sources only; it was soon clear that an impressive programme of scholarship was forming in his mind. It was time
for him to become a full University teacher. He was
appointed Assistant in 1963 and Lecturer in 1965.' 'As
for published scholarship we have, alas, only fragments
from his pen, in the form of articles appearing in Britain
and in Sweden. But it may well be that his manuscripts will
yield a larger memorial. His study *The Relations of Scotland
and Sweden 1500–1625* was his major scholarly work; it
exists in draft. So too does his *Letters of James Spens of*

Wormiston. A bibliography of Labour History in Scotland, to which he made a major contribution, is complete. Collaborative work with others, especially a volume of readings in the economic and social history of modern Scotland, will no doubt appear. It is an impressive list for an active teacher of so short a span. Scotland was his base; looking outward he believed that Scotland has something to offer the world today, and that this can best be understood from historical studies.'

Another friend of mine, animated by the same belief and believing that what Scotland has most to offer lies in the independent Scottish educational system, at the furthest remove from English education, the encroachments of which have gone far to erode the Scottish tradition, but may yet be arrested and indeed reversed, since it seems that here, in a return to the Scottish principles, is the solution for which the world is seeking. This is Dr. George Elder Davie, a friend of mine for over thirty years. He is now a Lecturer in the Logic Department of Edinburgh University. Over these years of our friendship we had discussed most of the ideas which he finally published in a massive tome, *The Democratic Intellect*, in 1961.

Dr. Davie says in his Introduction: 'F. W. Maitland seems to have understood fairly well the central paradox of Scottish History from 1560 onwards. The outstanding fact, he implies, is that the Reformation broke down the barriers between England and Scotland in one way only to re-establish them in another. Between the sixteenth century and the eighteenth, "two kingdoms are drifting towards a 'personal' and then a 'real' union. But two churches are drifting into discord and antagonism." Hence while it might appear as if, with the ending of the Franco-Scottish alliance, "a new nation, a British nation, is being born", in the sequel, religious considerations prevented a complete fusion. But while it was right to bring into prominence this Heraclitean rhythm of a simultaneous drawing towards, and away from, England, it is probably misleading to identify the differentiating factor with reli-

gion, and to imply, as Maitland seems to do, the absence of
a serious secular division between North and South. On
the contrary, the Great Britain of the 1707 Union is surely
best regarded not as an arrangement of two state-churches
in one state, but rather as a unity in politics combined with
a diversity in what may be called social ethics. The principle
of centralisation was confined to the Parliamentary and
fiscal spheres, and local autonomy remained intact not
only in the church, but also in the judicature, and, what is
equally important, in certain fundamental institutions in
which legal and clerical interests met, such as, above all,
the educational system. Hence, from the beginning of the
eighteenth century to the end of the nineteenth, the
distinctive code regulating the Scottish way of life was
based not simply on a religious separation but on a distinctive blend of the secular and the sacred. It may be
argued, moreover, that, under post-Union conditions, it
was the secular component rather than the sacred which
was chiefly responsible for the continuing foreignness of the
Scottish ethos. After all, the egalitarianism of the Presby-
terians always made a certain appeal over the Border,
although to be sure it was unEnglish in an official sense.
On the other hand, the ratiocinative approach of Parliament
House, looking as it did to Roman and Continental law,
was out of line with the inherited English practice; and
still more alien and uncongenial was an educational system
which, combining the democracy of the Kirk elders with
the intellectualism of the advocates, made expertise in
metaphysics the condition of the open door of social
advancement. Thus, the barrier between North and South
was proverbially located in the contrast between rationality
and rule of thumbs between principle and precedent, and
the English with their tolerant good humour, could refer
to the complex sister-nation as "metaphysical Scotland".
It was, then, this intellectual-secular element in Union
Scotland which Maitland apparently underestimated. However, in his case, the oversight was neutralised by the
illuminating presentiment that the distinctiveness of the

Scots was due to their carrying over into the modern world some of those mediaeval values which had lapsed in the South. The great continuities, he pointed out, were not wholly on one side of the Border, and the relevance to the pre-Reformation legacy comes home to us when, in studying the nineteenth century, we are brought up against those balanced tensions of Church and State, of faith and reason, on which depended the precarious stability of Scottish society. This common exaggeration of the religious monopoly in Scotland, though restrained within limits in the case of earlier scholars like Maitland, or again Buckle, seems unfortunately to be carried to a new extreme by historians of the modern school. The long episode of "Metaphysical Scotland", considered in abstraction from its laical side and as a merely clerical manifestation, has become the dark age of modern British History, and its un-English code of social ethics, no longer seen as a carry-over from Continental nationalism or from mediaeval ideals, is turned into an aberration of provincial nonconformity. According to Dr. Gordon Donaldson's recent influential book, (*The Scottish Reformation*, published in 1960), the distinctive Northern system was an exotic growth kept alive less by internal principle than by external circumstances. "It is hard to see", he says, "how any development originating in Scotland itself could have interrupted, far less reversed, the trend towards conformity with England." Apparently, the great continuities of which Maitland spoke existed only on one side of the Border! In an admiring notice of Dr. Gordon Donaldson's book, Professor Trevor Roper goes one better, insinuating that the operative ideals of the Presbyterian epoch were not just exotic, but even plain absurd, representing the triumph of evangelical metaphysics over a politic empiricism. At the Reformation "practical men" worked for "conformity with England". At one time, they nearly got it. Why did they fail? Why, in the next generation, did a rigid system—imported immediately from England, ultimately from the Continent,—prevail over this empirical

Q

spirit? In this way, the programme of Scottish research is defined by the Oxford Professor of History in abstraction from the intellectual-social background in terms of a perhaps largely artificial problem as to why victory rested with "clerical extremists", like "the grim and pedantic Andrew Melville and the grimmer more pedantic Covenanters", and no account is taken either of the Humanist, educational component of Presbyterianism as mediated by the great Buchanan, and by Melville himself, or with the inter-connection of the Reformation with Scots and Continental Law, as represented by the ratiocinative ex-advocate, the Rev. Robert Bruce in his classic sermons. No doubt, the historians of modern Scotland are achieving wonders in the way of pure research, but the pity is that their "scientific" procedure of studying the religious sector in isolation from the legal and the educational spheres makes nonsense of the Scottish story by obscuring the sociological background to the prolonged spiritual resistance against being completely assimilated to the South.'

In a footnote to his reference to Buchanan in the above passage Dr. Davie brings out a point which shows how deeply based the line taken by the Scottish Renaissance Movement has been. 'To clear up the common confusion in this matter,' he says, 'we might refer to Buchanan's often translated (both then and since, and into many languages) brace of tragedies—the *Jephtha* and the *Baptist*. Read in the pseudo-Shakespearian English of routine Victorian translations, these plays do indeed sound "pedantic and grim", whereas in the recent lively version (by the poet Robert Garrioch, published in 1960) we find the starkness of moral conflict presented with grim humour.'

The tract of history and scholarship Dr. Davie covers is *terra incognita* to almost all Scots today, but his book is essential reading for anyone seriously concerned with Scotland. The issues seemingly remote from our thoughts and interests today are on the contrary absolutely vital and of the utmost contemporary urgency. While writing this I have listened to two broadcasts, one given on behalf of the

Scottish Council for Development and Industry and the other by one of the leaders of the Scottish National Party. They expressed diametrically opposed opinions as to Scotland's condition and prospects today, but they had common ground in the fact that neither penetrated to the real issues. Spokesmen for Scottish political, cultural, and all other matters are almost all confined to this worthless superficiality simply because they have not inherited our national heritage. Dr. Davie's book may consequently be found 'hard reading' but every chapter in it is worth more than all that emanates from the innumerable 'prophets of easy things'.

Dr. Davie is not alone, however, in his deep understanding. The reference above to the 'interconnection with Scots and Continental Law' should be followed up by reading Professor T. B. Smith's little book, *British Justice*, which shows how peculiar to England and how divorced from Roman Law, and Continental Law generally, the English legal system is, and how unscrupulously and for how long a time it has been attempted to assimilate Scots Law to this isolated, inferior and much less humane system. It will be a veritable eye-opener to most readers. It is a fitting counterpart on the particular subject with which it deals to Dr. Davie's wonderfully comprehensive demonstration of the way in which 'in the case of Dr. Gordon Donaldson, the doctrinal separation of the Scots perhaps assumes the guise of an exotic and unnatural doctrinairism, largely because an arbitrary abstraction has kept out of the picture the "Continental" bias fostered by the country's central secular institutions. Or, again, the Scotland of the seventeenth century would hardly pose Professor Trevor Roper the problem of a land denuded by metaphysical punctilio, if the Scottish point of view had been comprehended by him not in the narrow sense of exclusive fanatical sectarianism, but as a complex of social aspirations, secular as well as religious, which, in a fashion perhaps foreign to the Anglo-American world, combined metaphysical intellectualism of an anti-empirical sort with a certain measure of democratic sympathies. Thus a one-sided approach obliterates the ancient image of Scotland as a balancing-ground in which Latin principles of civilisation encounter Saxon, until finally the high intellectual drama, glimpsed by Maitland and more than glimpsed by Buckle, has become a closed book to the younger historians who in the year 1960 automatically write off the story of seventeenth-century Scotland as "barren of the ideas which, stemming from ambition alone give interest to history".'

It is on this inoppugnable basis that Dr. Davie goes on to say: 'In order to discredit briefly these notions of total assimilation in favour of the rival formula of *unification in politics, separation* in *ethics*, it is sufficient to take note of certain outstanding differences in the seventeenth-century development of law and education in Scotland as compared with England. The crucial fact is that, by about 1700, the continuing Scottish efforts to reorganise law and education on rational lines had achieved a considerable measure of success, whereas the corresponding movement in England for a utilitarian reform of law and education had failed lamentably and was being forgotten. This superior state of Scottish institutional arrangements presumably accounted for the remarkable reservations introduced into the Treaty of Union, and throughout the eighteenth century the Scots at the same time as they congratulated themselves on the advantage of a common market with England, equally congratulated themselves on the advantage of their well-ordered progressive system of law and education (and of religion too) as compared with the stagnant and ill-ordered state of affairs in the South. In this way, submergence in the political-economic system of England was combined with a flourishing, distinctive life in what Marxists conveniently, if not perhaps aptly, call the social superstructure, and in Scotland, which was still national, though no longer nationalist, continued to preserve its European influence as a Spiritual force, more than a century after its political identity had disappeared.

Throughout the nineteenth century, too, in spite of increasing assimilation of political and economic life, the Scots stuck to this policy of apartness in social ethics. However, amid the recurrent tensions of the time, industrial and democratic, the old confident grip on the situation was noticeably slackening. Instead of the steady rhythm of independent institutional life, a new pattern emerged of alternation between catastrophe and renaissance, in which the distinctive natural inheritance was more than once brought to the very brink of ruin only to be saved at the last minute by a sudden burst of reviving energy.'

It is to that my own life has been devoted and I am glad to think that, in the view of a very large number of highly qualified commentators all over the world, this effort has secured so large a measure of success as to guarantee its continuance and increasing strength now. It has however hardly more than begun. There is need for a great deal of research and study: and the results of these must be incorporated into our educational curricula, and there is little likelihood of that unless (as was clearly realised at the outset) there are matching political developments which give the Scottish people control over their own affairs and resources.

How deep the necessary researches—and action based on them—must go is clearly and conclusively brought out in Dr. Davie's book. As David Masson said just over one hundred years ago: 'A Scotsman, when he thinks, cannot so easily and comfortably as the Englishman repose on an upper level of propositions co-ordinated for him by tradition, sweet feeling, and pleasant circumstance. . . . It amazes Scotsmen at the present day to see on what proximate propositions even Englishmen who are celebrated as thinkers can rest in their speculations. . . . Quietism, mysticism, that soft meditative disposition which takes things for granted in the co-ordination established by mere life and usage, pouring into the confusion thus externally given the rich oil of an abounding inner joy, interpenetrating and harmonising all—these are, for the most part,

alien to the Scotsman. No, his walk, as a thinker, is not by
the meadows and wheatfields, and the green lanes, and the
ivy-clad parish churches, where all is gentle and antique
and fertile, but by the bleak sea-shore which parts the
certain from the limitless, where there is doubt in the sea-
mews' shriek, and where it is well if, in the advancing tide,
he can find a footing on a rock.'

As R. M. Wenley said: 'Twentieth century Scotland is
shedding the substantial qualities transmitted from the
days of John Knox and George Buchanan, and maintained
even to the late Victorian era.' Or, as Dr. Davie points
out, 'the democratic intellectualism which had distinguished
Scottish civilisation was being allowed to disappear and the
peculiar polymathic values it supported were, increasingly,
at a discount among the cultural leaders. As Wenley said,
there has been a marked reaction in twentieth-century
Scotland against the historic heritage, but one will mis-
understand the situation unless one sees it not as a collapse
but a slow surrender. The ideal of a balanced breadth of
mind still remained entrenched in wide educational
sectors; what was being swept away was rather the intellectual sharpness required to secure its survival. . . . There
had been a failure of intellectual nerve among the Scots,
and the educated class of the new century, though still
loyal enough to inherited principles in a quiet way, had
become increasingly chary of public demonstrations of
national pretensions to intellectual independence. . . .
Thus, at the very time when other neighbouring countries
were becoming increasingly "history-minded", the Scots
were losing their sense of the past, and their leading
institutions, including the Universities, were emphatically
resolved—to use a catch phrase fashionable in Scotland of
the early twentieth century—"no longer to be prisoners of
their own history." And yet, characteristically, a certain
moderation set bounds to this attempt to break loose from
the past, and the result was an unstable compromise which
attempted to retain, in education at least, principles
associated with the nation, while at the same time refusing

the responsibility of large-scale initiative. The massive sanity remained fundamental to the Universities, but was now no longer offset by a social and cultural venturesomeness.'

One of my friends, though I fought against him (unsuccessfully) in his seat, the Kelvingrove constituency of Glasgow, the late Walter Elliot, wrote: 'In the early 1840's everything changed in Scotland at once. The distinctively Scottish tradition was broken. There came the Disruption. The Disruption was more than a quarrel about church government. It was the fall of a regime. The democratic intellectualism which had lasted for so many centuries was challenged because it could not with sufficient swiftness adapt itself to the conditions of the time. Power and machines were transforming Scotland over night. England, with its traditions of great houses, half-country, half-city absorbed the new stream of energy and directed it along her ancient channels in which it has flowed, although not without some straining at the embankment, even to our own day. But in Scotland its torrent burst its banks altogether and spread out in a submerging flood.'

This aperçu of Walter Elliot's, as Dr. Davie says, 'puts into proper perspective the much misunderstood crisis of the Scottish nineteenth century. In the 'forties (and 'fifties) a sudden provincialisation of the country took place which swept away the remarkable constitutional compromise instituted at the Union of 1707. The civil expansiveness of the new century, summed up in the Reform Bill of 1832, upset the delicate social balance required for the efficient operation of the peculiar institutional inheritance of Scottish Democracy, and, after a prolonged and desperate crisis, the Scots gave up the struggle to adapt their system to modern conditions, and quickly allowed it to lapse.

'W. E. Aytoun's class was responsible for the rise to prominence in the Scottish Universities of "Eng.Lit", which was an easier option. Aytoun argued that there is a connection between the Scottish tradition of poetry as natural and the democratic basis of Scottish society. The

English devotion to artificial poetry is due to the strati-
fications and segregations of Southern society. 'There is
nothing national,' he said, 'in either Spenser or Milton or
Pope, or Dryden, or Byron, or Wordsworth, or many more.
They are great poets, no doubt, but the people don't
sympathise with them, though portions of the intellectual
and educated classes may do so; and taking them altogether,
what kind of congruity either of sentiment or form do you
find in their work? But take Burns and Scott and Hogg,
and Motherwell and Allan Cunninghame, with their predecessors David Lyndsay and Allan Ramsay and Robert
Fergusson—they are adored by the people. And why?
Because they are minstrels and because they embody in
vivid strains the emotions, thoughts—nay, prejudices, if
you will—which are those most rife in the national bosom.'

The nub of the whole matter—of all that concerns the
real Scottish tradition as against what has progressively
weakened and de-Scotticised it and led directly and
inevitably to the deplorable state of Scottish education,
politics, and literature today—is brought out when Dr.
Davie goes on to say: 'Much of what Aytoun says here is in
line with the Northern cultural tradition, but the distinctive tendency of his criticisms obscured the intricate
balance of the national ideal of democracy *plus* intellectualism, by stressing the former to the exclusion of the
latter. He did indeed maintain the national values up to a
point, as when he insisted that "most of the English poets
want universality" in the sense of their being unable to
appeal simultaneously (as the Scottish poets can) both to
the unlearned many and to the learned few. But he left one
with the impression that the limited appeal of the English
poets was due to their employment of philosophical ideas
and of elaborate diction whereas the Scottish poets reached
a wider audience only by avoiding intellectuality and
artistry. Thus in the very circles responsible for pioneering
this new British subject of English Literature a convention
arose of refusing the traditions of Scottish learning credit
for the distinctive excellence of Scottish poetry.'

Dr. Davie brings out most thoroughly and convincingly the way by which 'ruthless public pressure on academic electors soon silenced the high metropolitan philosophy of the Hamilton-Ferrier era in the interests of a provincial-ising philistinism'. This was the atrocious state of affairs the Scottish Renaissance Movement was started to combat and in the hope of restoring the *status quo ante*. Whatever it has achieved, the decline of Scottish standards generally has continued unabated and in many connections has surely reached its nadir today, impelling the present Moderator of the Church of Scotland (the Very Rev. Dr. Archibald Watt) to say just the other day, when he gave a warning not to become concerned with the material advantages of education and lose sight of the quality of the men and women our schools and colleges produced: 'Should the light of their minds be made artificial by the fake promises of an irresponsible affluence and distorted in a ruthless rat-race for selfish aggrandisement, then we shall be producing a generation which may be clever but not cultured, and a leadership which is neither educated in the best sense of the term, nor responsible.'

That is indeed the stage we have reached in Scotland. If it is felt that Dr. Davie's book is 'too difficult', then it is clear that I was right in choosing as one of the realisations under which I thought the Scottish Renaissance Movement should proceed this passage from W. B. Yeats: 'Nations, races, and individual men are unified by an image, or bundle of related images, symbolical or evocative of the state of mind, which is of all states of mind not impossible, the most difficult to that man, race, or nation.'

Every Scotsman is faced with just the same position as in Russia confronted Chaliapin. It was Dmitri Andrevitch Ousatov who at Tiflis gave Chaliapin his first insight into musical characterisation, and he did so through examples from Moussorgsky's *Boris Godounov*. 'Now,' he would say, 'you see how music can react on the imagination. You see how silence and a pause are able to give the subtle effect of characterisation.' This was the lesson which evoked in

Chaliapin the qualities which made his art unique. 'Don't
take any notice,' the other singers of Ousator's class said,
'all he says may be true but "*La donna e mobile*" is the
right stuff for singers. Moussorgsky with his Varlaams and
Mitiouks is literally poison for the voice and singing.'
Chaliapin declared he was torn in two. 'Sometimes I was
so racked with doubt that I lay sleepless. Which should I
choose—"*La donna e mobile*" or "*In the big town of Kazan*"?'
This was the one critical moment in his career, the one
moment when he had to choose his party. Beside it all the
later adulations of the great, the angling for his adherence,
the fawning of the crowds, were of no importance whatsoever. Which should he choose? If he had chosen 'the right
stuff for singers' there would have been, no doubt, one
more highly successful singer in a world full of them, but
there would have been no Chaliapin—none of that secret
of his art, a secret everyone knows but no one else can
possess.

So far Scotland in every connection has chosen 'the right
stuff for singers', and the whole influence of our leaders in
every walk of life, of our Anglo-Scottish newspapers, of the
B.B.C. and other mass media, all our M.P.s, all our ecclesi-
astics, and even of the National Party of Scotland itself is
on that side and against any attempt at inducing Scotland
to realise its *Ur-motives*. If the so-called Nationalists among
these succeed there will be another small country in Europe
with a measure of autonomy and a somewhat better but
not essentially different administration as a consequence,
but Scotland will again betray its native genius and fail to
make that unique contribution which it ought to make
and, beside the mere possibility of which nothing else it
can do is of the slightest consequence.

No greater honour has been—or could be—paid to me
than that paid by Moray MacLaren when he deals in his
books, *The Wisdom of the Scots* and *If Freedom Fail*, with
the Declaration of Arbroath, and quoting the passage which
reads '*Quia quandiu certum viri remanserint . . .*' (*Anglicé*
'For so long as a hundred men of us remain alive we shall

never under any conditions submit to the domination of the English. It is not for glory or riches or honours that we fight, but only for liberty, which no good man will consent to lose but with his life.') asks 'but are there still one hundred?' and names me as at least one man faithful to that vow.

The late Lord Cooper, Lord President of the Court of Session, in his book *Supra Crepidam*, was certainly right when he said: 'If you compare the Declaration as a piece of rhetorical Latin prose with the surviving records of the period in the charters and state papers of England and Scotland you will find extraordinarily little worthy of comparison with it.'

I have found nothing at all.

So one of my first reviewers, in the early 'twenties, said of me: 'I write in the faith without which there can be no conquest; the belief that Scotland has still something to say to the imagination of mankind, something that she alone among the nations can say, and can say only in her native tongue.'

No wonder, in a long review in the *New Statesman* of Dr. Davie's book, C. P. Snow (now Lord Snow) said: 'For over 200 years, from the end of the sixteenth century to the beginning of the nineteenth, there were four universities in Scotland and two in England. Further, the content and intention of Scottish University education differed deeply from that of the English. Scottish education was much more like European, or the university education growing up in eighteenth-century New England . . . This admirable book by Dr. Davie is an account of how, in the nineteenth century, the Scottish universities were persuaded, coerced, bullied and argued into something like English *pastiche*. Not that this process was straightforward. It is still not quite complete. Scottish education has taken a long time to become *gleichgeschaltet*, and the universities preserve vestiges of an intellectual system and policy radically dissimilar from the English. At its core, the English policy is (a) to allow very few students into universities at all, (b) to

subject those few to courses of intense specialisation. The
Scottish policy—in this respect like the American or
Russian policy, or in fact the policy of all advanced
countries except England—is (a) to regard university
education as the normal thing for a high proportion of
students (b) to provide courses of considerable generality.
Dr. Davie firmly believes that (a) and (b) are linked. That
is, if you really believe, as a matter of social faith, as
Scotch, Russians, and Americans do, that university
education should be a democratic affair, then the education itself will inevitably become wider. If you believe, as
the English do, alone in the world, that university education ought to be restricted, then equally inevitably the
disciplines of study will become narrower and more
professionalised.'

Lord Snow digs down to the root of the whole matter
when he says of Sir William Hamilton, the Scottish
metaphysician (not to be confused with the other Sir
William Hamilton, the great Irish mathematician)—
nothing shook his conviction that English academics were
not only indifferent to, but actively disliked, any hint of a
general idea or any sign of the generalising intellect.
Curiously enough, in their criticisms of each other, the
English and Scots were pretty near right. On the particular
issue of the teaching of mathematics, they were both wrong.
It was, and still is, hard not to be wrong: for we are faced
with a conflict or opposition which can by its nature be
mediated, but not finally reconciled. This being so, an
adequately trained mind can do two things. The first is to
follow the *inner dynamic* of a subject as far as the mind
can go. This means thinking about one thing in depth for
a long time. The Cambridge mathematicians were right in
seeing that the inner dynamics of mathematics was going
to find its way through analysis: and that a mind wasn't
going to get experience-in-depth through a mathematics
which creative persons had abandoned (they were wrong
in detail, though. G. H. Hardy used to say that the Cambridge mathematical tripos, through its competitiveness

and its emphasis on mechanical tricks, killed mathematics in England during the whole of the nineteenth century). The second thing which the mind can do is diametrically opposite to the first. It is the ability not to think of one thing alone for a long time, but of one thing in relation to many others. In training and encouraging this ability, the Scots were dead right, and it accounts for the density and massiveness of the intellectual statements of Hamilton and his friends. In almost all formal English education, it has been singularly neglected; and its absence is responsible for a good many of our faults and mistakes. A foreign friend of mine used to say, rather sadly: 'You are an empirical people, and that I like. You are a clever people, at least as clever as anyone else. But so many of your clever people seem to have no substance in their minds. There is less intellectual exchange than in any country I know. Sometimes you think you are exchanging ideas; but all you are exchanging is intellectual gossip. Nothing but that.' Our entire educational system tends to suppress this talent. But even in societies less specialised, more intellectual, than ours, no one is certain of the best way of training it. There is not much doubt that it flourishes most when there is a common system of intellectual conviction. One finds good examples of it among, say, Benedictine philosophers or scholars at the Gorki Institute of World Literature. To a lesser extent, but still effectively, Scottish metaphysics in the early nineteenth century served to glue the country's intellectual culture together. Clearly we cannot revive Scottish metaphysics, period 1800. But, though we can patch and mend our educational system and remove its more anti-social follies, we shall still find it difficult to avoid educating for a set of skills, since a society like ours does not possess any common ground of intellect. One of the lessons of Dr. Davie's book is that we had better recognise our disadvantages, if we are going to stand a chance of coping with them. There is another lesson which applies to me personally. I happen to have been thinking and talking about some of the topics which, over 100

years ago, preoccupied the Scottish professional men.
They too were worried about divisions in the intellectual
life, the relation of intellectual people to society, and so
on. Well, they delivered themselves at greater length than
I should think appropriate: but, though I had not so much
as heard of most of them until I read this book, there is
precious little that I have managed to say on these matters
which they did not say before.'

Hardly anybody in Scotland today has 'heard of most
of them' unless they too have read Dr. Davie's book
(which ought to be compulsory reading for every Scottish
student). Unless they have done so, the basis of my propaganda for a Scottish Renaissance, and much of the essence of
my own poetry, will be unintelligible to them; and they will
fail to understand why I regard Dr. Davie as one of the
most important of living Scotsmen, or why, conjuring up
the many scores of professors I have known, I can only
think of two or three worthy to be named alongside him.
Anyhow, if readers will refer back to my first chapter and
remember the qualities I seek in friends and correlate that
with which Lord Snow quotes above about mere 'intellectual gossip', my own disposition may be understood and
sufficient light thrown on the service I have attempted to
render to Scotland.

In a subsequent article on 'Robbins and the schools',
Dr. Davie has said of the Robbins Report: 'Today, just as
in 1858—the Robbins documentation brings home—the
crowded lectures still furnish an institutional means of
propagating *idées generales* for which, apparently, there is
still no accepted equivalent in the more personal and
intense tuition of the South. If we are to continue this
distinctive intellectual culture, if we are not "to close it,
or to merge it with England" (Lorimer), then surely there
is still need of the interlocking system which was developed
in its defence by the generation of Lorimer, Forbes, Inglis
etc. But here too the Robbins Committee wants to keep the
end—general classes and general ideas—but to discard the
means. "The Scottish Universities", it says, "are right to

say that their standards and characteristics should be preserved. But there are other and better ways of achieving these ends." What *are* these ways then? The Committee, however, gives no answer, and this silence makes us supect that some of its members do not appreciate the precariousness of our position. The reception of Robbins in some academic circles, for example, vividly brings home the continuing influence all over Britain "of these numerous corporations who have disregarded every system of ideas but their own (Lorimer)—who on this question of the general approach versus the specialist, the lecture and the seminar versus the intimate tutorial, still consider the French, Germans, Russians, Americans, Dutch, etc., to be "lesser breeds". In any case, it is not difficult to demonstrate practically how precarious is the situation of these general studies in Scotland itself, once the social sanctions which support them are removed. We need only look at what happened in Glasgow, at the Royal College of Science and Technology, when as a condition of getting University status, it was "liberated" from the "restrictive" Northern ethos, as conceived by the Robbins Committee. Under the old dispensation, a most promising experiment in general studies had got under way: lectures on general ideas and their application were greeted by the engineers with rising enthusiasm. Then suddenly, as soon as the institution began to move out of the Scottish orbit, the whole atmosphere altered. General studies came under the fumbling influence of those who fear first principles, and where before there had been successful intiative in adapting philosophy for technologists, there was now anxious imitation of banal expedients already unsuccessfully pioneered elsewhere.'

13

Strange bedfellows

I HAVE mentioned how A.E. (George Russell) thought at first he had found a kindred soul in me, but speedily discerned I was a spiritual enemy instead—not that that prevented our continuing to be 'friends'. But, as A.E. went on to say: 'I keep always some instinct of what precious gifts our contraries hold for us. It is the temptation of idealists like myself to imagine our Paradise too swiftly out of the gold and jewels of thought, and to forget the earth, the common clay, which was the matrix which held those jewels. But earth itself, and the earth-born, those who revolt against our heavens, those whom we shrink from as rough and ungentle and think of as outposts of the Hosts of Darkness, hold for us, if we only knew it, secrets of powers which are exiles from the soul, but without which our Paradise would be strengthless and jerry-built. Our foes, our opposites, become in eternity our friends. The end of the long road of hate is adoration, and the Secret of Satan, as Carpenter told us in his finest imagination, is that the Adversary makes us strong.'

Not only have I received a great deal of help and kindness from people on the opposite side to myself in almost everything—men like the Duke of Hamilton, his brother the Earl of Selkirk and others—but take the case of my relations with John Buchan and Walter Elliot. John Buchan wrote a preface to my first volume of Scots lyrics. It is difficult today to imagine with what bated breath as if they were Immortals he and Neil Munro were regarded in the early years of the century, as great Scottish writers. I

did not think so. When I launched my annual anthologies
of contemporary Scottish poetry, *Northern Numbers*, I
included them, but this was not a matter of using them to
climb up on and then kick away; it was because I wanted
on the one hand to represent what was generally considered
to be the best of current Scottish poetry, and on the other
hand set against it the work of younger poets determined
to supplant these elder writers and supply poetry of a very
different kind. The difference was not perhaps very obvious
at first, but it became progressively more marked, and, as
it did, I discarded the older contributors in favour of the
new. This has been condemned as a treacherous and ungrateful proceeding. I do not think so. I made it clear from
the very beginning what I was setting out to do. The older
writers who figured in my anthologies were not induced
to do so under any false representations. What happened
is clear enough now and, I am sure, abundantly justified in
the outcome.

Buchan was not a poet of any consequence, nor did I
think him a novelist of consequence either. I told him so,
and he wrote agreeing with me, and said that he had
hoped, if circumstances permitted, to have been, rather
than a novelist, a philosophical writer in the tradition of
Sir William Hamilton's philosophy. I could only feel it was
on the whole better that he should have been constrained
to be the novelist he was. But I also thought his *Northern
Muse* by far the best anthology of Scottish poetry available
at the time. The preface and notes, as well as the selection,
showed a great knowledge and love of Scottish poetry.
Like myself, Buchan was a Border man and I knew how
much that meant to him. That Buchan is best known by
his thrillers (his best novel to my mind, however, is *Witch-
wood*, where he used a great deal of Scots, of which he had
a very thorough knowledge) does not confute but rather
exemplifies the truth of my statement that the curse of
Scottish life and literature and other arts in modern times
had been an appalling infantilism. One of Buchan's
obituarists told the exact truth when he wrote: 'John

R

Buchan wrote some of the best thrillers ever published in English and some of the best popular historical biographies. Some of his books sold by the hundred thousand, but like some greater men, he always hankered after success in spheres not suited to his talents. Just as Cicero wanted to write poetry so John Buchan wanted to be a statesman. He was obsessed with the idea of "greatness". Those who knew him will tell that he had no political gifts of any kind. As a result his achievements were mainly ceremonial. When he was Lord High Commissioner of the General Assembly of the Church of Scotland he wore splendid robes and was radiantly happy in their magnificence. The House of Commons led him not to Cabinet Office, but to the Governor Generalship of Canada. Here was the perfect honorific post. If one cannot achieve real political success, to be the King's representative is surely the best possible substitute.'

Burns was of a very different cast of mind. On the subject of titles he would have agreed with the Australian paper that wrote: 'Since St. Michael and St. George are both dead and buried, to be the companion of two corpses is just about the same as being brother to a quantity of stale fish or uncle to an ancient egg', and he would certainly have treasured the story of how, when a former Governor, Lord Carrington, returned to England and told the Duke of Clarence, that 'Australia would for ever remain loyal to England', *The Bulletin* exploded in a fury of invective, in the course of which it referred to His Royal Highness as 'the flabby little duke, whose face is as expressionless as an African's feet'.

Walter Elliot was another great lover of Scotland and wrote better essays about some of the aspects of its history than anyone else has done. But he was a disappointment, not least to himself, I think. Sir Colin Coote in his biography of Elliot says: 'I have often been asked why he never became Prime Minister.' Sir Colin says Elliot's inability to be punctual, and the extent to which that reflected a strong element of indecision in him, prevented Elliot rising to the topmost top. In my view, he was a split personality. He could not square his knowledge and love of Scotland with service in the Westminster Parliament. His head and his heart were at variance. It was that inability to come out wholeheartedly for Scotland and against England that not only inhibited or distorted Elliot's career but prevented my seeing more of him and being friendlier towards him, much as I respected his high qualities, and precisely the same considerations operated to delimit my friendship with Elliot's friend, 'James Bridie' (Dr. O. H. Mavor) and many other notable Anglo-Scots.

In much I have written there is Anglophobia (and indeed, *Who's Who* for forty years has given that as my hobby), and in what I have quoted from Dr. Davie's book *The Democratic Intellect*, anti-English feeling—the sense of ineradicable opposition—crops up continually. This is far more frequently to be found in notable Anglo-Scots than may be generally imagined. One of the early contributors to my *Northern Numbers*, was Sir Ronald Ross, with whom I remained on terms of friendship from the time we first corresponded till his death years after. Sir Ronald, who discovered the cure for malaria, describes an interview with Joseph Chamberlain: 'Neither he nor his officials had understood in the least what we meant. As usual with politicians, he deprecated expenditure, not recognising that sanitary expenditure is an insurance against the much greater expenditure caused by sickness, as that on fire-engines is against fires. On the other hand, he was "prepared to consider" a travelling commission of three business men and one scientific expert, all of whom would have to be paid by the Chambers of Commerce for doing the business of the Colonial Office. The proposal was characteristic of British administration. Instead of doing cheap and necessary work it spends large sums on expensive and worthless talk. The proceedings now closed with more compliments. Chamberlain had done some good (and won much political capital) by suggesting the schools of tropical medicine, but, in my opinion, his refusal of a proper sanitary organisation for the colonies largely cancelled, then and since, the benefits which might have accrued. I suppose I was the only one present who had any real knowledge of tropical sanitation; and I remember thinking to myself angrily as I left stately Whitehall: "These people are no longer fit to hold the hegemony of the world." '

If we turn to a very different personality, Ross's great co-worker, Sir Patrick Manson, we find again and again— more quietly stated—the same complaints against the stupidities of officialdom and the freemasonries of mediocrity, and we see again the Scottish rebellion against the British system. Manson, like most of the better type of Scotsmen abroad, had a very much better attitude to the 'damned foreigners' than is usually found in the Englishman abroad; and was animated by a very different spirit than that of the typical Empire-builder. This different attitude with regard to such matters of the Scotsman as compared with the Englishman finds magnificent exemplification again and again in Manson's biography. Dr. Abraham in *The Surgeon's Log* depicts a Scot far more typical in his attitude than the English care to recognise, or Anglo-Scottish quislings dare admit, when, discussing the treatment of the Kling powers in Malaya, he tells of a Scotsman, Guthrie, who looked at him and said: 'You think it very high-handed?' I nodded. 'Man,' said the Scotsman, 'if you come to think of it, our mere presence in this country is the most insufferable high-handedness. We haven't a moral leg to stand on!'

This Scottish spirit, so utterly different from anything English, was never better shown perhaps than in the character of Sir William MacGregor of Fiji. Captain C. A. W. Monckton, in his *Some experiences of a New Guinea Resident Magistrate*, tells how Sir William came to be appointed on New Guinea:

'Sir William, at that time Doctor MacGregor, was attending, as the representative of Fiji, one of the earlier conferences regarding the proposed Federation of Australasia; he had already made his mark by work performed in connection with the suppression of the revolt among the hill tribes of that Crown Colony. At the Conference, amongst other questions, New Guinea came up for discussion, whereupon MacGregor remarked: "There is just the last country remaining, in which the Englishman can show what can be done by just native policy." The remark struck the attention of one of the delegates, by whom the mental note was made: "If Queensland ever has a say in the affairs of New Guinea, and I have a say in the affairs of Queensland, you shall be the man for New Guinea." When, later, New Guinea was declared a British Possession, Queensland had a very large say in the matter, and the man who had made the mental note happening to be Premier, he caused the appointment of Administrator to be offered to MacGregor, by whom it was accepted!'

Another tremendous advantage the Scots have over the English is in their flair for languages. That is why all through our history we have thrown up great linguists like Sir James Grierson, who compiled the dictionary of Indian dialects, and Sir Edward Denison Ross, and scores upon scores of men who have done far more for native languages and literatures than any of their English colleagues. Katherine Tynan in her *Twenty-Five Years; Reminiscences* has several delightful paragraphs about the then Chinese Professor at Oxford—a very dear, charming old man, with snow-white hair, bushy eyebrows, and side-whiskers, the blue eyes and pink and white complexion of a child. 'Lovely as a Lapland night.' Well on in the seventies he used to rise at four o'clock every morning, make himself a cup of tea, and work away through the quiet hours at his Chinese folios. His study, hung with Chinese scrolls, was walled about with his lifework in the shape of Chinese classics which the Oxford wits used to say might or might not be genuine, since none but the Professor himself knew anything about them. And she mentions his 'strong Scottish accent', his 'appalling' moments of frankness, and the fact that he was 'justly proud that he had refused a chair at a Scottish University in his young manhood because he would have had to conform in some way'. Another typical Scot in fact!

And I think next of E. J. W. Gibb of Glasgow who devoted the whole of his life to the study of Ottoman poetry. When Gibb died, only one volume of his monumental *History of Ottoman Poetry* had appeared, if most of the matter for the other five volumes had been gathered in; as a labour of love Professor E. G. Browne took upon himself the onerous task of seeing the whole work through the press, completing the unfinished parts, and this involved an immense amount of research, for every quotation had to be verified, and the originals of many poems translated by Gibb had to be traced to their sources, often in rare manuscripts, and copied for the printer. It fell to Browne, too, to establish with five other scholars and Gibb's widow the 'E. J. W. Gibb Memorial' founded with a sum of money given by the scholar's mother. This Trust has published upwards of thirty texts and translations of Turkish, Arabic, and Persian authors.

The Scottish gift of languages was held in high measure by Sir William MacGregor too, and Captain Monckton, after showing Sir William's ability to deal with surveyors, engineers, and others on their own ground and surprise them, says: 'The same sort of thing occurred with Sir William in languages; he spoke Italian to Giulianetti; German to Kowold; and French to the members of the Sacred Heart Mission. I believe if a Russian or a Japanese had turned up Sir William would have addressed him in his own language. Ross-Johnston, at one time private secretary to Sir William, once wailed to me about the standard of erudition Sir William expected in a man's knowledge of a foreign language. Ross-Johnston had been educated in Germany and knew German, as he thought, as well as his own mother tongue. Sir William, while reading some abstruse German book, struck a passage the meaning of which was to him somewhat obscure; he referred to Ross-Johnston who, far from being able to explain the passage, could not make sense of the chapter. Whereupon Sir

William remarked that he thought Ross-Johnston professed to know German. Ross-Johnston, feeling somewhat
injured, took the book to Kowold, who was a German.
Kowold gave one look at it, then exclaimed: "Phew! I
can't understand that. It's written by a scientist for
scientists".'

Let me drive to the heart of the matter and ask what is
the secret of the Scot's universal acceptability and success,
so different from the attitude evoked by the Englishman.
It can be illustrated perhaps by what Miss Freda White
has said in discussing Margery Perham's and J. Simmon's
book, *African Discovery, An Anthology of Exploration*
(1943), which deals with the ten great African explorers
namely, Bruce of Abyssinia; Mungo Park, Clapperton,
Lander, Baikie, all four explorers of the Niger; Burton,
Speke, Livingstone, Baker and Stanley, travellers in East
and Central Africa.

'Professor Joad', says Miss White, 'once madly committed himself on the Brains Trust to the opinion that the
Scottish Nation had contributed little to the foundation of
the British Empire, even in exploration. What about
Livingstone? I would recommend to the Professor's notice
the fact that five out of these ten—and by far the greatest
one, were Scots. . . . Livingstone towers above this very
considerable company. It is not easy to define why. His
writing in his journals is plain to dryness. He has no charm,
and is indeed terrifying in the ruthlessness in which he
pursued his object, and which he himself admits with shame.
Other missionaries have served God as faithfully, and loved
humanity as well. It may be his extraordinary honesty,
wedded to the statesmanship which planned not only the
abolition of the slave trade, but a happier future for the
Africans; it may be the regard which to the end saw every
man truly as a person, not as a type or a race. There is all
that, but it does not in itself constitute greatness, and no
one can read his writing without knowing that this was a
great man. Stanley felt it, and *his* skin was thick enough.
The passages where he shows his reverence and love for

Livingstone redeem his usual assurance and render him momentarily likable. Next to Livingstone, in my estimation, comes Bruce. Partly because he writes excellently well in the easy graphic prose of his date (he is the only definitely eighteenth-century member of this volume). Partly because he is a man with whom one would love to travel. He preserves his own standards—the cruelty of the Abyssinian war sickens him—but he does not expect isolated African communities to share European habits, as some travellers do even today, and he is entirely free from race snobbery. It does not enter his head that he should not regard himself as a guest of the Ethiopians, and there is not even any deliberate thought in his acceptance of their customs. He prostrates himself before the king as is fitting, stands his long and weary watch as a chamberlain when he is appointed to office, and in consequence wins a liking which allows him much closer insight and much more liberty than the assumption of superiority could have gained. He was given every facility to visit the source of the Blue Nile, and indeed only found difficulty in gaining permission to leave the country. When his patron was defeated in civil war and he met the queen, his friend, in exile, he recorded the meeting as "one of the happiest moments in my life." This capacity for liking people, and his natural proper behaviour, are in sharp contrast to Burton's constant sneer and in utter opposition to the ill-breeding of Speke who wrote: "Now I have made up my mind never to sit upon the ground as the Arabs and natives are obliged to do, nor to make my obeisance in any other manner than is customary in England. . . . I felt that if I did not stand up for my social position at once, I should be treated with contempt during the remainder of my visit, and thus lose the vantage-ground I had assumed of appearing rather as a prince than as a trader, for the purpose of better gaining the confidence of the kings." '

These examples of Scottish internationalism could be multiplied a hundred times over, but I content myself now by showing that the matter works both ways—at home as well as abroad. Most people today, I think, would deem it very unlikely that learned men, commanding many languages and travelling the world over, would find, and confess, that their lack of receiving in over-Anglicised Scotland a knowledge of Scotland's own languages, Gaelic and Scots, afflicted them as a sorely felt handicap. Yet it is so. The late Sir Donald MacAlister, Principal of Glasgow University, and a great linguist making verse-translations of poems of many languages, told in a remarkable passage how lack of Gaelic had retarded and mutilated his mental development. Mr. Ivan Sanderson, the brilliant scientist author of *Animal Treasure* and other books, artist too, and explorer of the upper reaches of the Amazon, testified to the same effect and wishes he had been able to escape an English education.

Readers who have had just an English education, and have practically no knowledge of anything Scottish except the little—and that often wrong—allowed through the English filter, are apt to imagine that I am a solitary Anglophobe. That is not the case. By the death in 1951 of Cecil Gray, Scotland lost (characteristically without any appreciation of the loss) one of her most distinguished sons of the century and her ablest music critic—indeed, the only music critic of any consequence she has yet possessed. While he lived mainly outside Scotland and took no active part in Scottish affairs—any thought of the present horrible condition of Scottish culture throwing him at once into blistering fury—it is not surprising that a man of his rich aesthetic sensibilities and great intellectual gifts should nevertheless by an independent path have reached many of the basic conclusions upon which the Scottish Renaissance Movement was founded.

This was admirably exemplified in one of the brilliant essays in his volume *Predicaments* in 1936, when he wrote: 'Present circumstances and conditions are uniformly propitious to creative activity in this country (i.e. Great Britain), save only one which unfortunately also happens to be a very important one; namely, the attitude of mind

and code of aesthetic values which largely dominate
English life today, and are mainly responsible for all its
worst features, and for our complete inability to induce
other nations to take us seriously in literature and the arts
—*the cult of the English gentleman*! It permeates every aspect
of our national life. It may well be true that our military
triumphs have all been won on the playing fields of Eton;
but it is very certain that most of our artistic failures have
been sustained there. This spirit stunts or oppresses or
forces into a pusillanimous compromise every potential
native talent and is the absolute antithesis of everything
that we call art, and *must be fought as one fights the devil,
without rest and without quarter*. There can be no hope for
English culture until this fatal confusion of artistic with
false social and ethical values has broken down.'

The late William Power, a great friend of mine for many
years, in his excellent little volume *Literature and Oatmeal*
said: 'Gaelic has had a far bigger and longer run in Scotland
than Scots or English. Teutonic speech is still a comparative
upstart, and its sweeping victory did not begin till well on
in the seventeenth century. A conscientious Chinaman who
contemplated a thesis on the literary history of Scotland
would have no doubt as to his procedure. "I will learn a
little Gaelic, and read all I can find about Gaelic literature,
from the oldest Irish poets down to Ban Macintyre, and
nearly a third of my thesis will be on Gaelic literature." He
would be rather mystified when he discovered that historians of Scotland and its literature had known and cared as
much about Gaelic as about Chinese, and that they had
gone on the remarkable assumption that the majority of
the Scots were Anglo-Saxons and that their literature
began with Thomas the Rhymer in the reign of Alexander
III.'

Very much to the point is what Power says of the Scottish
attitude today to our literature and history, and the different attitude of the English people to theirs (for, of course,
while we accord a virtual monopoly to English literature
that is a one-way traffic—there is no reciprocal interest in

Scottish literature in England, and if some of us are Anglophobes that is nothing to the continual disparagement and sneering at Scottish literature and Scottish matters generally—and usually on the basis of utter ignorance—in English papers and periodicals). 'In the compartment of the Flying Scotsman, roaring north along the central rockridge of the Merse, I began', says Power, 'to dilate to a companion on the part that the Canyon of Pease Dean, near Cockburnspath in Berwickshire had played in Scots history. I spoke of Cromwell and the Battle of Dunbar, Scott and *The Bride of Lammermoor*. A man in a landward corner of the compartment broke in: "Ugh! That's history. An' literature, I suppose." He was burly and fiftyish, with a bristly moustache. He wore a good suit of rough brown tweed, and there was a horseshoe pin in his ugly tie. His boots had cost a good deal. I guessed him to be a prosperous contractor and general merchant in a country town, grazing beasts on a couple of "led" farms. "Don't the history and literature of your own country mean anything to you?" "Not a bit. Just nonsense. The stuff we used to get in school. Ugh!" His contempt was beyond articulate expression. In the attitude of this man, I reflected, there was more than mere indifference. There was a positive hostility. History and literature, particularly those of Scotland, were somehow inimical to his way of life. He had a bad conscience concerning them. The outlook in such matters that usually confronts one in England is curiously different. It is one of amiable nescience. Anyone who begins to talk of history or literature in a chance company is listened to with polite inattention, as if he were a foreigner who was inadvertently speaking his own language. The terms seem to have no connotation. But nobody is ever rude about it.'

The late Professor Denis Saurat, at one time head of L'Institut Française in London and Professor of French at King's College, was one of my best friends for many years. He published a great number of books and though towards the end he became increasingly preoccupied with occult and supernatural matters for which I had no use, I think he has been greatly underrated. One of his best contributions to imaginative literature—*La Fin de la Peur*—is a work of profound imagination and most powerfully concentrated expression. His greatest and much too-little-known work is *The Three Conventions*, which A. R. Orage declared had no rival for concentration outside certain untranslatable Sanskrit works. Other important books by him are *Literature And The Occult* (an extraordinary demonstration of the extent to which all great European poetry derives a high proportion of its greatest stuff from little-known occult and anti-Christian writings —to which the sequence of great poets with whom he deals had not themselves direct access, but which they inherited from each other without first-hand examination at all, and thus we have the amazing fact that all the greatest European literature is really a vehicle for the uninterrupted transmission of a body of ideas alien to European civilisation as generally understood, and at complete variance with all the Christian and other beliefs most Europeans have professed throughout the centuries) and *A History of Religions*. Much better known are his books on Milton and Blake—on the *ideas* in their poetry; Saurat had little aesthetic sensibility.

A reviewer of *A History of Religions* said: 'His writings on the esoteric elements in European literature have shown his tremendously wide knowledge of the bypaths of religious history; he has read prodigiously; and he knows the boundary between knowledge and guess-work. His faculty of condensation is remarkable, as a glance at his footnote references brings home. He does not write popular history, but popularises history. His précis of the historical evidence bearing on the origins of Christianity, for example, is a model of care and concision. He has a mordant, incisive style, and it is interesting to compare—rather, contrast—his method with H. L. Mencken's. Whereas the American is shallow, angry, and facetious by turn when writing on the Gods, the Frenchman wastes no time in abuse, and allows himself only an occasional excursion into irony, never a guffaw. "The Roman . . . had the feeling that the gods had taken an advantage of a contract that was unfair. . . . The Sibylline books demanded that two young couples should be buried alive: Greeks and Gauls were chosen: no great loss."

'Professor Saurat treats philosophies as fragments of religious systems, and we can recall no more clear-headed account of the philosophical preoccupations of post-renaissance times than his. Looking to the future, he foresees a certain progress in philosophical thought, since, for the first time since the Greeks, philosophers are tackling their problems with no presuppositions. "A first-rate philosopher like the German Husserl, for instance, does not even consider religious probabilities at all.' As for religion, he sees no more intellectual future for the off-shoots of Protestantism than he does for occult pantheism, the "wisdom of the east". While recognising the unlimited intellectual resources of the east, he sees them burdened by the false cosmology, the false history, and false oriental religions. "We can do nothing with oriental religions. The more the east will become civilised, the more it will rid itself of the religions which . . . contradict its own natural impulses by negating life." In the West, Catholicism is the only remaining virile religion. "It has adapted itself to so many changes that it may adapt itself further." And looking into the remote future: "One cannot escape the thought of God; one escapes only this or that form of it. . . . Flowers, and even trees, are still growing on the ruins of religions and philosophies. That is all the historian can tell, on reaching the verge of the present. He cannot but see, besides, that, in the human soul, round the ruins and the flowers and the trees, there is the menace of the desert."'

Saurat was one of the most delightful men I ever met. A terrifically hard worker, he had always time for everything, and he had not only the great French gifts of 'netteté, clarté, and ordonnance', but was full of bonté. We were good friends for over twenty years. Incidentally, in an early essay on my work, he coined the descriptive phrase, 'The Scottish Renaissance Movement', which has been so persistently gibed at by small minds affecting to believe that it represented an inordinate claim as to what the group associated with me had actually already achieved, whereas, of course, it only defined our general hope and purpose. Saurat, too, did me a high honour by being one of the earliest translators of my Scots lyrics, half a dozen or more of which he did into French very well.

Saurat was a splendid *conferencier*, and rendered great service to the International P.E.N. as one of its Vice-Presidents. He was also very active in trying to organise Western Europeans concerned with minority languages and literatures. His causeries on literary topics appeared regularly in the little periodical, *Marysas*, issued by his friend (and mine), Sully André Peyre. *Marysas* was devoted to Provençal, Catalan, and Basque poetry, and for years its monthly arrival was one of the most welcome elements in my mail.

With reference to what I have been writing about anti-English feeling, it is interesting to note that Saurat wrote that unless the Second World War was to prove to have been fought in vain there must be a profound change in English mentality (and he did not mean that availability to Yankee trash-culture which has developed apace!). Saurat used his terms with scrupulous care. He pointed out that he was not referring to Scottish mentality but strictly to English mentality. Everything that has happened since—and is happening now—has shown how right he was. Saurat knew Scotland and Scottish Literature well, and was a close friend not only of mine but of F. G. Scott and many other Scots. He perfectly understood why I agreed with Henry Miller's statement in his book, *The Cosmological Eye*, namely, 'as for English literature, it leaves me cold, as do the English themselves; it is a sort of fish-world which is completely alien to me. I am thankful to have made a humble acquaintance with French literature, which on the whole is feeble and limited, but which, in

comparison with Anglo-Saxon literature today is an unlimited world of the imagination.' And he would have
endorsed Cecil Gray's statement, which I have said should
be hung up in large print in the vestibule of every library
in Scotland, namely: 'Even today the whole hierarchy of
the English novelists from Fielding and Smollett, through
Dickens and Thackeray up to Hardy and Meredith means
precisely nothing to me. I simply cannot read them. I have
tried hard, I have read several books of each. I have given
them all a fair trial, but it is no use.'

I was put in touch with *The New Age* and its editor A. R.
Orage when I was still at school by a very remarkable
school-master, George Ogilvie. I still think it is the most
brilliant journal that has ever been written in English,
and small though its circulation was it reached all the
liveliest minds in Great Britain and further afield. In this
respect it was like another influential publication, Claud
Cockburn's roneo'd *The Week*, which literally kept me
alive in the Shetland Islands. I subsequently met Cockburn in London and he is one of the most delightful, well-
informed, and wittiest men I have known. When Orage
gave up *The New Age* and went to America to promulgate
the doctrines of Ouspenskey and Gurdjieff I took over the
literary editorship of *The New Age* and was a prolific
contributor to it over my own name and various pseudo-
nyms for several years—until, in fact, Orage returned to
England. When news got about that he was back, a
mutual friend offered to motor me down to the out-of-the-
way Sussex farmhouse where he was living. Great secrecy
was enjoined upon me and the visit was given all the
trappings of melodrama. But I was not disappointed.
Orage was well worth meeting under any circumstances. A
little later I saw a great deal of him in London.

He died very suddenly just after a broadcast on Douglas
Social Credit on 5th November 1934. In its issue of 15th
November, the *New English Weekly*—which had succeeded
The New Age—published more than forty tributes to
Orage. As has been said, these tributes, however diverse the

outlook of their authors, all emphasised Orage's personal
charm, his freedom from materialism, the wide range of
his intellect. The writers included Ezra Pound, Richard
Aldington, Herbert Read (not yet Sir Herbert), Will
Dyson, Holbrook Jackson, Middleton Murry, Anthony M.
Ludovici, Clifford Bax, Augustus John, H. G. Wells,
Roland Kenney, Henry W. Nevinson, S. G. Hobson, the
Very Rev. Hewlett Johnson, Eric Gill, Llewelyn Powys,
G. D. H. Cole, Ashley Dukes, Maurice Browne, Frank
Swinnerton, St. John Ervine, Thomas Burke, Ruth Pitter,
C. H. Norman, E. H. Visiak, T. Sturge Moore. It all
constituted one of the most remarkable and impressive
tributes ever made on the death of an English writer.
Orage wrote nothing really substantial—for the most part
only paragraphs commenting on general issues of the day
and on books and authors. One of the contributors for *The
New Age* in its heyday was Beatrice Hastings, who wrote
over the pseudonym of Alice Morning. A couple of years
after Orage's death she published a pamphlet entitled *The
Old 'New Age', Orage and others*. Paul Selver has commented, very stupidly I think, on this pamphlet in his
book *Orage and The New Age Circle* (1959). Only an expert
psychiatrist could, he opines, deal adequately with it. To
me, on the contrary, it rings absolutely true. It is certainly
a devastating debunking of Orage, and no franker dealing
with a man's sexual life (and its relation to his writings) has
probably ever been penned. It should stand on the shelf
beside Dunbar's *Twa Mairyet Wemen And the Wedo*, that
searing revelation of the feelings of women about the
sexual prowess and proclivities of their husbands.

Mrs. Hastings—whom I knew as well as Paul Selver—
says, inter alia, 'Orage, who had not a particle of genius,
hated creative writers.' I think he almost certainly envied
them very bitterly. I think too that there is justice in Mrs.
Hastings' claim that she did far more than Orage himself
to encourage new writers. That Orage should take credit
for the brilliance of the paper he edited was natural enough,
but it is undoubtedly the case that certain of the regular

contributors should have shared that credit to a far greater extent. J. M. Kennedy, A. E. Randall, Roland Kenney, and one or two others have never received a fraction of the recognition they deserved, and it would still be an excellent idea to bring out an anthology of extracts from their articles. But Beatrice Hastings was right when she alleged that 'Orage, the new Socrates, the Light-bringer of the Age, according to some, certainly suffered from paranoiac mystagoguery'. This is a shadow that has fallen across not a few of my most prized friendships—A.E., Yeats, even at the end Saurat himself. Philip Mairet in his biography of Orage (1936) quotes A.E. as saying: 'What I continually met in Orage was a mind whose range and depth could not be manifested fully even in the most brilliant journalism,' and Mairet adds: 'Besides his intellectual and relatively practical ambitions—which were not small—he was driven by an ardent will to some unknown, ultimate goal of en-lightenment. At certain crises, this divine discontent would overwhelm him to the misprision of all the attain-ments others most admired in him. That spiritual strife in Orage, doubtless obscure even to himself, can never be fully explained, but his story could not be told without relation to it; for this was the essential man, the secret of his gifts and his magnetism, as well as of his sudden changes of purpose, his recurrent crises, perhaps of the dignified silence with which he took his final departure.'

I prefer Mrs. Hastings's explanation, which in no way conflicts with a recognition of Orage's genuine qualities. I deplored Orage's relationship at the end with another Eastern European mystagogue, Metrinovic, and the general atmosphere of hocus-pocus, with Fascistic overtones, that hung about the publications with which Orage was con-nected towards the end—*New Britain, The New Atlantis.* The great days of *The New Age,* when Shaw, Wells, Chesterton, Belloc, and Arnold Bennett, were all contri-buting and arguing with each other were already lost in a past that seemed infinitely more remote than the actual number of years involved warranted. Selver's book is

S

incredibly silly in many respects. One has only to read some of his own poems, which he quotes with great pride, to be reminded of a lack of judgement as stupefying as was Upton Sinclair's when he praises some of his wife's appallingly bad poems in terms of the most extravagant eulogy. The whole history of Orage and his colleagues and *The New Age* must, I think, be regarded so far as English literature and literary journalism is concerned, as the final brilliant flare-up of a guttering candle.

The last of these men who were friends in A.E.'s sense of the 'attraction of opposites' was T. S. Eliot. We can have had few opinions in common. I was utterly opposed to his religiosity and near-Fascism. His self-definition as a 'neo-classicist, Anglican, and Royalist' was at the opposite pole from my own position, yet we got on very well together and he certainly helped me in many ways. He published my *Second Hymn to Lenin* and my *Cornish Heroic Song* in *The Criterion* and also many book reviews by me, as well as my essay *English Ascendancy in British Literature*. Eliot himself came out strongly on behalf of the attempt to revive Scots as a literary medium, insisting that this was invaluable to English Literature itself and that many things could be said in Scots that could not be said in English at all—and that it was vitally important that these things should be said. He corrected Matthew Arnold's unfortunate misunderstanding of Burns, and insisted that Burns was 'the decadent representative of a great alien tradition' (i.e. alien to English literature). In a word, he supported the most essential planks in the platform of the Scottish Renaissance Movement. He also mightily encouraged me in regard to my *In Memoriam James Joyce*. Succour, I felt, had again come from a most unexpectable quarter—Saurat, Orage, Pound, Eliot, and Dylan Thomas; the kind of propaganda I have been engaged in for over forty years certainly brought me many strange bedfellows. But how do any of the opponents of the Scottish Movement size up set against men like these?

14

Epilogue

O<small>N THE</small> heels of what I have called 'the great break-through' which attended my seventieth birthday, it was inevitable in Scotland that there should come a characteristic anticlimax. Modern Scots are adepts at disparagement —there is nothing they hate more than a man getting 'a little above himself' and rising above the ruck. They are quick to prick the balloon of any such pretensions, and Lewis Grassic Gibbon and many other Scottish writers have had bitter cause to complain of the way in which the deadly phrase 'I kent his faither' is used to reduce them to their proper level, the implication being that coming from the background they did it was impossible that they should become of any more consequence than any other people.

My native town of Langholm, with a population of some 1500, was the instrument of my correction. A journalist friend of mine thought it would be a good idea in connection with my seventieth birthday that I should be given the Freedom of Langholm, which up to then had never been conferred on anyone. The proposal was warmly supported by a local minister, the leading textile-mill proprietor, and several people, in Canada and elsewhere, who claimed to have been at school with me. But the Langholm Town Council turned it down flat—on the ground that some twenty years earlier I had told in *Lucky Poet* a couple of rather scandalous stories about Langholm people. The stories were not only slightly *risqué*; they were also really amusing. And as was still well known in the burgh they were true. Besides, it was pointed out that I had not been much in

Langholm for many years (no account being taken of the economic reasons which had for the most part located me in distant places) and that I had done nothing for the burgh. What that meant was that I hadn't presented Langholm with a couple of park benches or something of that sort.

I pointed out that I was not so destitute of honours as to care very much what a handful of local Bumbles who knew nothing about my work and were quite incompetent to assess its value might think, and while I loved Langholm and returned there whenever I could I would never in future accept any gesture meant to honour me at the hands of a group of citizens ignorant of my work. The future would determine which of us had brought distinction to the town. And there the matter rested.[1]

So, in concluding this volume, I think I have made it clear that my life-story has been actuated throughout by a sense of the truth of what another Scottish writer, Norman Douglas, has said. Namely:

'Consider well your neighbour, what an imbecile he is. Then ask yourself whether it be worth while paying any attention to what he thinks of you! . . . Were the day twice as long as it is, a man might find it diverting to probe down into that unsatisfactory fellow-creature and try to reach some common root of feeling other than those physiological needs which we share with every beast of earth. Diverting; hardly profitable. It would be like looking for a flea in a haystack or a joke in the Bible—they can perhaps be found; at the expense of how much trouble!

'Therefore the sage will go his way, prepared to find himself growing ever more and more out of sympathy with

1. Mr James Finlayson, of Hawick, as guest speaker proposing 'The Immortal Memory' at the Eskdale Burns Club's Supper in Langholm (January 1966), expressed the hope that a reconciliation might be effected between the author and his birthplace and that Langholm might not delay too long in honouring him, as Hawick had done in the case of the distinguished artist, Anne Redpath. Mr Finlayson's remarks were greeted with cries of 'Never! Never!' and 'Away back to Hawick'.

vulgar trends of opinion, for such is the inevitable development of thoughtful and self-respecting minds. He scorns to
make proselytes among his fellows: they are not worth it.
He has better things to do. While others nurse their griefs
he nurses his joy. He endeavours to find himself at no
matter what cost, and to be true to that self when found, a
worthy occupation for a lifetime.'

Index